COSMOPOLIS II

COSMOPOLIS II

MONGREL CITIES OF THE 21ST CENTURY

LEONIE SANDERCOCK

Images by
Peter Lyssiotis

continuum
LONDON • NEW YORK

Continuum

The Tower Building
11 York Road
London SE1 7NX

15 East 26th Street
New York
NY 10010

Text © Leonie Sandercock 2003
Images © Peter Lyssiotis 2003

British Library Cataloguing-in-Publication Data
A catalogue record for this book is available from the British Library.

ISBN: 0826470459 (hardback) 0826464637 (paperback)

Typeset by RefineCatch Limited, Bungay Suffolk
Printed and bound in Great Britain by
MPG Books Ltd, Bodmin, Cornwall

for John

CONTENTS

ACKNOWLEDGEMENTS

This book began as a second edition of *Towards Cosmopolis* but, over the space of the year I spent working on it, became a new book. It was written in the inspiring physical and cultural environment of my new home, Vancouver. I feel very fortunate to be teaching now at the University of British Columbia and my first thanks go to all my colleagues in the School of Community and Regional Planning at UBC, and especially to Tony Dorcey, the School's Director, for creating a sane, productive, and convivial environment. I am also grateful to UBC for a small Hampton Research Grant which provided me with the excellent research assistance of Maged Senbel.

I spent five years in Australia, from 1996 to 2001. A chance encounter in a poetry bookstore in Melbourne led to a friendship with the artist Peter Lyssiotis. Peter provided the images for *Towards Cosmopolis*, and I had no hesitation in turning to him again, this time in a long-distance collaboration, for this new book. His insight, irreverence, and commitment to my project have been a blessing. Peter, it's a privilege working with you. What's next, mate?

The nourishment of friendship, near and far, has always provided the vital counterbalance to this obsession with writing. My heartfelt thanks to Tony and Plu Dorcey, Norma-Jean McLaren and Nathan Edelson in Vancouver; Heather Ellyard and Alex Broons in Melbourne; Wendy Sarkissian in Brisbane; Lizzie Vines in Adelaide; Liv Torgerson and Richard Chew, Bob Andrus, Manuela Friedmann and James McKissick in Los Angeles; Robin and Ron Cobb in Sydney and Los Angeles; Bent Flyvbjerg in Aalborg; Klaus Kunzmann and Wang Fang in Berlin: Bob Beauregard, Eleanora Tevis, and Janet Abu-Lughod in New York; Margaret Crawford and Marco Cenzatti, Bish Sanyal and Dianne Davis in Boston; Jim Throgmorton in Iowa; John Forester in Ithaca; Ute Lehrer and Roger Keil in Toronto; Iain Borden in London; Maria Cerreta in Naples; Raffaele Paloscia in Florence; Dino Borri in Bari; Oren Yiftachel and Tovi Fenster in Israel; Tanja Winkler in Johannesburg and Vancouver; and Amy Ruth, a wonderful kinesiologist in Vancouver, who has shown me how to take care of a back injury in a very empowering way. The 'Friedmann clan', Martin and Laila, Aloysia and Jackie, and their hospitality on Orcas Island, have added immeasurably to our pleasure in moving to the Pacific North West.

Some friends also happen to be incredibly generous colleagues. Bob Beauregard and Jim Throgmorton sacrificed chunks of their summer in 2002 to give detailed critical readings to the first draft. I can't thank them enough. Patsy Healey, as a non-anonymous reviewer, provided many suggestions and comments that were of great assistance in the final polish. She is also an inspiration, a warm and generous colleague with a wonderfully critical, innovative, and open approach to cities, planning, and scholarship. A second reviewer, this one anonymous, challenged me on a number of issues and caused some necessary sleepless nights, for which I am perversely grateful. S/he will see his/her imprint in the final draft, in terms of what I spent time re-thinking and re-writing.

Tristan Palmer was the editor who first contracted *Towards Cosmopolis*, and who kept in touch as both of us went through several relocations and changes of employers in the intervening seven years. I am very grateful to him for encouraging this project, and his flexibility as what began as a second edition turned into a new book.

Most important, on the home front, I have this irritatingly persistent critic and sparring partner, diligent reader of my words, and always constructive commentator on them. He also provides music, meals, poetry, and many other joys. This book is dedicated, again, to John Friedmann – my beloved.

I acknowledge Ashgate Publishing Limited for permission to use 'Difference, Fear and Habitus: A Political Economy of Urban Fears', which appeared in *Habitus: A Sense of Place*, edited by Jean Hillier and Emma Rooksby, 2002. A revised version of this chapter appears here as Chapter 5.

I am also grateful to Routledge, publishers of the journal *Planning Theory and Practice*, for permission to use parts of 'When Strangers Become Neighbours: Managing Cities of Difference', which appeared in *Planning Theory and Practice*, 1, 1 (2000). Arguments and research from that paper appear here in Chapters 6 and 7. To the same publisher, of this same journal, thank you for permission to use 'Out of the Closet: The Importance of Stories and Storytelling in Planning', *Planning Theory and Practice*, 4, 1 (2003), in an expanded form as Chapter 8 of this book.

Finally, I acknowledge John Wiley, publisher of my *Towards Cosmopolis* (1998), for permission to use revised versions of Chapters 2 and 3 of that book.

PREFACE

If you've read *Towards Cosmopolis* and are wondering whether you should read this 'sequel', here (in one sentence) is why I hope you will. Eight of its ten chapters are new, and there is a brilliant set of new images created for this new volume by Peter Lyssiotis.

The first edition of this book was written in the mid–1990s and influenced by the events and debates of the previous decade as well as by my location at the time, Los Angeles. In 1995 I accepted a job in Melbourne. One of my reasons for wanting to return to Australia was its apparently remarkable progress as a multicultural nation, and its recent recognition of indigenous land rights. The Labour Government at that time, under Prime Minister Paul Keating, expressly spoke of Australia as a nation of cultural diversity, a hybrid nation with a dynamic and heterogeneous identity. By the time I arrived there a year later, the Keating Government was already history and, under the new conservative regime of Prime Minister John Howard, multiculturalism became (unofficially) a taboo word in government circles. Beyond those circles there were both right-wing grassroots backlashes against official multicultural policy and left-wing critiques. I began to research the effectiveness of multicultural policies on the ground, still believing in their importance, in principle, yet at the same time feeling the need to understand the range of critiques, and the backlash. What I learned through that research, and that questioning, has partly shaped this new book.

More recently, my attention has shifted to European cities and to the rising levels of anxiety about immigration. Questions of tolerance and peaceful co-existence seem ever more urgent in what I am calling the 'mongrel cities' of the 21st century. I've appropriated 'mongrel' from Salman Rushdie (1992) and use it in the same spirit as he does: as both provocation and term of approbation for the kinds of changes that are happening in cities the world over, as they become more multiethnic and multicultural. This book is a manifesto of sorts: a radical multicultural manifesto for 21st century cities.

The new Introduction sets out my agenda for 'mongrel cities and the 21st century multicultural project' – a project that is now, as ever, hotly contested, imperfect, a work in progress. My central question is how we stroppy strangers might live together in these cities without doing each other too much violence (Donald, 1999). The operational question is what kind of challenge this is for citizens, city governments, and the city building professions of architecture, urban design, planning, landscape architecture, and engineering. Answering these questions has forced me to think a lot more about fear, as it relates to identity and difference, to home and nation, to belonging and freedom. I've had to ask whether multiculturalism is another defunct twentieth-century ideology, part of the problem rather than part of the solution. I've had to question the sacred cow of 'community', asking about its relevance in the globalized localities of multicultural cities.

I've engaged directly with the operational challenges of integrating migrants in countries that have not, until recently, thought of themselves as countries of immigration, and compared that with the continuing challenge of de-segregating American cities. I've thought a lot about the uses of story and the importance and meaning of creativity in planning. I've moved beyond the five literacies (technical, analytical, multicultural, eco-logical, and design) that I developed in *Towards Cosmopolis*, talking now about the five qualities or sensibilities of a 21st century urban imagination: political, therapeutic, auda-cious, creative, and critical. I've shifted my focus from Los Angeles (where I had lived for 11 years at the time of writing *Towards Cosmopolis*) to a wider range of cities (Birming-ham, Rotterdam, Frankfurt, Berlin, Sydney, Vancouver, Chicago, East St. Louis, to name a few), chosen for their experimental, innovative approaches to cultural diversity and social inclusion.

'*Cosmopolis*' remains the goal of this work: a construction site of the mind and heart, a city in which there is genuine acceptance of, connection with, and respect and space for 'the stranger' (outsider, foreigner . . .), in which there exists the possibility of working together on matters of common destiny, of forging new hybrid cultures and com-munities. But this book goes beyond dreaming *cosmopolis*, to the practical challenges of creating it. In the wake of the events of September 11th 2001 this is an even more daunting, even more necessary project.

Leonie Sandercock
Vancouver, Winter 2003

CITY OFFICE OF THE MEDICAL EXAMINER

Case No _1463 - 02_

Name _X (Refugee)_   Age _27_ Race _Arabic_ Sex _F_

Tagged at _the border_

Tagged by _Rick Deckard_   Time in _1:30 am_

F14

INTRODUCTION

A love song to our mongrel cities

If the *Satanic Verses* is anything, it is a migrant's eye view of the world. It is written from the very experience of uprooting, disjuncture and metamorphosis (slow or rapid, painful or pleasurable) that is the migrant condition, and from which, I believe, can be derived a metaphor for all humanity. Standing at the centre of the novel is a group of characters, most of whom are British Muslims . . . struggling with just the sort of great problems that have arisen to surround the book, problems of hybridization and ghettoization, of reconciling the old and the new. Those who oppose the novel most vociferously today are of the opinion that intermingling with a different culture will inevitably weaken and ruin their own. I am of the opposite opinion. The *Satanic Verses* celebrates hybridity, impurity, intermingling, the transformation that comes of new and unexpected combinations of human beings, cultures, ideas, politics, movies, songs. It rejoices in mongrelization and fears the absolutism of the Pure. Melange, hotchpotch, a bit of this and a bit of that is how newness enters the world. It is the great possibility that mass migration gives the world . . . The Satanic Verses is for change-by-fusion, change-by-conjoining. It is a love song to our mongrel selves.

(Rushdie, 1992: 394)

A decade ago, in this defence of his controversial novel, Salmon Rushdie staked out some of the territory that I want to cover in this book. Movement and migration are, arguably, among the defining socio-historical conditions of humanity. In these movements, Rushdie sees a metaphor for the human condition, and I see in them also a metaphor for the urban condition that came into being in the late twentieth century, in the era of late modernity. I will use the metaphor of the mongrel city to characterize this new urban condition in which difference, otherness, fragmentation, splintering, multiplicity, heterogeneity, diversity, plurality prevail. For some this is to be feared, signifying the decline of civilization as we know it in the West. For others (like Rushdie and myself) it is to be celebrated as a great possibility: the possibility of living alongside others who are different, learning from them, creating new worlds with them, instead of fearing them. My project is to provide a better understanding of the emergence of cities of difference in the context of globalization and other, related, social forces; and to reflect on the challenges which these mongrel cities present in the 21st century to the city-building professions (architects, planners and urban designers, landscape architects, engineers), to city dwellers, and to conventional notions of citizenship. My central question is how can 'we' (all of us), in all of our differences, be 'at home' in the multicultural and multiethnic cities of the 21st century.

For as long as there have been cities, there have been women and men seeking to define and then perfect the art and science of city-building. Artists and designers, inventors and theologians, vegetarians and philosophers are among the many who have turned their thoughts to perfecting the pattern of human settlement. From architectural to political, technical to religious, social to spiritual to environmental solutions, we have juggled with the elements of the city – its political economy, its built, social and natural environments – dreaming its perfection many times over, but never realizing the dream. The utopian impulse at the heart of so many experiments in city-building has always proved disappointing, if not downright disastrous, in the actual flesh and stone. Much has been written about why this is so – perhaps enough to discourage any further attempts at utopian thinking about the city. But the utopian impulse is, and will hopefully remain, an irrepressible part of the human spirit. This author is not ashamed to take her place in a long line of utopian thinking about cities. I am *dreaming cosmopolis*, my utopia, a construction site of the mind, a city/region in which there is genuine acceptance of, connection with, and respect and space for the cultural Other, and the possibility of working together on matters of common destiny, the possibility of a togetherness in difference. But I also want to *practise utopia*, a city politics of possibility and of hope. I want to outline a planning imagination for the 21st century that is utopian and critical, creative and audacious.

Around the turn of the nineteenth century and into the first decade of the twentieth, a new profession emerged, staking out a claim for itself in relation to city-building. The profession of town and country planning, these days more usually referred to as urban and regional planning, emerged at that particular time in response to the perceived ills of the western industrial city, and among its founding ideas, and always contested, was a distinct stream of utopian thinking. This utopian stream found its most powerful expression in the paradigm that came to dominate planning in the twentieth century, the so-called modernist paradigm, with its foundation in scientific and technical reason. One of the stories this book tells is of the life and death of modernist planning. The ability of this paradigm to endure, despite attacks from many directions, is one reason for examining it. Another is the damage it has done to the environment, to community, to cultural diversity, and to the human spirit. Yet another reason for scrutiny is that although the pillars of modernist planning have been crumbling for at least three decades, there is still no agreement as to what might replace that grand social project. What lies beyond the modernist paradigm?

This book is not the first to notice that the understandings and world views on which the city-building professions were constructed and the problems they were designed to solve have changed dramatically in the last three decades. But it is the first to give systematic attention to the crumbling pillars of modernist planning, and to suggest a way out of the impasse, a way of advancing a progressive planning practice in the 21st century, based on the insights of feminist, postmodern and postcolonial thinking. With a certain exhilaration, I write in Chapter 1 of the death of the 'Rational City' – that is, of modernist notions of technical rationality providing order, coherence, regulation, homogeneity – and celebrate instead the spaces of insurgent citizenship, the rise of civil society in the form of organized social movements which confront modernist planning with its anti-democratic, race- and gender-blind, and culturally homogenizing practices.

In the postwar rush to turn planning into an applied social science much was ignored

– the city of memory, of desire, of spirit; the importance of place and the art of place-making; the local knowledges written into the stones and memories of communities. Modernist architects, planners, engineers – Faustian heroes all – saw themselves as experts who could utilize the laws of development to provide societal guidance. The hubris of the city-building professions was their faith in the liberating potential of their technical knowledge and their corresponding belief in their ability to transcend the interests of capital, labour, and the state, and to arrive at an objective assessment of 'the public interest'. Modernist architecture has been under the critics' microscope for at least three decades. Modernist planning has encountered something more like border skirmishes. This book focuses a number of critical lenses on the pillars of modernist planning, specifically on the attributes of rationality, comprehensiveness, scientific objectivity, the project of state-directed futures, and the notion of the public interest. If we want to assist in the realization of cosmopolis, we need to deconstruct these pillars of modernist planning wisdom and rebuild them with reconsidered concepts of democracy, social justice, citizenship, multiculturalism, and multiple publics, and along with these, new qualities of planning imagination.

That we are increasingly living in global cities, and that forces of global economic integration (usually assumed to be beyond the control of any one region or nation) are drastically restructuring cities and regions, is now a familiar refrain. While urban and regional researchers busy themselves studying the processes and consequences of globalization, the planning profession around the world finds itself marginalized by urban political regimes rushing to embrace the global investors, terrified that their city/region will drop off all the relevant maps. These economic forces of global integration have spawned an important new literature on urban and regional restructuring, on deindustrialization and reindustrialization, postfordism (the shift that began in the 1970s from mass production of manufactured goods to more varied forms of production: see Amin, 1994), flexible production, and so on.

I have nothing to add to that literature. I do, however, feel that by concentrating all our attention on the economic, we are missing something of equal importance that is also occurring on a global scale. I refer to the demographic restructurings which many cities and regions in the industrialized countries have been experiencing for the past several decades[1] and, more broadly, to four major socio-cultural factors which have been and will continue to re-shape cities and regions in the 21st century.

These socio-cultural forces, which I discuss in Chapter 1, include international migration (Castles and Miller, 1998) and an accompanying new politics of 'multicultural citizenship' (Kymlicka, 1995); the discourse of postcolonialism, and an as yet unresolved postcolonial condition in the West; the resurgence of indigenous peoples and an associated politics of reclaiming their land; and the rise of organized civil society, and the new politics of social movements. Each of these is having a profound effect on the shaping of the cities and regions of the 21st century, leading to the central importance of a new 'cultural politics of difference' that has further undermined the modernist paradigm. When these socio-cultural forces are ignored, it is easy to fall into an analysis in which the economic forces of globalization are seen to be shaping everything (Harvey, 1989; Jameson, 1991; Castells, 1996).[2] This leads us to accept as inevitable that which is not yet so. It turns us into theoretical couch potatoes in a nihilistic postmodern scenario – death by paralysis.

Cities and regions of the 21st century are multiethnic, multiracial, multiple. The cultural diversity which has emerged in cities in the West, and will continue to insert itself as a distinguishing characteristic of cities the world over, is also producing what I call a new world disorder. The multicultural city/region is perceived by many as more of a threat than an opportunity. The threats are multiple: psychological, economic, religious, cultural. It is a complicated experiencing of fear of 'the Other' alongside fear of losing one's job, fear of a whole way of life being eroded, fear of change itself. These fears are producing rising levels of anxiety about and violence against those who are different, who are seen as not belonging, 'not my people'. This fear is as great a threat to the future stability of cities and regions as the much more talked about economic forces. In the first two years of the new millennium, such fears have produced race riots in three British cities; the re-emergence of Le Pen in France as the standard-bearer for a coalition of the fearful; the strengthening of right-wing, anti-immigrant parties in most European countries; and in Australia, an immigration backlash which has given rise to the 'Pacific Solution', the notion of buying a small island away from the mainland on which to dump unwelcome refugees – out of sight, out of mind.

The dilemmas of difference, in all their cultural, social and spatial manifestations, are a challenge to the current ways of thinking of the city-building professions, to city dwellers, and to ideas of urban governance and urban politics. Contemporary cities are sites of struggles over space, which are really two kinds of struggle: one a struggle of life space against economic space (Friedmann, 1988), the other a struggle over belonging. Who belongs where, and with what citizenship rights, in the mongrel cities of the 21st century? The 'new cultural politics of difference' (West, 1990), or what James Tully (1995) has called the 'politics of cultural recognition', that emerged in the 1980s, did not fade away by the end of the century. On the contrary, these new voices and new demands for rights – rights to the city, rights to a voice, to participation, and to co-existence in the actual physical spaces of the city – have become louder, more insistent, even as (or because) populist and fundamentalist opposition mobilizes against them. City governments in Europe, North America and Australia have become more and more involved in addressing these new realities in their neighbourhoods, through accommodation or repression, or often both. The most progressive city regimes, however, are asking how peaceful co-existence might be possible, what policy responses are necessary, and whether some new notions of urban identity and citizenship might be called for. Part II of this book addresses these practical, operational questions.

Two points about the scope of the book. While the metaphor of the mongrel city is intended to encompass and embrace all forms of difference, and to acknowledge the reality of our co-presence in the city, there is no way that one book can address the policy issues of all the groups thus embraced. I do think that the theoretical, epistemological and process arguments in this book are relevant to all forms of difference in the city, but I have given my most detailed policy attention to the issue of ethno-cultural differences that arise from the 'age of migration', because at this moment in history it seems to be the most contentious and, in Europe at least, the most potentially destabilizing. Second, my focus is on western metropolises, which I conceptualize as 'racialized liberal democracies' (Hesse, 2000: 13), rather than on the non-Western world, although I believe these issues are becoming increasingly salient (while still repressed) in countries like Indonesia, China, Singapore and Malaysia, as well as Japan (which will increasingly have to depend on immigrant labour) and South Africa (which attracts large numbers of immigrants from the rest of the continent).[3]

The concept of racialized liberal democracies is an important one in helping us to connect multicultural discourse with postwar labour migrations, and that, in turn, with an unresolved postcolonial condition. This is particularly important for understanding contemporary conflicts around immigration in formerly imperialist European countries, but it is also relevant in understanding the limits of multiculturalism in so-called settler societies such as Canada, Australia and the United States. While not all European nations were involved in empire-building projects from the fifteenth to the twentieth centuries, most have defined themselves, as nations, in racially and/or culturally exclusive ways, which has inevitably produced social conflict as those nations have moved towards accepting immigrants and refugees from different cultural backgrounds. The 'multicultural project' then, is neither innocent nor pure, but implicated in and complicated by these histories.

Part II will unravel the many, evolving, and contested meanings of multiculturalism. My goal is to unsettle accepted meanings of the term before coupling it with more radical and plural notions of an agonistic democracy. I have been influenced in this project by the work of Stuart Hall (2000) and Bhikhu Parekh (2000) on multiculturalism and power; James Tully (1995) and Ash Amin (2002) on interculturalism; Chantal Mouffe (2000) on agonistic democracy; Tully (1995) and Iris Young (1990) on a politics of cultural recognition; William Connolly (1991, 1995) on identity and difference, and extending the democratic pluralist imagination; and James C. Scott (1998) on the modern state.

*

The book is organized into three parts. Part 1 looks back at the twentieth century and critiques the modernist urban project without entirely abandoning it. I begin with a sketch of Birmingham as 'the city of everyman', an archetypal industrial city of the second half of the twentieth century, and trace the upheavals faced by that city and many others. What follows is an outline of the four major socio-cultural forces reshaping the cities and regions of the next century. The chapter concludes paradoxically with the argument that planning has never really been modern – whether modernist is associated with the rational and scientific, or with doubt and emancipation (each important parts of the dialectic of modernity). I then propose six elements of a hybrid postmodern planning practice, radically democratic and responsive to cities of difference. Chapter 2 looks at how the modernist historical narrative of planning as the progress of the profession and its practices – 'the Official Story' – has omitted the 'noir' side of planning, its racist and sexist effects, as well as erasing the insurgent or alternative histories of, for example, women, blacks, gays and lesbians, and indigenous peoples as they relate to city- and community-building. The task of revisiting and retelling the past is to recover, to make visible, these stories that have been rendered invisible by the official, heroic narrative.

Chapter 3 asks what kinds of knowledge are regarded as valid, and who possesses these knowledges. The roots of modernist planning are deep in the soil of the eighteenth-century Enlightenment and its faith in the scientific method. The social sciences have been dominated by a positivist epistemology which privileges scientific and technical knowledge over an array of equally important alternatives – experiential, intuitive, local knowledges; knowledges based on practices of talking, listening, seeing, contemplating, sharing; knowledges expressed in visual and other symbolic, ritual, and artistic ways rather than in quantitative or analytical modes based on technical jargons that by defin-ition exclude those without professional training. We need to acknowledge the many ways of knowing that exist in culturally diverse populations, and to discern which are most useful and in what circumstances.

Looking Back at the last two decades of the twentieth century from the vantage point of the 21st, we can see the confluence of several elements: the collapse of Communist states; a post-Marxist appreciation of energies in civil society exceeding the unity and power of command economies; an acceleration of population flows accompanying the globaliza-tion of economic life, as affluent members of a new managerial class enjoy transnational mobility and impoverished postcolonials migrate to the centre of former empires; the eruption of new claims to positive identity among constituencies whose previous iden-tifications along lines of race, gender, sexuality, religion or disability were experienced as injurious or degrading; and the increasing porosity and uncertainty of territorial bound-aries and national identities. These drives to civil society, multiculturalism, the return of the colonial repressed, transnational mobility, and pluralist tolerance in turn encounter their dialectical opposite, a series of bellicose responses that demand a return to a unified faith, race, reason, nation, gender duality or 'normal' sexuality (Connolly, 1995). With a little help from the events of September 11th 2001, real and metaphorical border patrols appear to be tightening in the early years of the 21st century as this battle between the impulse to fundamentalism and the impulse to pluralization and tolerance plays itself out in our cities in complex ways. While fundamentalist terrorists attack what they see as the manifold decadence of the West, there are powerful fundamentalist forces within western nations seeking to purify their own societies of all that is seen as Other or 'unnatural' – feminists and homosexuals, atheists and Muslims, immigrants and multi-culturalists. This book necessarily engages in these broader debates, for the radical, pluralist and democratic planning imagination I seek to outline must draw on broader notions of democracy and citizenship that reconceptualize difference while acknowledg-ing and working through the fears and anxieties that difference generates.

Looking Forward, Part II, dives deep into the question of how we might live together in the mongrel cities of the 21st century. In Chapter 4, the task is to rethink multicultural-ism as a form of democratic politics and as a perspective on human society, and thereby to elaborate the components of a revivified 21st-century multicultural project. Such a project acknowledges the cultural embeddedness of all human beings; the inescapability, but also desirability, of cultural diversity and intercultural exchange; the right to the city, which is part of the right to difference; political community (rather than ethno- or any

other sub-cultural identity) as the basis for belonging in multicultural societies; and social recognition, as well as a just sharing of economic and political power for all cultures, as a necessary basis for a stable, yet dynamic multicultural society.

The 21st century is indisputably the century of multicultural cities and societies. It will also be the century of struggle for multiculturalism, and against fundamentalism, which is a belief in cultural (and/or religious) purity. The following chapters turn to how this struggle plays itself out in cities and neighbourhoods and what citizens, city governments, and the city-building professions can do, and are doing, to advance the project of multiculturalism. Chapter 5 discusses fear in contemporary cities, specifically fear of outsiders, strangers, foreigners, and how that fear is linked to notions of home and nation, and to 'nation as home', metaphorically. There are numerous practical questions to be addressed in developing practices and policies that are responsive to various kinds of difference. For example, how can migrants be integrated into cities that are unused to thinking of themselves as multicultural? How might intersecting material and psychological fears be mediated? Chapter 6 explores how some cities (Frankfurt, Berlin, Rotterdam, Sydney and Vancouver) have become involved in positive ways in addressing the challenge of integrating migrants from different cultures, engaging in the active construction of new ways of living together. This is a long-term process, during which fears and anxieties cannot be ignored, but need to be worked through. Efforts in some American cities (like Oak Park, on the edge of Chicago) to actively promote residential racial integration, and in Vancouver, to establish truly inclusive neighbourhood-based institutions, offer some guidelines about a process of mobilizing civil society, block by block, neighbourhood by neighbourhood, and institution by institution, around *the project of intercultural co-existence.*

The effort of building *cosmopolis* is a necessarily combined effort, by residents, planners, social movements and politicians at local, provincial, and national levels, and this book is written for all these actors in the ongoing drama that is urban life. Part III explores the possibilities and realities of transformative planning practices. Chapter 7 dissects three stories of planning activity: the first concerns a land-use conflict between indigenous Australians and their non-indigenous neighbours in an inner Sydney suburb; the second tells of a community mobilization in partnership with a university research effort in East St. Louis, USA, that was successful in reversing structural and political processes of abandonment; the third is the unfinished story of the attempt of the city of Birmingham, UK, to reinvent itself as a *cosmopolis*, a city in which dynamic new sources of growth might be enjoyed across culturally diverse neighbourhoods in a more inclusionary approach to urban regeneration. The larger purpose is to understand how and why cities change, and who and what are the key change agents.

What Part III underlines is that *building cosmopolis* is not only about mobilizing resources and power, but also about organizing hope, negotiating fears, mediating collective memories of identity and belonging, and daring to take risks. In this effort, the role of imagining alternative stories and futures is critical. Chapter 8 discusses the importance of story, metaphor, and ritual in the work of planning for *cosmopolis*, and Chapter 9 outlines five qualities of a new planning imagination for dealing with the mongrel cities of the 21st century: critical, creative, therapeutic, political, and audacious.

I want to suggest a different sensibility from the bureaucratic (or regulatory) planning that dominated the twentieth century – a sensibility that is as alert to the emotional economies of the city as it is to the political economies; as alert to city senses (of sound, sight, touch, smell, taste) as to city censuses; as alert to the soft-wired desires of citizens as it is to the hard-wired infrastructures; as concerned with the ludic as with the productive spaces, indeed seeing these as inseparable and complementary; a sensibility as curious about the spirit of place as it is critical of capitalist excesses; and above all, a sensibility which can help citizens wrest new possibilities from space, and immerse themselves in their cultures while respecting those of their neighbours, and collectively forging new hybrid cultures and spaces. That is my love song to our mongrel cities.

PART I

LOOKING BACK: MODERNIST PLANNING AND ITS DISCONTENTS

1

MODERNIST CITIES AND PLANNING

Oh what a lovely paradox!

Where 'we' are today globally is a situation in which every 'we' discovers that it is in part a 'they': that the lines between 'us' and 'them' are continuously redefined through the global realities of immigration, travel, communication, the world economy, and ecological disasters.

(Benhabib, 1995: 244)

Habermas and his disciples hold on to the modern project only by abstaining from all empirical inquiry – not a single case study in the 500 pages of his master work . . .

(Latour, 1993: 60)

INTRODUCTION

From the vantage point of the early 21st century, we can look back on the last three decades of the twentieth and give some coherence to the massive changes occurring in cities in the West, a coherence that was far more chaotic as lived experience. Interdependent economic, demographic, and socio-cultural forces have been reshaping these cities since the late 1960s from industrial to postindustrial landscapes, accompanied by new geographies of exclusion. That much seems straightforward. More contested has been a parallel restructuring of our thinking about cities and planning, and about the modern state. Have we moved from a modernist to a postmodern age? Are these labels descriptive or normative? Are there good reasons for speeding up the passing of the modernist city, celebrating its demise? Are there things worth preserving? Have we, as Bruno Latour (1993) suggests, ever really been modern?[1] I return to these questions at the end of this chapter.

This book is particularly interested in the demographic and socio-cultural re-shapings of Western cities and the challenges that these pose to city governments, citizens, and the city-building professions. Specifically I'm interested in the 'cities of difference' whose dynamics have been produced by four demographic and socio-cultural forces: international migration, the discourse of postcolonialism, the resurgence of indigenous peoples, and the rise of organized civil society. How we understand and think about these changes affects our capacity to respond to them. Have the intellectual, emotional, and political tools been adequate? Has the modernist paradigm that guided the city-building professions as well as the administrators of the modern state had its day?

No city can stand as an archetype for all cities. Nevertheless, as a narrative device, I ask the city of Birmingham to serve as my springboard in exploring these questions, partly because I see Birmingham as a 'City of Everyman', a typical industrial (and masculine) twentieth-century city that has undergone massive changes in the past 30 years, and is still struggling to understand 'what hit it', and how to respond. So I begin (with Latour's critique of Habermas in mind) with the concrete city of Birmingham, setting out the book's project through that example. Then I make a broader argument about the four demographic and socio-cultural forces that have been neglected in urban analysis because everyone has been preoccupied with the forces of economic globalization (Scott, 2001; Sassen, 2002). I explain why we need to pay more attention to these four forces. In the third section I interrogate the articles of faith of modernist architecture and plan-ning, and, more broadly, the modern state, asking what was missing, what was concealed, and what was lost in designing, building, and administering the Rational City. I navigate between the radical magnificence of the modernist project, and its inherent lacunae.[2] I want to reimagine the mythical modernist urban project as a radical postmodern project, a response to the mongrel cities of the 21st century.

BIRMINGHAM: CITY OF EVERYMAN, 1950–2002

TAKE ONE: THE 1950S

Let's begin, then, with the concrete. Literally. The concrete collar of freeways around downtown Birmingham, second largest city in the UK. If there is one popular symbol of the modernist city, it is the city of freeways and of motor vehicle dependence, sometimes described as the city of mobility and freedom. In the rebuilding and expansion of European and New World cities after World War II, freeways were that mandatory symbol of social progress and individual freedom. People abandoned the streetcar or train and drove newly acquired cars into the city centre or across the metropolitan area to their place of work. City centres thus became ringed with a concrete necklace, or collar, like Birmingham's. The project of modernizing cities was always both a physical and a symbolic project, expressing and conveying speed, democratization (a chicken in every pot, a car in every garage . . .), dynamism, change, moving on to better worlds in which technologies would set us free. The mass appeal of this modernist vision was simultaneously material and spiritual. Alongside material abundance, Everyman would have the opportunity to better himself, to shake loose the chains of the past, of tradition and custom, to invent himself anew – while Everywoman, well, she would remain where she had always been, taking care of hearth and home, but liberated in her own small way by modern appliances which would transform household chores into a technological pleasure. It was heady stuff, a heady moment in history, heady, at least, for 'everyman', and at least in the history of the West.

Birmingham, mid-twentieth century, was 'a city of everyman', an honest, hardwork-ing, unpretentious, unglamorous city. The city of a thousand trades, the city of metal bashing, of cars and assembly lines, of pubs and football. A masculine city of sweat and swearing. It was also a city of immense pride in its own history of technological and social innovation. The engineer/inventor Matthew Bolton; the politician of liberal social values Joseph Chamberlain; the philanthropist industrialist George Cadbury, who dared to dream of reconciling the pursuit of profit with the provision of decent living standards for all, and built a model town (Bourneville) to prove it could be done. The people of Birmingham, known to each other affectionately as Brummies, had many things to be proud of and were proud of many things, not least of which was being British, with all that that meant about empire and God and country and being white, and yes, being somehow better than those (non-white) folks in the colonies.

In the decade after World War II the assembly lines expanded and the future was golden. There weren't enough 'hands' (that is, male white bodies) to do the assembly line work, so immigrants from the empire's former colonies became the new factory fodder.[3] And for a time, everyone knew their place in this 'us' and 'them' world, and many people were doing better than before. Difference was accommodated by residential segregation and enclaving. Out of sight, hopefully out of mind. In Birmingham, the middle ring of Victorian and Edwardian bylaw housing became the new homes of West Indian and Asian populations, the former north-west of the city centre, the latter east and south-east. These middle ring houses were large enough for multi-family occupancy but, because they lacked garages, were rejected by upwardly mobile whites. Different ethnic groups occupied discreet spaces in the city. But that couldn't, and didn't, last.

TAKE TWO: THE 1980S

Gradually there is leakage, spillover, contamination. Impurity in the urban fabric. And crisis in the urban economy. Those who had been contained in specific parts of the city begin to make wider claims on and in the spaces of the built environment. Whole streets, even neighbourhoods, proclaim themselves through signage and human presence, as Asian streets or West Indian villages. Indian and Pakistani immigrants have now owned businesses for several decades, and become landlords. The ethnic neighbourhoods elect their own people to join the Labour-dominated city council. Suburban homes become small mosques, flaunting local land-use codes. Ethnic religious communities become organized, and seek to build larger mosques and temples, apparently flaunting their different religious practices in the faces of the 'indigenous' Anglo community. They even set up their own schools. Now there is a pervasive unsettling of the common understanding of what it means to be a Brummie.

Meanwhile in the inner ring, the modernist public housing estates that were a symbol of social compassion, of a benign state, when they were built in the 1950s and 1960s are already deteriorating because the poor (Anglo and non-Anglo) families who have been contained there, side by side, (no 'luxury' of segregation here), have seen a generation grow up without life prospects improving, so there is bitterness, resentment, the need to blame someone, the need to strike out at someone or something. The folks of the inner ring have never been included in the postwar prospering of Birmingham. They survived on the paternalism of the welfare state at the same time as they were injured by that same state, trapped in cycles of dependency and poverty, and given their identities by that same state's classification systems, identities as failures, misfits, unable to fend for themselves, to adapt to modern society.[4]

The metropolitan economy is splintering. Between 1971 and 1987 150,000 jobs disappear in manufacturing, 46 per cent of the sector (Henry, McEwan and Pollard, 2000: 3). The inner areas are the worst hit. There is 20 per cent unemployment across the city. The multiethnic neighbourhood of Handsworth erupts in 1985. Two Asian shopkeepers die in the flames of their burning shops. The national press prints a picture of a young Afro-Caribbean throwing a firebomb, even though a white male was arrested for the murders. The (white) national press seeks to racialize the problem. It's them, not us. Birmingham's race relations problems had surfaced in crudest form in the 1964 General Election with the loss of the Smethwick seat, formerly held by the Labour Party, to a Conservative candidate campaigning openly on the race issue – with the slogan 'A Vote for Labour is a vote for a Nigger' (Slater, 1996: 143). But Birmingham's race relations problems were really Britain's problem of racism, in turn related to still unresolved issues of postcoloniality. The desire for immigrant bodies as factory fodder bumping up against the desire for an unreconstructed British (and Brummie) identity. 'No multiculturalism please; we're British' (Hesse, 2000: 3). We will return to these issues in Part II of this book, in Birmingham and far beyond.

The City Fathers (city politics still being an almost entirely male affair) were confounded by the unravelling of the urban fabric and the urban economy, but were swifter than most industrial cities in similar predicaments in taking action. Reflecting a long-standing tradition of cross-party support for major urban initiatives and public-private partnerships (Loftman and Nevin, 1996), these City Fathers put together a new vision for Birmingham. Their early 1980s inspiration was a postindustrial vision of the physical regeneration and beautification of downtown that, it was hoped, would change the image of the city into a more seductive place, a place where international investors, tourists, and conventioneers would want to come, stay, and spend. A new story began to be told, about Birmingham as an attractive alternative to (and more affordable than) London – a city of cafés and canals and walking paths, a pedestrian, fun downtown. Marketing campaigns promoted the city as the 'Meeting Place of Europe' (Henry, McEwan and Pollard, 2000: 4).

Jaded as we are now by 20 years of almost identical visions for decaying industrial cities in the old and new worlds, it would be too easy to dismiss Birmingham's achievement, and the energy, focus and initiative it embodied. That is not my intention. Within a decade, four flagship postindustrial projects had been completed – an International Convention Centre (ICC) and new home for the City of Birmingham Symphony Orchestra, a four-star Hyatt Hotel, a National Indoor Arena for entertainment and sports, and Brindley Place (a major leisure development of clubs and pubs, restaurants, shops, offices, and luxury housing in the old canal basin) – all at a direct cost to the Birmingham City Council of £276 million.[5] And, even more symbolically powerful, the concrete collar had been broken (for the Brindley Place development) on the western side of downtown, literally demolished, and there were plans to do the same on the east side. The jackhammers of construction staccatoed Birmingham's new identity as a postindustrial city to be reckoned with.

TAKE THREE: THE 1990S

But, of course, the panacea of downtown physical regeneration, as successful as it had been in creating an attractive built environment, masked a more enduring set of problems. A decade after this amazing physical transformation had begun, 83,000 homes were declared unfit for human habitation and the repair bill for the public housing stock stood at an estimated £980 million. Birmingham was graded by the national government as falling 28 per cent below the average performance of English local authorities in housing expenditure (Loftman and Nevin, 1996). There had been similar capital under-spending on education in the previous decade and another national ranking showed Birmingham's schools to be suffering from low morale among teachers and students, and falling grades that matched rundown buildings. The opportunity costs of all this flagship expenditure had been born directly by these social sectors. The human capital of the city had been sacrificed. And local employment gains were few. Jobs in cleaning, catering and security, related to the ICC and the hotels built in the late 1980s, paid below the Council of Europe's 'decency threshold', and disadvantaged areas had gained least from all this investment, especially the poor inner-city neighbourhoods immediately adjacent to the downtown. Ethnic minorities had missed out altogether (Loftman and Nevin, 1996).

In 1994 Theresa Stewart became the first woman Leader of the Birmingham City Council. Here was another change of huge symbolic import in this masculine city, the presence of a woman in the public sphere in a position of power signifying further changes in the city's social relations. With Stewart's election came some new spending priorities and social goals that were reflected in an immediate increase of £40 million for the education budget. But Birmingham's problems were deeper. The link between the urban economy and the urban fabric in the 1980s regeneration vision had ignored the ethno-cultural complexity of the 'metropolis of the Midlands' (Bhattacharyya, 1999). It took the death of a young black man, not in Birmingham but in London, to crystallize that issue in the local political consciousness, and precipitate action.

The murder of 18-year-old Stephen Lawrence in 1993 in the south London borough of Greenwich deeply affected public perceptions of race relations in British cities. Stephen was stabbed to death by five white youths. The Metropolitan Police spectacularly failed to treat his death as a racist murder, ignoring many witnesses who indicated the identities of the assailants, preferring instead to question Stephen's black companion on the night. Between 1993 and 1998 Stephen's parents spearheaded a campaign to bring the killers to justice. In 1997, following the election of a Labour government, the Home Secretary, Jack Straw, agreed to establish a public inquiry into Stephen's death and the subsequent police investigation. The inquiry, conducted by Sir William McPherson throughout 1998, reported in February 1999. Its condemnation of the police's failure to investigate Stephen's death effectively, to treat racism seriously, and the subsequent police cover-up of this failure was unprecedented, as was its identification of institutionalized racism in the Metropolitan Police Force. This marked the first-ever public acknowledgement of institutional racism in a major state institution in Britain (Hesse, 2000: 30).

A year earlier Britain had celebrated the 50th anniversary of the arrival of the SS Empire Windrush, the ship bringing the first of what was to become a steady stream of Caribbean migration to Britain. Windrush as a symbol had always had multiple readings in British society. For most of the previous 49 years it had predominantly signified 'the originary moment' of Britain's national implication in the colonial demarcation of race relations, and the ensuing problems of 'race' and the racialized Other in the public sphere. In the nationalist fears of the white racist imagination it also symbolized a 'strange coloured trickle of immigration that became a Black flood of undesirability into British cities' (Hesse, 2000: 98). The constant repetition of the Windrush symbol reiterated that black citizens and their children were 'newcomers, aliens forever' (*ibid.*). The celebration of the anniversary of the arrival, however, was presented as 'the irresistible rise of multi-racial Britain' (Hall, 2000: 239). The juxtaposition of this event followed by the release of the McPherson Report drew the following comment from Stuart Hall, one of Britain's most distinguished commentators on race relations:

Both these events are deeply paradigmatic of the contradictory state of British multiculturalism and their appearance together, in the same conjuncture, is essential to an understanding of Britain's confused and problematic response to 'the multicultural question'.

(Hall, 2000: 239).[6]

TAKE FOUR: BIRMINGHAM 2001

The 1980s economic development vision of the City Fathers had been a leap of faith into a postindustrial future via a transformed physical environment. That new environment, in turn, was the platform from which to tell a new story about the city, a city which was now opening itself to the outside, purveying an image of a lively and attractive metropolis, open to the 'new economy'. But this new vision reproduced not only the socio-economic exclusions of the previous era but also the socio-cultural exclusions. Birmingham's multiethnic, multiracial society was not part of the new image. Its two generations of ethno-cultural diversity, now bleedingly obvious on the streets, in the schools and so on, remained invisible in official representations of the city. That began to change around the turn of the new century. The event that symbolized at least the desire for a new direction was Highbury 3, a three-day workshop organized by the City Council with the help of consultants Charles Landry and Phil Wood of Comedia. This extraordinary participatory event (over 100 locals were invited from all sections of the community) was, amongst other things, a form of public confession on the part of the Council that the economic development vision of the early 1980s had failed on two counts. It had not created economic prosperity beyond a narrow range of middle-class beneficiaries, and it had not provided a culturally inclusive representation of the city, which left many of its communities feeling invisible and resentful. The challenge, then, was to work together to create a new vision and set of policies that would shift attention from downtown regeneration to the neighbourhoods, and that would involve and acknowledge Birmingham's empirically changed identity as a multicultural, postcolonial city.

It was at this point that I became involved as a consultant to the city, and began to learn about its heart and soul. And I confess to a fondness for the city, though I've never lived there: a fondness for the Brummie spirit of determination, for the life on its neighbourhood streets, the city pride of its citizens, and the willingness to be critical about itself. Having spent time there, talking with a wide variety of its citizens, (politicians and planners, young people, community activists, artists, rock musicians, entrepreneurs, academics, of Anglo, South Asian, Afro-Carribean and other descents) I have a more empathic take on the city than I would if I'd read about it in the case study literatures of urban economic geographers, political economists, or planners.[7] Face to face, one is confronted with hard human choices, the fugitive abundance of life in spite of hardship, and the refusal of real places to conform to preconceived systems.

Chapter 7 resumes where this story now leaves off. There I will talk about what it takes to reinvent or transform a city-region, and whether Birmingham is headed in the right direction, in terms of its own espoused ideals. Let me now reflect on the historical narrative so far, which I intend as an illustration of the dilemmas and challenges facing the multiethnic and multicultural cities of the 21st century. No city can stand as an archetype for all cities. That would counter my belief in the paramount importance of context, of specificity of time and place. Nevertheless, as a narrative trope, I do ask Birmingham to serve as my springboard, as a lesson in the lineaments and stress fractures of late capitalism, postcoloniality, and cultural pluralism in all of their inseparable dimensions . . .

What Birmingham shared with other western industrial cities in the latter half of the twentieth century (Melbourne, Toronto, Rotterdam, Los Angeles, Chicago, Cleveland . . .) was a Fordist economic base (mass production, assembly lines, unionized workforce, decent wages); a welfare state umbrella; a modernizing urban fabric (freeways, car dependence, separation of land uses, increasingly monofunctional downtowns); an expanding immigrant population with cultural backgrounds distinctly different from the dominant culture; residential segregation by class, race and ethnic markers; a patriarchal political and social order and masculinist popular culture; and a modernist belief that this was the best of all possible worlds. But the City of Everyman began to be unsettled in the 1970s by economic and socio-cultural forces that began to reshape the urban economy, the fabric of the built environment, and the fabric of social relations. This unsettling, this destabilizing, has been in train for more than three decades and shows no sign of abating.

It takes time to get a clear view of the changes we are collectively living through. How we understand and think about these changes and their associated challenges obviously affects our capacity to respond to them. Ultimately this book is focused on the domain of the city-building professions and on cities themselves. In this chapter I am establishing the groundwork: both what has been happening in western cities,[8] and how architects and planners and urban policy-makers and politicians have responded. Have the intellectual, political, and emotional tools been adequate? In the next section I outline in more general terms four major socio-cultural forces at work in the reshaping of western cities: international migration; the discourse of postcolonialism; the resurgence of indigenous peoples; and the rise of civil society. In the section following, I argue that the economic and demographic restructurings since the 1970s – the transformation of an industrial and modernist landscape into a postindustrial and postmodern one – requires a parallel restructuring of our thinking about cities and planning, and about the modern state. Slowly the paradoxes of modernization and of modernism will unfold.

THE SOCIO-CULTURAL RE-SHAPING OF CITIES AND REGIONS

INTERNATIONAL MIGRATION

'The closing years of the twentieth century and the beginning of the twenty-first will be the age of migration'.

(Castles and Miller, 1998: 3)

International migration is not an invention of the late twentieth century, nor even of modernity in its twin guises of capitalism and colonialism. Migrations have been part of human history from the beginning. But there has been a growth in the volume and significance of migration since 1945, and again since the mid-1980s. An ensemble of factors has contributed to this: growing inequalities in wealth between North and South impel people to move in search of opportunities for work; political, ecological and demographic pressures force some people to seek refuge beyond their homeland; ethnic and religious struggles, like those in Sri Lanka, Ethiopia, and the former Yugoslavia, lead to mass exodus; and the creation of new free trade areas causes movements of labour. In some developing countries, emigration is one aspect of the social crisis that accompanies integration into the world market and modernization (Castles and Miller, 1998: 4). The result is cities and regions of extraordinary cultural diversity and the attendant problems of living together in one society for ethnic groups with diverse cultures and social practices. Migrations can change economic, demographic and social structures, and the associated cultural diversity can call into question long-standing notions of citizenship and national identity. Influxes of migrants lead eventually to the spatial restructuring of cities and regions, in which sometimes the very presence of new ethnic groups leads to the destabilizing of the existing social order. In this new 'ethnoscape' (Appadurai, 1990: 7), ambivalent new communities are thrust together with anxiously nostalgic old ones, and xenophobic fears can quickly turn into territorially based racist politics as the new mix of cultures projects itself onto the urban landscape (Jacobs, 1996; Cross and Keith, 1993).

When residents with different histories, cultures, and needs appear in 'our' cities, their presence disrupts the taken-for-granted categories of social life and urban space. The urban experiences of new immigrants, their struggles to redefine the conditions of belonging to 'their' new society, are reshaping cities the world over, and not only the so-called 'world cities' (Knox and Taylor, 1995) or 'global cities' (Sassen, 1995) of the advanced capitalist economies (Los Angeles, London, New York) but also the second- and third-order cities (Melbourne, Vancouver, Birmingham, Rotterdam, Berlin . . .). As new and more complex kinds of ethnic diversity come to dominate cities, the very notion of a 'shared interest' may come increasingly into question. These struggles over belonging take the form of struggles over citizenship, in its broadest sense, of rights to and in the polis. James Holston (1998) has called the sites of these struggles 'spaces of insurgent citizenship'.

Citizenship changes as new members emerge to advance their claims, expanding its realm, and as new forms of segregation and violence counter these advances, eroding it. The sites of insurgent citizenship are found at the intersection of these processes of expansion and erosion.
(Holston, 1998: 48).

These sites vary with time and place. Today they include ethnic neighbourhoods, suburban migrant labour camps, sweatshops, places of worship, and the zones of the new racism (which does not exhaust the list). The multicultural (multiethnic, multiracial) city is continually creating these sites of struggle. They are part of *the landscape of postmodernity, which is a landscape marked by difference.* Negotiating these spaces, claiming them, making them safe, imprinting new identities on them, is today a central sociocultural and political dynamic of cities, a dynamic in which the planning system is deeply implicated.

The twentieth-century role of planning has been to regulate the production and use of space. In this state-designated role, planners have acted as spatial police, regulating not only land uses but, often, who – that is, what categories of people – might use that land; thereby regulating *bodies* in space, administering who can do what and be where, and even, when. There are at least four different ways in which multicultural, polyethnic cities challenge existing planning systems, policies and practices. First, the values and norms of the dominant culture are typically embedded in the legislative frameworks of planning, in planning bylaws and regulations. *The planning system thus unreflectively expresses the norms of the culturally dominant majority, including the norms of how that majority likes to use space.* Second, the norms and values of the dominant culture are embodied in the attitudes, behaviour and everyday practices of actual, flesh-and-blood planners. If planners believe that immigrants should adapt as quickly as possible to the life-ways of the dominant culture, then they are unlikely to be sensitive to or sympathetic regarding new ways of belonging in the city, new forms of place-making. Third, the xenophobia and racism that can exist in any neighbourhood of any city may find an expression or outlet through the planning system, in the form of a planning dispute over, say, the location of a mosque or Hindu temple, the nature and location of burial practices, retailing practices, recreational preferences, and so on. How can the planning system, and planners, respond in constructive ways to such conflicts? Fourth, and most intransigent, what happens when citizens and planners come up against cultural practices that are incompatible with their own deeply held values? (Sandercock, 2000a). Chapter 6 deals at length with these issues, outlining a number of possible ways of responding to such challenges. That chapter also tackles what are arguably the two most underexplored questions in the public discourse on international migration and its urban impacts: better and more meaningful opportunities for immigrants to become full members of host societies, and far greater emphasis on effective intergroup relations – 'goals that are at the very heart of successful pluralist democracies' (Papademetriou, 2002: 10).

THE DISCOURSE OF POSTCOLONIALISM: OLD AND NEW WORLD POSTCOLONIALITIES

Consider some recent events from five different countries, Old World and New:

- In the summer of 2001, three northern British cities (Burnley, Oldham, and Bradford) were the sites of so-called race riots of sufficient magnitude of personal injury and property damage that the national government established an independent inquiry, an inter-departmental Ministerial Group on Public Order and Community Cohesion, which asked how these fractured communities might become more cohesive.[9]

- In the spring of 2002, the 'candidate of the people', Jean-Marie Le Pen, earned the right to challenge Jacques Chirac for the presidency of France. Le Pen's politics – France for the French, a strong French state free of the European Union, overseeing a system to benefit 'native' French and excluding immigrants – might be described as appealing to a 'coalition of the fearful'. He argues that if France stopped immigration and expelled its illegal immigrants, unemployment and crime would cease to be problems.[10]

- In May 2002, in the Netherlands, a rising political star, Pym Fortuyn, was assassinated in Rotterdam. Fortuyn, who was openly gay, had risen quickly to public prominence by being openly critical of Muslim immigrants in the Netherlands, arguing that their values threatened to undermine Dutch tolerance and liberalism. He worried that Islam was anti-feminist and anti-gay. His message to immigrants was 'The Netherlands is Full', and he believed that asylum seekers should be given no more than a tent and some food.[11]

- In May 2002, Denmark, a country which had prided itself as an immigrants' haven, dumped its liberal asylum policies in favour of a law designed to prevent all but a few foreigners from settling there: thereby ending its reputation as a pioneer of multiculturalism.[12]

- In mid-2001, the Australian prime minister, John Howard, refused to allow a boatload of refugees from the Middle East to set foot on Australian soil. His hard-line stance won his party the national election months later. Subsequently, he has proposed (what the media immediately labelled) a 'Pacific solution' to the refugee problem. Australia should buy or lease an island in the Pacific and deposit all refugees there while they await adjudication of their claim – a zero tolerance attitude to uninvited refugees.[13] There is a line item in the 2002 federal budget to cover this expense. Australia's reputation as a tolerant multicultural society has plummeted accordingly.

The first three of these episodes all flag a link between immigration and a prior colonial history. Since granting independence to their colonies, each of these European heartlands has been the site of immigration of former colonial subjects from the periphery. But the Australian case (as well as Canada, New Zealand, and the USA) is different. Each of this latter group was once a colony subordinate to the rule of Great Britain. Each has been a country that has officially welcomed, indeed depended on, immigration for its growth, while always strictly controlling the kinds of immigrants who were welcome. For most of the twentieth century, skin colour was a key criterion (for example, the 'White Australia' immigration policy was not ended until the late 1960s), thereby reproducing the exclusions and segregations of the former empires of which they were part. In what sense, then, is it accurate to talk of an age of postcolonialism?

We need to establish an empirical distinction between the colonial and the postcolonial. Empirically speaking the 'colonial' comprises the formal, institutional, racialized governmentalities of the imperial 'Age of Europe 1492–1945' (West, 1990). The empirical 'postcolonial' refers to the formal disestablishment of the colonial institutional arrangements, the official moments of decolonization and racial desegregation (Hesse, 2000: 12). But clearly a colonial mentality, and governmentality, has lingered on in other forms. It therefore makes sense to talk conceptually of an unresolved postcolonial condition in the former heartlands of empire (the European capitals) as well as in New World settler societies. The transition from western imperialisms to the ostensible universalism of western democracies has in fact been a transition to *already racialized* liberal democracies in which the persistence of institutionalized racism, not to mention individual prejudice, has enormously complicated the politics of immigration and the social integration of immigrants, let alone the treatment of indigenous populations. The racism implicit in the eighteenth-century Euro-American Enlightenment project of 'civilizing' the supposedly uncivilized parts of the globe endures, and in that sense we have not arrived at an age of postcolonialism.

What has to be acknowledged, then, is the enduring historical connection between empire, immigration, labour markets, and racism. What has to be remembered in discussing the dilemmas of multiculturalism in the mongrel cities of the 21st century is that these cities are embedded in already-racialized western liberal democracies, countries in which there is a history of regarding the cultural/racial/ethnic Other as inferior, less civilized – in popular parlance 'not like us' and 'not one of us'. In the economic expansion of the 1950s, British, French, Dutch and other European societies manned their factories with immigrant labour from their former colonies, but were less than comfortable about the presence of those strange immigrant bodies in their streets and neighbourhoods. In all of these countries, 'race relations' became a problem that needed managing, and a sequence of policies ensued, from assimilation to multiculturalism, none of which were entirely successful because none dealt with the residues of colonialism, the lingering colonial mentality. Other European countries such as Germany with its expanding postwar economy, as well as countries in the New World, experienced similar issues (albeit with different policy responses) because each and every one of these had been predicated, albeit unconsciously, on a founding identity as a White Nation.[14]

In the last decade of the twentieth and into the 21st century, the same issue – of integration, of intercultural co-existence at close range – reappears in European, Japanese, and New World cities where, now because of aging population profiles (Papademetriou, 2002), there aren't enough young workers in the service industries to physically take care of aging baby boomer bodies, and not enough young working tax payers to economically maintain the pension benefits for these aging populations. Thus are long-held notions of national identity – notions that assumed affinity, shared history, homogeneity – being profoundly unsettled. And this unsettling has its most concrete expression in cities and neighbourhoods, in the form of conflicts over space itself, and over services, signage and symbols in the urban environment.

This book takes it as a given that this migration trend is politically and humanly irreversible in the medium to long-term, even if there are short-term resistances.[15] The challenge then, for urban populations, is to co-exist with difference, finding better pathways to integration, adjusting notions of citizenship and national as well as local identity – what it means to be a Brummie as well as what it means to be British, for example.

THE RESURGENCE OF INDIGENOUS PEOPLES

In New World settlements the world over, in the era of colonialism, settlers usually occupied space at the expense of existing inhabitants, who were referred to as 'native' and regarded as 'primitive'. While the details of colonial occupations vary, the process of city-building and the clearing of regions for farming and other extractive industries required an ordering of urban and regional space by a whole range of spatial technologies of power such as the laws of private property, the practices of surveying, naming, mapping, and the procedures of urban and regional planning. The effects of these various sorts of legal and/or violent arrangements and appropriations were the effective dispossession and exclusion of indigenous peoples – the original inhabitants of these lands. The desire to establish settler colonies depended upon 'the will of erasure' or, when that failed, the 'systematic containment' of the original inhabitants (Jacobs, 1996: 105). In the United States and Canada, 'treaties' were struck with Indian nations, who were then forced onto reservations. In Australia, 'this erasure was inaugurated by the notion of *terra nullius*, land unoccupied, which became the foundational fantasy of the Australian colonies' (*ibid.*). Spatial segregation of indigenous peoples was the almost universal intent of colonizers, but that intent was only ever imperfectly realized – not least because the colonized, the indigenous peoples, were at various times essential as guides for colonists' explorations of 'the interior' and then as labour for farms, stations, mines, and construction projects, in times and places of labour shortage. So segregation quickly gave way to more disorderly and permeable spatial arrangements in which individuals or groups found their way into cities and settled areas, occupying what came to be the 'unseen' or unincorporated parts of the city, or the fringes of urban areas or country towns (*ibid.*: 106).

The dominant settler culture's land-based interests were represented by the emerging planning practices of the colonial era, practices which asserted non-indigenous control over aboriginal domains and concepts of space and place. Research by Jackson (1998) in Broome and Darwin, two towns in north Australia, has demonstrated how land use discourse has identified, mapped, and delimited representations of aboriginal people's socio-spatial relations through processes of closure, containment and regulation. Practices that began in the nineteenth century were still at work in the late twentieth,[16] and 'as indigenous communities attempt to negotiate or contest planning systems, fundamental aspects of their modernist and colonial origins are brought to the foreground (Jackson,

1998: i). The invisibility of aboriginal aspirations from contemporary land use plans (such as those for Broome and Darwin), far from being an innocent or unfortunate oversight, is central to the cultural politics of the area and says much about planning's complicity in excluding aboriginal people from access to decision-making processes (*ibid*.: 226). Equally profoundly, this invisibility raises the question of whether planning's practices have ever been decolonized, in this supposed age of postcolonialism.

Since the 1970s, there has been a global movement on the part of indigenous peoples to reverse these foundational injustices and dispossessions. At the heart of this movement are land claims that are potentially destabilizing of established practices of land use planning, land management, and private property law – all of which are found at the core of planning practice. While most of these land claims have been lodged and contested in relatively remote regions,[17] where they may clash with mining and farming interests, there are also urban implications and sitings of these postcolonial struggles. Jacobs (1996) details a case in Perth, (a city of almost one million, capital of its province, on the West coast of Australia), in the late 1980s, in which a former brewery came to be seen by the then state government as a heritage site and as a perfect opportunity for recycling the existing structures for use as a tourist/leisure centre featuring restaurants, retail outlets and galleries. This vision was confounded by aboriginal claims that the site was the home of the Waugal serpent; that is, an aboriginal site of significance which must be protected.[18] For almost a year aboriginal people from the Perth region occupied the site and residents and urban authorities were confronted with the unexpected presence of the aboriginal sacred in the city.

The aboriginal sense of the sacred is deeply antagonistic to urban modernity's need to keep the sacred apart from the secular and to regulate it as if it were just another land use. While aboriginal protests failed on this occasion, and development proceeded, subsequent events on the national stage in the 1990s – what has come to be known as the Mabo decision and the subsequent Native Title Act of 1993 – have even more profoundly unbound existing laws governing the ownership and use of land, 'dismantling the established spatial architecture of existing land rights provisions . . . which comfortably placed a spiritualized, "tribalized", lands-rights deserving, Aboriginality well away from the urban centers' (Jacobs, 1996: 112).

In the claims of indigenous peoples for the return of, or access to, their lands, planners are confronted with values incommensurable with modernist planning and the modernization project which it serves, a planning which privileges 'development' and in which exchange value usually triumphs over use value. If the voices and desires of indigenous peoples are to be respected, acknowledged, and *honoured*, the foundations of the modernist planning paradigm itself must be drastically revised. This story continues with a case study in inner Sydney in Chapter 7.

THE RISE OF ORGANIZED CIVIL SOCIETY

Beginning in the 1970s, a new wave of feminist writing and activism began to deconstruct the city as it had come to be understood in modernist thought. The spatial order of the modern industrial city came to be seen as a profoundly patriarchal spatial order; that is, an arrangement of space in which the domination of men over women was written into the architecture, urban design, and form of the city. Cities built and planned by men for men, confined women to the suburbs, to the home, to the private sphere, and then, having segregated them, doubly disadvantaged them by not recognizing that their needs in the city were different from those of men, based as they were primarily around home, neighbourhood and caring for children and the elderly. From the routes of public transport to the location of key educational, cultural, and health facilities in downtown urban centres, cities and their planning processes could be seen as excluding women from participation. Not surprisingly then, urban social movements advocating women's needs in the city – needs for more and better public transport, for child care, for community facilities, for safety, for a right to occupy public space, day and night, and so on – have flourished since the 1970s. This critical onslaught, combined with social activism, and subsequent demands to engender planning practices,[19] at first seemed containable within a modernist paradigm. Feminist planners working within the planning system addressed themselves both to raising the consciousness of male colleagues and to the identifiable demands of the feminist urban social movements described above. We swapped 'war stories' and gave each other support at conferences, and in coffee shops. We made some progress, and shared many disappointments and frustrations.

But then, as of the early 1980s, something profoundly destabilizing happened. The 'we' of feminist urban analysis was challenged by 'Other women' who argued that the 'we' had never included 'them'. These were the voices of women of colour, of lesbians, and of the physically challenged, who claimed that the voices who had hitherto represented 'women' were really only representing the white, middle-class, able-bodied, heterosexual and nuclear family-oriented, and metropolitan-based women who actually already lived relatively privileged lives, and whose very privilege was usually built on the 'backs' of women of colour/third world women who cleaned their houses, did their shopping and sometimes cooked for them, and looked after their children. These 'voices from the borderlands',[20] the voices of women who are in one way or another on the margins (Sandercock 1995a, 1998a), are part of the fourth major challenge to the modernist planning paradigm – the rise of civil society.

The re-emergence of the women's movement in the past 30 years is simply one among a number of important social movements that have arisen in this period – to combat racism and homophobia, to prevent the destruction of natural and built environments, to reverse the discrimination against the physically challenged, and more.[21] This rise of civil society has radically altered the political and cultural climate in which we work as planners (Douglass and Friedmann, 1998). It presents a countervailing force to the power of the state and to the planning ideology of technical rationality. It challenges previous notions of social planning which had revolved around top-down provision, design, and delivery of community services. Insofar as spatial public policy impacts adversely on the concerns of any of these social movements, they have mobilized against it, against both the policies and the processes of modernist planning. The voices from the borderlands inhabit and embody the new cultural politics of difference, complicating that politics with their intersectionalities of race, class, ethnicity, gender, and sexual preference formations of 'difference'. Together they suggest that social justice in post-modern cities and regions is inseparable from a respect for, and an engagement with, these social movements, and with the politics of identity and difference. That politics constitutes a challenge to the theory of democracy underpinning twentieth-century western racialized liberal democracies. The nature of this challenge will be further explored in Chapter 4.

Each of the socio-cultural changes discussed so far has helped to re-shape modernist cities by contesting taken-for-granted uses of space and challenging accepted notions of who belongs where, doing what, in the public spaces of the city. Each of them is also intricately interwoven, as cause and effect, with the crisis of modernization itself, which is a crisis not only of Fordist industrialism but also of a whole system of belief – modernism – and its related social order. How might planning praxis – that is, a theoretically informed practice – engage with all of the transformations described above? To answer that we must journey further into the modernist mindset and explore its relations with the city and with the articles of faith and the practices of the city-building professions.

THE MODERNIST CITY, THE MODERN STATE, AND MODERNIST PLANNING

A few years ago I flew over the city in a helicopter with fellow city planners. Why couldn't all this be different, we asked: why should this house, this street, stay where it is? An unjustifiable, irrational city – untidy, crowded, anarchic. Let's put air ducts into its gasping lungs: let's relieve its clogged arteries and cut through its concentric circles. Traffic is choking its inner core: it is cowardly and sentimental to want to spare its undulating and redundant mysteries. This is the eleventh hour, time for major surgery. We managed to rearrange the city down to the last grain of sand. Upheavals of imagination erupted under our fingers. Then we came down and saw under our giant dragonfly mountains of smoke, whirling dust.

(Konrad, 1977)

Oh, what a lovely paradox! By means of the critical spirit, the moderns have invented at one and the same time the total system, the total revolution to put an end to the system, and the equally total failure to carry out that revolution – a failure that leaves them in total postmodern despair! . . . the critics have imagined that we were incapable of tinkering, reshuffling, crossbreeding and sorting.

(Latour, 1993: 126)

A dozen years before the fall of the Berlin Wall signalled the symbolic end of the hopes that had been invested in Socialism, and the system of central planning that was its core, the anti-hero of Hungarian George Konrad's novel, *The City Builder*, endures his own crisis of conscience. In a harrowing monologue that runs the length of the novel, this unnamed anti-hero, this twentieth-century architect/city planner in an unnamed East European city, considers his life, his work, and the many-layered history of the city he and his family – architect/planners all – have contributed to shaping. The narrator/anti-hero carries on an impassioned dialogue, in his mind, with the city, cursing and praising, excusing and lamenting. This city-builder's ruthless honesty and intelligence, his awareness of having contributed to a system whose inhumanities he can neither condone nor deny, make him, in a sense, the battleground where modernist ideas (and idealism), always looking to the future, are locked in confrontation with what James Holston calls the heterogeneous and ethnographic present (Holston, 1998).

The modernist city, as both achievement and failure, has always been fraught with ambiguity. How – as a child of the Enlightenment, whose faith in progress through Reason led planners to dream of the Rational City – could it be otherwise? On the one hand, all the advantages of sanitation, engineering, electricity, factories producing goods for mass consumption; and the sheer exhilaration of speed, movement, change, freedom. On the other, destruction of the past, of continuity, community and tradition; freeways, air pollution, machines, noise, alienation, anomie. I want to do several things in the closing section of this chapter. One is to convey the radical magnificence of the Enlightenment or modernist project. Another is to trace its implications in the modernist city and in the articles of faith of modernist planning and architecture, to ask what was missing, what was concealed, and what was lost in (the intent and practices of) designing, building, and administering the Rational City. Finally I wrestle with what might be preserved, and what must be discarded of the modernist paradigm in city-building.

THE RADICAL MAGNIFICENCE

Three words: 'Dare to know!' The words of Immanuel Kant, the year 1784. Kant, in these three words, had thrown down the gauntlet to the authority of the Church, the State, the aristocracy, to tradition and superstition, and asserted the supreme power of human reason (as had others before him – Rousseau, Voltaire, Montesquieu, Diderot, Leibniz, among the best known). These gentlemen (and there were some gentlewomen, for example the magnificent Emilie du Châtelet, but that's another story) of the Enlightenment questioned what it meant to be human, what it meant to be a member of a society, and argued for the rights of man, for liberty, equality and fraternity, and for religious tolerance. The modernist project to which the Enlightenment gave birth was a project pregnant with immense possibility. Marshall Berman has captured this best in his account of the dynamic and dialectical nature of modernism, the contradictory forces and needs that inspire and torment us:

our desire to be rooted in a stable and coherent personal and social past, and our insatiable desire for growth, not merely for economic growth but for growth in experience, in pleasure, in knowledge, in sensibility – growth that destroys both the physical and social landscape of our past, and our emotional links with those lost worlds; our desperate allegiances to ethnic, national, class and sexual groups which we hope will give us a firm 'identity', and the internationalization of everyday life – of our clothes and household goods, our books and music, our ideas and fantasies – that spreads all our identities all over the map; our desire for clear and solid values to live by, and our desire to embrace the limitless possibilities of modern life and experience that obliterate all values; . . . a world where, as Marx said, 'everything is pregnant with its contrary' and 'all that is solid melts into air'.

(Berman, 1982: 35–6).

If this expresses the best of modernist thought, let us now turn to . . .

THE LACUNAE

Modernism has received a bad rap since the 1960s, since Herbert Marcuse, Michel Foucault, and many others put the boot in. Foucault's microscopic attention to modern technologies of power, particularly as exercised through state institutions and through the professions, is an utterly bleak account of the oppressions of modern life through the administrative ordering of society (Foucault, 1979; 1984; 1990). He exposes the dark side of the 'knowledge is power' mantra of the Enlightenment and shows how the tools of modern statecraft have locked us all in Weberian iron cages. An application of Foucauldian and other post-Enlightenment critiques to the city-building professions of the twentieth century paints a grim picture.

Through the nineteenth century the apparatus of the modern state began to be assembled, in tandem with the modernization project (industrialization) that was meant to liberate humankind. The new conception of the state's role that had emerged out of the Enlightenment was the idea that a central purpose of the state was the improvement of all members of society, their health, skills, education, longevity, productivity, even their morals and family life. An Enlightenment belief in the perfectibility of Man became, by degrees, a belief in the perfectibility of the social order. One avenue for achieving and expressing this transformation was the comprehensive planning of human settlements, the rational ordering of the modernist city. As James Scott (1998) has explained, modernist thinking about the city tended to see rational order in visual and aesthetic terms – an efficient, rationally organized village or city was one that looked regimented and orderly, orthogonal and geometric. The high priest of such thinking in the twentieth century, when the technology emerged to match the scale of the ambition, was Le Corbusier, and his organizational voice was CIAM, the Congrès Internationaux d'Architecture Moderne.

The CIAM manifestos from the 1920s to the 1940s, and particularly *The Athens Char-ter* (1941), identified lack of urban planning as 'the cause of the anarchy that reigns in the organization of cities and the equipment of industry'. CIAM doctrine was at its most radical in its intention of controlling land speculation and thereby abolishing the ultim-ate power of private interests to block planning initiatives. With the power of private property interests eliminated, architect-planners would be able to assume a position of unchallenged authority over the city's destiny. Their plans would become blueprints, based on the planner's presumed ability to control the future through rationally guided action, and protected by the authority of the central state. Their plans would treat the city as a machine, much as an engineer goes about designing an industrial process, breaking the city down into its essential functions (housing, work, recreation, and traffic) that would be standardized, eventually to be reassembled in the Master Plan as a totality. The totalizing scope of CIAM-style modernist planning derived from this conception of the city as a machine. The new architecture set out to redefine the social basis of each urban function, refusing any accommodation to existing urban and social, let alone environmental, conditions.

The break with the past was intended to be absolute. In Le Corbusier's 1925 plan for the reconstruction of central Paris, or in Hilberseimer's 1927 project for central Berlin, 'an enormous area has simply been leveled to make room for the insertion of a new and complete environment' (Holston, 1989: 53). This was to be a new style of planning, liberated from history. Although neither of these plans was implemented, they evoke images of post-World War II redevelopment, as well as of an earlier era of totalizing planning, Haussmann's rebuilding of Paris in the 1870s.[22] As James Holston demonstrates in *The Modernist City* (1989), principles of decontextualization, denial of history and of everyday life rhythms were central to the vision of these modernists, and techniques of shock and defamiliarization were to be used to achieve the vision. Underpinning the whole modernist enterprise was a faith in the state as the benign agency for implementation of master plans. It was through an all-powerful technocratic state that planners would realize their dream of a future dominated by Reason.

Holston's critique of modernist urbanism is a powerful one, but it is based on two extreme examples, that of Le Corbusier's thought as representative, and that of Brasilia as a built exemplar. There have been many other devastating critiques (Peattie, 1987; Scott, 1998; Hooper, 1998). One of the earliest came from Jane Jacobs, whose *Death and Life of Great American Cities* (1962) was really a critique of the damage that Robert Moses (a latter-day Hausmann) was doing to the urban and human fabric of New York, from the Bronx to her beloved Greenwich Village. Her argument for urban diversity and complexity, for apparent visual chaos or jumble, was a diatribe against the modern planners' practice of separating land uses and thereby separating housing from shops from places of work from recreation; in other words, a critique of postwar American suburbia. A decade later, sociologist Richard Sennett wrote of the city as a necessarily anarchic system which planners were far too obsessed with ordering and controlling. Sennett accused planners of being afraid of, or uncomfortable with, life's ambiguities, and therefore of overly 'disciplining' (to borrow from Foucault) the city. He argued that the accepted ideal of order generates patterns of behaviour that are stultifying, narrow, and violence-prone, and he proposed a city that can incorporate diversity and creative disorder to bring into being adults who can openly respond to and deal with the challenges of life (Sennett, 1970).

Feminists too have had a field day with the masculinist symbolism and spatial arrangements of the modernist city. Barbara Hooper, for example, writes of Haussmann and other urban reformers of late nineteenth-century Paris, and continuing through to Le Corbusier, as inventing a discipline (urban planning) in which mind is at war with the thwartings of body (Hooper, 1998). Further, body is always gendered as female. In Paris, Hooper writes, 'in the texts of planners, public hygienists, sanitation engineers, city fathers ... female, female body became synonymous with that which disorders, threatens, undoes the work of Man, the idea of the plan'. In the dominant binary tradition of the West in which planning is located,

... order has been authored as Reason's order, with reason set forth as something real, something that proceeds from mind, something different from and superior to the chaotic sensings and respondings of body, the realm of female and female's analogical correlates: the lower orders, savages and primitives, desires, animals, irrationality, dreams, magics, confusions, and most dangerously, uncontrolled sexuality.

(Hooper, 1998: 247)

Holston's and Hooper's readings of the origins of modern planning doctrine, in both nineteenth-century Paris and the later manifestos of Le Corbusier and CIAM, clue us in to one source of twentieth-century inspiration for city-building, a source that was most influential in the training of architects and urban designers. The parallel source for the profession of urban planning (in North America)[23] was the approach that emerged in the immediate post-1945 era at the University of Chicago, whose social-science-based Program of Education and Research in Planning became the model for planning education for the next 40 years. The Chicago model, as developed by its first luminaries, teachers and reformers like Rexford Tugwell and Harvey Perloff, was a comprehensive, rational model of problem-solving and decision-making to guide state intervention. The intent of the modernist planning project, institutionalized as a form of state intervention, was to ameliorate the excesses of industrial capitalism and to mediate the intramural frictions among capitalists that had resulted in a city inefficiently organized for production and reproduction. Underlying these reformist intentions were 'procedural assumptions and substantive commitments that sealed the fate of planning as a modernist project' (Beauregard, 1989: 384).

The seminal expression of the Chicago model is Perloff's *Education for Planning* (1957), which defines planning as 'optimization and allocation of resources among various public activities according to objective standards rather than solely on the basis of political pressure' (Perloff, 1957: 143). Employing these 'objective standards', which were seen as generically and globally applicable to any and all of the developmental problems of cities and regions and 'less-advanced countries', planning would master the environment, 'shaping the habitats of urban man and bringing natural resources into the service of man's own needs' (*ibid.*: 141). The planning process was meant to triumph over both politics and nature with its rational decision-making and problem-solving techniques, grounded in rigorous social analysis. Knowledge in planning would precede and shape the actions taken by investors, households, and governments. Knowledge and reason would liberate societies from ideologies, superstitions, prejudices. 'The aim of modernist planners was to act as experts who could utilize the laws of development to provide societal guidance' (Beauregard, 1989: 385).

We can summarize the Chicago model as containing six pillars of planning wisdom.[24]

1. Planning – meaning city and regional planning – was concerned with making public/political decisions more rational. The focus, therefore, was predominantly on advanced decision-making, on developing visions of the future, and on an instrumental rationality that carefully considered and evaluated options and alternatives.

2. Planning was most effective when it was comprehensive. Comprehensiveness was written into planning legislation and referred to multifunctional/multisectoral spatial plans as well as to the intersection of economic, social, environmental and physical planning. The planning function was seen as integrative, coordinative, and hierarchical.

3. Planning was both a science and an art, based on experience, but the emphasis was usually placed on the science. Planners' authority derived in large measure from a mastery of theory and methods in the social sciences. Planning knowledge and expertise were thus grounded in positive science, with its propensity for quantitative modelling and analysis.

4. Planning, as part of the modernization project, was a project of state-directed futures, with the state seen as possessing progressive, reformist tendencies, and as being separate from the economy.

5. Planning operated in 'the public interest' and planners' education privileged them in being able to identify what was in the public interest. Planners presented a public image of neutrality, and planning policies, based in positivist science, were believed to be gender- and race-neutral.

6. Planning stood apart from politics, and was regarded as value-neutral.

We might call this the heroic model of planning. It invoked the spirit of a Daniel Burnham, with his exhortation to 'make no little plans', or a Robert Moses, who argued that 'sometimes you have to hack your way through the city with a meat axe'. It was a vision of planning in the service of modernization, industrialization, of material growth as progress. But since the mid-1960s, these 'pillars' experienced a series of seismic shocks that began to undermine them. Processes of socio-cultural change began to reshape cities and regions in ways not dreamt of in the Chicago model of the rational, orderly, homogeneous city. Citizens increasingly rebelled against both the process of planning embodied in this model, and many of its outcomes. Developments in social theory across the humanities and social sciences challenged some of the fundamental assumptions of the modernist project and its epistemological foundations.[25] And many city dwellers grew angry as they sensed a loss. Modernist city builders, imbued with the CIAM metaphor of the city as a machine for living, had turned their backs on the city of memory, the city of desire, and the city of spirit. In a cosily complicit alliance with capital, they were ripping the heart and soul out of cities and neighbourhoods in the name of progress, of modernity.[26]

And yet, in spite of all this talk of being modernist, or perhaps precisely because of it, the *actual practices* of planning remained rather obscure. Could there have been a gap, all along, between the ideal and the reality? Indeed, when researchers looked at the actual practices, rather than the espoused ideal, what they discovered (and then rediscovered, decade after decade since at least 1955), is that as a profession (and to appropriate Bruno Latour), 'we have never been modern' – that is, planning practices have always been deeply interested rather than disinterested, deeply implicated in politics and in communicative acts. Martin Meyerson and Edward Banfield, of the (very same) Chicago School of

Planning, were the first to make this 'discovery', in *Planning, Politics and the Public Interest*, published in 1955. Bent Flyvbjerg, in his *Rationality and Power* (1998), a study of the operations of power 'distorting' environmental planning goals in Aalborg, Denmark, is perhaps the most recent.[27] This discovery, however, is potentially liberating. Far from merely 'reducing' planning to political interests, it allows us a new freedom, if we are prepared to grasp it. Planning is not reducible to 'political interests' because it does not simply *reflect* social forces. Rather, as a relatively new player, it redefines politics, producing new sources of power and legitimacy, changing the force field.[28] Here indeed is a lovely paradox. Planning, as part of the apparatus of the modern state, makes its own imprint, has its own powers for good *and* evil. Its competing visions of the good city, its rival ideologies, therefore do matter. Unmasked as nakedly political, planning activity can now accept the challenge of becoming *transparently* political.

It remains for me to ask how the properties of the now-defunct modernist planning paradigm might be transformed in light of this discovery, and this new challenge. And what might we call the result? Inspired by Rushdie, cautioned by Latour, I arrive at the notion of cross-breeding, mongrelization, hybridity. The following chapters do not reject the Enlightenment project *in toto*. But they begin with a more humble attitude. Gone is the modernist certainty about what's right for others. In its place is just one radical postmodern certainty – a belief in the virtues of a participatory, inclusive and always agonistic democratic process.[29] The following is a condensation of what will be developed in the rest of the book: fragments of a *Radical Postmodern Planning Practice*.

1. Means-ends rationality continues to be a useful concept – especially for building bridges and dams – but we need greater and more explicit reliance on *practical wisdom*.

2. Planning is no longer exclusively concerned with comprehensive, integrated, and coordinated plans but more with negotiated, political, and focused planning. This makes it *less document-oriented and more people-centered: deliberative as well as analytical*.

3. There are different kinds of appropriate knowledge in planning. Local communities have experiential, grounded, contextual, intuitive knowledges, manifested through speech, songs, stories, and various visual forms (from cartoons to graffiti, from bark paintings to videos). Planners have to learn to access these *other ways of knowing*.

4. The modernist reliance on state-directed futures is not misguided – we cannot do without the state – but it is not the whole story either. Community-based planning, geared to *community empowerment*, is an essential complement to and control over the hubris of top-down processes. But . . .

5. We also have to deconstruct both 'the public interest' and 'community', recognizing that each tends to exclude difference. We must acknowledge that there are *multiple publics* and that planning in this new multicultural arena requires new kinds of *multicultural literacy*. And . . .

6. Planning with multiple publics requires a new kind of democratic politics, more

participatory, more deliberative, and also more agonistic. Planners, and planning activity, are embedded in this politics and therefore operate in conjunction with citizens, politicians, and social movements, rather than standing apart from them.

The next two chapters of Part I lay the groundwork for a radical, postmodern practice, by recovering hidden histories of resistances to modernist planning and alternative histories of indigenous and progressive practices; by revising planning's knowledges, in the light of feminist, postmodern, and postcolonial critiques, in order to outline an epistemology of multiplicity, of many ways of knowing, for the mongrel cities of the 21st century; and by challenging the wisdom of planning's accepted traditions. My argument is directed at today's cities, not yesterday's. That means we need a different model of politics, action, participation, and imagination than the ones written in the last two centuries. Parts II and III take that on.

2

REWRITING PLANNING HISTORY

Official and insurgent stories

Subversive historiography connects oppositional practices from the past and forms of resistance in the present, thus creating spaces of possibility where the future can be imagined differently – imagined in such a way that we can witness ourselves dreaming, moving forward and beyond the limits of confines of fixed locations.

(bell hooks, 1994)

THE POWER OF HISTORY

Professions, like nations, keep their shape by moulding their members'/citizens' understanding of the past, causing them to forget those events which do not accord with a righteous image, while keeping alive those memories that do. Novelist Milan Kundera has said that the struggle of people against power is a struggle of memory against forgetting (Appleby, Hunt and Jacob, 1994: 270). For historians, the struggle of particular memories against particular exercises of omission or suppression also involves power. Stories about the past have power and bestow power. The impulse to tell new stories about the past points up the fact that time itself is a perspective in the construction of histories. Successive generations of scholars revise historical knowledge, investing it with contemporary meaning.

This chapter sets out to revise planning history, to offer not one 'official history' but many histories, to diversify both the themes and the subjects of these histories. If diversity, or difference, is a defining characteristic of multicultural cities, why is that not reflected in our accounts of city-building? For planners there is a further challenge. There are several senses in which history has power and bestows power. In constructing histories of itself, the planning profession is moulding its members' understanding of past struggles and triumphs, and simultaneously creating a contemporary professional culture around those memories, those stories. And in choosing to tell some stories rather than others, a professional identity is shaped, invested with meaning, and then defended. What are the erasures and exclusions implicit in the process of forging a professional identity? What are some of the hidden meanings and practices of planning, its *noir* face? In taking the planning dimensions of these debates further in this chapter, I concentrate primarily on the United States, for the sake of a single historical and geographical focus.

But because my argument is that the line of questioning is internationally pertinent, I will offer two examples of recent work, from Australia and South Africa, which tell radically different stories from the mainstream planning histories of those countries.

I begin with 'the official story' of planning history, the story that we desire to believe about ourselves. It is a heroic story. But is it a true story? Or is it a myth, a legend? At the very least, there is a *noir* side to this story, which also needs to be told. Further, the official story is the story of planning by and through the state, part of a particular tradition of city-building and nation-building. But there are, and always have been, alternative traditions of planning, existing outside the state and sometimes in opposition to it. These *insurgent planning histories* (Sandercock, 1995b; 1998) challenge our very definition of what constitutes planning. They also provide a foundation for an emerging alternative (to the modernist) paradigm for planning in multicultural cities. In that sense, they provide us with a 'future imaginary'.

THE OFFICIAL STORY

In the United States, a course in planning history is a required part of any professionally accredited planning programme. But what is it that students read in such courses? The sub-field of planning history has emerged as part of the discipline of planning (rather than as a sub-field of history, like urban history) only in the last 30 years. Since the first major works in the 1960s – J. W. Reps' *The Making of Urban America: A History of City Planning in the United States* (1965) and Mel Scott's *American City Planning since 1890* (1969) – interest in the field has grown and its scope has broadened. There are now many volumes of essays on the subject – the best-known and most widely used of which are those edited by Donald Krueckeberg, *The American Planner: Biographies and Recollections* (1983b) and *Introduction to Planning History in the United States* (1983a), and Daniel Schaffer, *Two Centuries of American Planning* (1988). There is a more recent bestseller by Peter Hall, *Cities of Tomorrow. An Intellectual History of Urban Planning and Design in the Twentieth Century* (1988), the scope of which goes well beyond US planning history. And there are a host of historical case studies of particular pieces of planning history, covering an era, an agency, a city, or a theme. Almost without exception these studies come from within planning,[1] and are unabashedly modernist in their orientation. What does this mean?

What is planning history? What constitutes its proper field of inquiry? The answer given by the historians identified above is a fairly simple one: to chronicle the rise of the planning profession, its institutionalization, and its achievements. There are various strands to these histories: from the emergence of the profession itself, to accounts of the key ideas and/or people (always great men) shaping the emergence of planning, to histories of specific policies within the field, housing, transportation, garden cities, and so on. All of these works employ a descriptive approach in which the rise of planning is presented as a heroic, progressive narrative, part of the rise of liberal democracy with its belief in progress through science and technology and faith that 'the rational planning of ideal social orders' can achieve equality, liberty and justice (Harvey, 1989: 11–13). The choice of individual hero or heroes in these narratives is quite eclectic, with some championing Ebenezer Howard, others Patrick Geddes or Le Corbusier, as the founding fathers of the profession, and most giving prominence to such local heroes as Daniel Burnham, Frederick Olmsted and Robert Moses. But beyond these individuals, planning itself is the real hero, battling foes from left and right, slaying the dragons of greed and irrationality and, if not always triumphing, at least always noble, on the side of the angels.

In these modernist portraits of planning, which I have referred to elsewhere as mainstream planning history (Sandercock, 1995b; 1998), planning has no fatal flaws. If battles are sometimes, or even often, lost, it is not the fault of the hero but of the evil world in which he must operate. Common to these mainstream histories are the following characteristics. The role of planning and of planners is unproblematic. It is assumed that planning is 'a good thing', a progressive practice, and that its opponents are reactionary, irrational, or just plain greedy. It is assumed that planners know what is good for people and possess an expertise that ought to prevail (in a 'rational' society, at least) over politics. It is taken for granted that planners have agency – that what they do and think has autonomy and power. It is seen as natural and right that planning should be 'solution-driven', rather than attentive to the social construction of what are held to be 'urban problems'. There is no scrutiny of the ideology, the class or gender, race or ethnic origins or biases of planners, or of the class, gender, or ethnic effects of their work. The rise of the profession is a cause for celebration rather than critical scrutiny.

For example, Mel Scott's *American City Planning Since 1890* outlines what have become the traditional themes of US planning historiography: beginning with the attempts to grapple with issues of urban sanitation, slum housing, and population concentration on the part of late nineteenth-century reformers and settlement house workers; followed by transformations in the city's built environment according to the standards of the City Beautiful campaign in the early part of the twentieth century; the development of a 'scientific' foundation for the profession under the crusade of the City Functional movement; the emergence of planning at regional and national scales by mid-century; and finally, a call for a renewed human-centred comprehensiveness. In this sweeping narrative, Scott offers the history of urban planning practice as an almost seamless evolutionary continuum in which ideas take root, mature into legislative proposals, which in turn give birth to planning agencies and institutions, which must then develop procedures of policy implementation. Along the way there are many obstacles, which the hero, with his 'will to plan', must overcome.[2]

Peter Hall's *Cities of Tomorrow* chooses a dozen major themes, rounding up all the usual suspects – slum and sanitation reform, the garden city, the City Beautiful, the birth of regional planning, the Le Corbusian city of towers, the automobile city, and more – and devotes a chapter to each. His method is to trace these themes to the ideas of a few 'visionaries', most of whom lived and wrote in the decades straddling the dawn of the twentieth century, and then to follow the fate of these grand ideas and visions as others (implicitly lesser mortals) seek to implement them. Hall's main theme, which he describes as 'the real interest in history', is individual human agency. He wants to show,

in the face of what he calls the economic reductionism of Marxist historians, that individuals can and do make a difference, 'especially the most intelligent and most original
among them' (Hall, 1988: 4–5). Hall's heroes are Ebenezer Howard and Patrick Geddes,
the 'fathers' of modern city planning – 'there were, alas, almost no founding mothers'
(*ibid.*: 7) – and their interpreters in the New World like Lewis Mumford, Clarence Stein,
Stuart Chase, Benton MacKaye, Rexford Tugwell, and Frank Lloyd Wright. But there is an
elegiac note to his narrative in his lament over the gap between the visionary quality of
the ideas and their diluted impacts 'on the ground', where sometimes these grand ideas
are 'almost unrecognizably distorted', and indeed, after 100 years of planning practice,
'after repeated attempts to put ideas into practice, we find we are almost back to where
we started' (*ibid.*: 11). What begins as an evolutionary tale, then, ends in a kind of
circular finale and lament. But Hall seems unable to offer any satisfactory explanation for
this gap between vision and reality, perhaps precisely because he chooses to focus on
individuals rather than on social forces. In his story, therefore, it is the *idea* of planning
which is the true hero, rather than the practice.

What is missing from these mainstream/modernist histories? At the most fundamental
level – ontological and epistemological – there has been a failure to address two basic
questions. What is the object of planning history? And who are its subjects? The boundaries of planning history are not a given. These boundaries shift in relation to the
definition of planning (as both ideas and practices) and in relation to the historian's
purpose. If we define planning as bounded by the profession, and its objective as city-
building, then we generate one set of histories. If we define planning as community-
building, we generate another. If we define planning as the regulation of the physicality,
sociality, and spatiality of the city, then we produce planning histories that try to make
sense of those regulatory practices over time and space. But in emphasizing planning as a
regulatory or disciplinary practice, we may miss its *transformative possibilities*, which in
turn may be connected to histories of resistance to specific planning practices and regulatory regimes. The writing of histories is not simply a matter of holding a mirror up to the
past and reporting on what is reflected back. It is always a representation, a textual
reconstruction of the past rather than a direct reflection of it. Mainstream planning
historians have typically seen their subject as the profession, and their object as describing (and celebrating) its emergence. There have been two significant consequences of this
approach. One is the absence of diversity in these texts. The other is the absence of any
critical/theoretical perspective. These sins of omission are the *noir* side of planning.

THE *NOIR* OF PLANNING HISTORY

In his critical history of Los Angeles, *City of Quartz*, Mike Davis delineates an earlier
tradition of boosterism in the writing about the city that parallels what I describe as the
mythologizing of the planning profession in mainstream planning histories. In the
absence of a critical tradition of historical writing about the city in Los Angeles from the
1940s through to the 1970s, Davis argues that this city came to understand its past,

instead, through a robust fiction genre known as *noir*, in which the image of the city is repainted as a deracinated urban hell. The *noir* novelists (James Cain, Horace McCoy, Nathaniel West, Raymond Chandler are the best known) created a regional fiction concerned with puncturing the image of Southern California as the golden land of opportunity and the fresh start (Davis, 1990: 38). Most interesting of all was the brief appearance of 'Black *noir*', embodied in the fiction of writers like Langston Hughes and Chester Himes, who portrayed Los Angeles as a racial hell in which blacks are destroyed or driven to self-destruction by the capricious and psychotic dynamics of white racism (Davis, 1990: 43).

What follows is a puncturing or de-mythologizing of the heroic image of planning history by means of injecting a series of critical themes. Perhaps the most glaring omission from the saga of the rise of planning is the absence of all but white, professional, males as the actors on the historical stage. Were there no women? No African Americans, Mexican Americans, Japanese and Chinese Americans? Were there no gays and lesbians? Where are they, both as subjects – engaged in planning, contributing to city and community building, researching urban problems – and as objects, victims, of planners' neglect of or desire to regulate these groups' particular existence, concerns, and needs in cities?

WOMEN?

Peter Hall justifies their absence from his study by the bold assertion that there were no 'foremothers of city planning', only forefathers (Hall, 1988). That is simply wrong, as the works of feminist scholars like Dolores Hayden (1981), Eugenie Birch (1983), Susan Wirka (1989; 1994), Barbara Hooper (1992), and Gail Dubrow (1998), among others, have clearly shown. Feminist approaches to city planning history range from the chronicling of the 'Great Women' (Jane Addams, Edith Elmer Wood, Mary Simkhovitch, Florence Kelly, Lillian Wald, Catherine Bauer); to the documenting of a whole tradition of feminist home design and community planning (Hayden, 1981; Wirka, 1989; 1994); to critiquing ways in which women's contributions have been memorialized (Dubrow 1992; 1998; Dubrow and Goodman, 2002). More recently, these white feminist historians have acknowledged the absence of women of colour from earlier accounts, and have begun to address that absence (Dubrow, 1998; Hayden, 1995). Some feminist historiographers are challenging the traditional periodizations of planning history (Sandercock, 1990); others are doing new textual readings of existing accounts in order to explore new themes – like the social control or disciplinary elements of planning practice (Wilson, 1991; 1992; Hooper, 1992; 1998). Wirka has argued persuasively for a redefinition of planning, to include the City Social as well as the City Practical, in order to appreciate the contributions of women social reformers and community builders (Wirka, 1989; 1994; Marcuse, 1980).

In the absence of such a (re)definition of planning, mainstream historians have failed to appreciate women's contributions. Mel Scott's work has two references to Addams and

Simkhovitch, each no longer than half a sentence. Addams is noted as the founder of Chicago's Hull House, the first Settlement House in the US, and as someone who, along with Jacob Riis, had an advanced insight into the social needs of the community (Scott, 1969: 72). But it is Riis to whom Scott devotes a paragraph, attributing Riis' insight into New York's housing problems to his recent immigrant status and empathy for the plight of poor immigrants. Yet it was Addams who, through Hull House, had been working with poor immigrants on the south side of Chicago since 1889 – well before Riis' study – and had pioneered social survey research among them. And what of Mary Simkhovitch, whom Scott also mentions, but only in passing, as an outstanding Settlement House worker, and as a member of the 1907 Committee on Congestion of Population, and who pops up again, in 1931, as president of the National Public Housing Conference? Despite her obvious longevity in the planning and housing movements, Simkhovitch never rates more than these fleeting mentions, while Benjamin Marsh is given all the credit for the work of the Committee on Congestion of Population. As Susan Wirka's research has shown, Mary Simkhovitch not only wrote extensively on housing and social planning issues, she also worked tirelessly as a public activist on these issues, and was the first to outline a comprehensive vision of neighbourhood planning, and to locate such a planning in its broader metropolitan context (Wirka, 1989; 1994). The work of recovering the contributions of individual women to mainstream planning continues, as does the task of reconceptualizing women's work in urban and social reform issues and in community development as another kind of planning, albeit at grass-roots level rather than through state agencies – planning as community-building.

INVISIBLE MINORITIES?

What of the absence of African Americans and ethnic minorities from mainstream accounts? There is the unspoken assumption here that there are no African/Mexican/Asian American forefathers or mothers of city planning. There is another implicit assumption in mainstream narratives – that planning has been race-neutral in its practices, rather than supportive of a white power structure's policies of segregation and discrimination. Joan Fitzgerald and William Howard have addressed the first assumption, making the case that there is indeed a black planning history, and that blacks were involved in planning around urban problems long before the civil rights era. They focus on the activist research of W. E. B. DuBois, beginning with his monumental study *The Philadephia Negro* in 1898, and continuing in his investigations reported in the Atlanta University Publications which provided a comprehensive portrait of urban African Americans. Through these publications, DuBois 'made a great contribution to urban research and community development planning, especially as such planning related to the black community' (Fitzgerald and Howard, 1993: 10–11).

Along with the work of the Urban League, black churches, and black women working in their communities (Gilkes, 1988), there is a body of research, political action, and urban social services that collectively represents a distinctively African American urban planning and community development tradition. Cheryl Gilkes (1988) and Gail Dubrow (1992; Dubrow and Goodman, 2002) are among a growing group of researchers who are documenting the role of black women in community-building. If we redefine planning to include the community-building tradition – planning 'from below' – then clearly we must include these narratives in our planning histories.

According to Fitzgerald and Howard, there are two reasons why this tradition has been ignored both by the emerging planning profession and by mainstream histories. First, the researches of DuBois and of the Urban League drew attention to histories of racial tension and strife in American cities. But in the emerging profession of city planning in the first half of the twentieth century, the matter of white racism was a taboo subject, and this continued to be the case at least until the challenges of the civil rights era. Second, the planning tradition that came to dominate the profession was based on shaping the physical environment – the city-building tradition – while the focus of the African American tradition was on employment and economic concerns, social work and urban service delivery, and collective political action – a community-building tradition.

The silence of mainstream historians on the subject of the racism that has been so prominent in American cities has led to an avoidance of the ways in which planning practice has often worked to reinforce racial segregation and discrimination. One needs to go to the work of the legal scholar C. E. Vose for a systematic study of the ways in which whites used the planning tool of restrictive covenants to exclude blacks (and Jews, and Mexicans) from their neighbourhoods for the first half of the twentieth century, until the NAACP (National Association for the Advancement of Colored People) and the ACLU (American Civil Liberties Union) took the matter to the courts (Vose, 1967). And we need to go to the 'new ethnic histories' (Hayden, 1995), like Ricardo Romo's *East Los Angeles: History of a Barrio* (1983), to get an account of the multiple ways in which minorities have been spatially excluded from large parts of American cities.

This theme of the racist consequences of urban and regional planning schemes receives full engagement in recent works by June Manning Thomas (1994; 1998), Clyde Woods (1998), and the edited collection by Thomas and Marsha Ritzdorf, *Urban Planning and the African American Community* (1997). Thomas (1994) argues for a more racially conscious perspective in planning history, one that is 'more sensitive to the history of African American urbanization'. She suggests a new, four-part periodization for city planning history to bring it into line with black urban experience. This would begin with the era during and immediately after World War I, which saw the first substantial migration of southern blacks to northern cities and, not coincidentally, the first major race riots of the twentieth century. This migration created industrial, civic, housing and religious issues for city officials. Their planning response was the creation of residential controls: zoning for social segregation by race, and restrictive covenants built into land titles (Thomas, 1994). The second stage in this story is the era of public housing, after the passage of the Wagner-Steagall Act in 1937, and including World War II housing and postwar urban renewal. This was a period in which residential segregation was reinforced and ghetto boundaries consolidated as local politicians and planners, responding to overt displays of white racism, used the planning system to keep black housing projects out of white neighbourhoods. This was also the time of the second great migration of southern rural blacks to the north and west, and of the clearances of 'black slums' for freeways. The third stage is the era of civil rights and civil rebellions, an era in which the planning profession developed a consciousness of, and conscience about, race and racism and when social planning and advocacy planning were responses to this new awareness (Thomas, 1994). In the era that Thomas describes as the 'racially separate metropolis' since the 1970s, the black community has experienced both an increase in political power (at least as measured by the number of black elected officials) and disastrous economic decline thanks to processes of deindustrialization and economic restructuring. Thomas describes how planning affects, and is affected by, race and racism, as well as showing the historical linkages between urban development and racial oppression of blacks by whites.

In a more recent essay, Thomas (1998) argues for making the issues of race and racism central to the history of urban planning in the United States. Criticizing existing histories for their dismissive treatment of African Americans as either invisible, or as passive victims of urban policies, or, worse, as the carriers of social pathologies, Thomas gives us a fine-grained account of the historical links between race, racism, and planning. While not avoiding the extent to which planners have been complicit with oppressive policies in the past, she also gives a subtle reading of the difficulties of urban improvement efforts in a social context of racial oppression. She describes the persistent struggle by African Americans to plan their own communities, emphasizing how these stories of struggle can empower present and future generations.

Similar studies are needed for other minorities, from the exclusionary nineteenth-century zoning actions against Chinese immigrants (Kayden and Haar, 1989) to the restrictive covenants against Mexicans and Jews through the first half of the twentieth century (Romo, 1983), to the whole system of 'planned reservations' for Native Americans as part of a broader reinterpretation of the work of planning as social control of (certain) bodies in space – women, 'minorities', the poor, indigenous peoples. This is indeed a *noir* side of planning history, something which planners would rather not acknowledge in their collective professional past. And yet, unless we discuss these hidden intentions and consequences of planning practices, we will continue to perpetuate them, as both Thomas (1998), and Beauregard (1998) – talking about South African planning – have argued.

Diversity in the multicultural city has many faces. Alongside the struggles for recognition and place-claiming by racial and ethnic 'minorities' are those of gays and lesbians, a minority with a long history of oppression and of resistance. Like other groups, gays and lesbians have stories to tell about the ways in which their lives in cities and neighbourhoods have been and are impinged on by planning's social and spatial policies, and how they, in turn, have contested certain policies. Making these stories an integral part of planning history requires us to address questions such as the following: have homosexuals, as individuals or as couples, been excluded from particular housing developments and certain neighbourhoods? How have planning and housing policies created or reinforced such barriers? How have policies affecting the design and use of public spaces impacted the ability of gays and lesbians to live openly and without fear of perpetual harassment? What assumptions about the 'normal' family/household are built into suburban planning codes and how does this discriminate against gay couples/households? How do public housing agencies and private landlords treat gays who are parents? How can planners help to create safer streets and neighbourhoods for gays and lesbians? How have gays and lesbians acted to create and protect their urban places? How have they made certain parts of cities their own? How have they interacted with planners in this pursuit?

Gay urban politics and social movements inevitably spill over into planning issues and into questions of who controls city councils and planning agencies. Gays and lesbians have become involved in electoral struggles precisely to influence the kinds of neigh-bourhood in which they live and to provide services specific to their economic, recre-ational, and health needs. Just as planning policies are neither gender- nor race-neutral (Sandercock and Forsyth, 1992; Grigsby, 1994; Mier, 1993; Thomas, 1994), nor are they neutral with respect to gay and lesbian communities.[3] We need to understand how planning policies, historically, have affected the quality of urban life of gays and lesbians, and indeed how they may have reinforced their broader societal oppression. Scholars like Moira Kenney (1995; 2001) and Eric Reyes (1993) have done pioneering work in these areas, employing cognitive mapping and other techniques to make visible the histories of gays and lesbians in American cities, their place-claiming, and the ways in which they have transformed the contemporary city.

In recent years, a wealth of scholarship about the history of gays and lesbians in the city has revealed, on the one hand, extensive and systematic practices of discrimination and oppression targeting them as 'threats' to the urban social order, and, on the other, a century of resistance to this oppression (Chauncey, 1994; Faderman, 1991; D'Emilio, 1983). Kenney (1995; 2001) asks planning historians to acknowledge the importance and relevance of this research as part of a broader shift away from the focus on institutional responses to urban inequalities, and towards the collective, street-level responses of those who are targets of discrimination. She also reminds us of the fluidity of the boundaries we have drawn around other divisions in the city – class, race, gender, age – and of how the gay and lesbian struggle crosses these other boundaries and compounds many of the difficult social and cultural questions we have only recently begun to consider. Kenney's work is important in yet another way, in drawing attention to the complexity of roles that marginalized groups have played in the development of American landscapes, as both subjects and objects. Our planning histories have yet to grapple with these complexities.

HISTORY AND THEORY

There is a fundamental critique embedded in drawing attention to some of the glaring absences in mainstream accounts of planning history. These absences are not innocent. They are systematic exclusions which emerge from the authors' epistemological positions concerning the proper subject and object of planning, concerning the writing of history, and concerning the relationship of planning to power and the power of systems of thought. In order to understand these systematic exclusions, we need theory. As a discipline, historians have acknowledged the importance of theory at least since the inception of journals like *History and Theory* (1961), *Radical History Review* (1974), and *Marxist Perspectives* (1978). Over the past two decades there has been a proliferation of 'new histories' – feminist, postcolonial, ethnic, queer, cultural, and more. The very titles of some of these works – *Remaking History* (Kruger and Mariani, 1989), *The New Cultural History* (Hunt, 1989), *Selected Subaltern Studies* (Guha and Spivak, 1988), and *Telling the Truth about History* (Appleby, Hunt and Jacob, 1994) – indicate the challenges across many fronts to 'traditional histories' not only of 'dates and greats' but of masculinist, white, and Eurocentric accounts. These new histories begin with the recovery of neglected, repressed, and forgotten cultures, the recuperation of names and faces erased from past accounts. This process of 'recovery' – what Joan Kelly (1984) has called 'compensatory histories' – is essential in disrupting mainstream accounts of planning history, and is also an important factor in the contemporary politics of identity. Recovering one's history is a first step in constructing or reconstructing both individual and group identity. But the process of recovery is not the end of the story. There are further levels of excavation and analysis.

The awareness of new voices with new stories to tell has produced, as Foucault described it, 'a new form of history that is trying to develop its own theory' (Kruger and Mariani, 1989). Over the past two decades a new American urban social history has begun to be written, taking ethnic diversity as a starting point and recognizing the disparate experiences of class and gender. Urban history was for many years dominated by what Hayden calls city biography, 'a single narrative of how city leaders or "city fathers" – almost always white, upper- and middle-class men – forged the city's spatial and economic structure, making fortunes building downtowns and imposing order on chaotic immigrant populations' (Hayden, 1995: 39). Planning historians seem to have taken their cue from this earlier genre of urban history, and, just as the early urban histories bore many similarities to the 'conquest' histories of the American West, so too have planning histories unfolded heroic stories of the great white visionary men who have shaped the planning profession and city-building processes in the twentieth century.

In the late 1980s, urban historians began to develop a more inclusive approach to the entire city, exploring the whole as seen from the perspective of different oppressed groups, while emphasizing the sharpness of spatial as well as cultural divisions and distinctions (Hayden, 1995: 40). The new urban histories not only draw attention to the contribution of different ethnic communities in the building of American cities. They also place women at the centre rather than at the periphery of economic and social life in the city. With a couple of notable exceptions – Christine Boyer's *Dreaming the Rational City* (1983) and Richard Foglesong's *Planning the Capitalist City* (1986) – planning historians throughout the 1980s remained immune to these new developments in related fields of history.[4] This began to change in the 1990s as new work, influenced by a range of critical theories, from Marx to Foucault, from feminism to postcolonialism, poststructuralism, and queer theory, began to re-present planning's histories (see Sandercock, 1995b; 1998; Yiftachel, 1992; 1996). These are 'insurgent planning histories'.

INSURGENT PLANNING HISTORIES

It is the argument of this book that planning in the multicultural cities of the 21st century requires a very different approach than that of the modernist paradigm. In order to imagine the future differently, we need to start with history, with a reconsideration of the stories we tell ourselves about planning's role in the modern and postmodern city. There is an important social sense in which history is, as Herodotus said several millennia ago, stories we tell ourselves around a campfire. In telling new stories about our past, our intention is to re-shape our future. If we can uncouple planning history from its obsession with the celebratory story of the rise of the planning profession, and demonstrate its multiple and insurgent histories, we may be able to link it to a new set of public issues – those connected with the challenge of planning for a future of multicultural cities and regions. The future multicultural city – *cosmopolis* – cannot be imagined without an acknowledgement of the politics of difference (which insurgent planning histories embody); a belief in inclusive democracy; and the diversity of the social justice claims of the disempowered communities in our existing cities. If we want to work towards a politics of inclusion, then we had better have a good understanding of the exclusionary effects of planning's past practices. And if we want to plan in the future for multiple publics, acknowledging and nurturing the full diversity of the many social groups in the multi-cultural city, then we need to develop a new kind of multicultural literacy. An essential part of that literacy is familiarity with the *multiple histories* of urban communities, especially as those histories intersect with struggles over space and place-claiming, with planning policies and resistances to them, with traditions of indigenous planning, and with questions of belonging and identity and acceptance of difference. What follows are some examples of insurgent planning histories: insurgent in their theoretical approach to understanding what constitutes planning history as well as in the particular stories they have to tell, about Native Americans, African Americans, women, and gays and lesbians.

There is a difference between rewriting history by adding the forgotten or repressed contributions of particular groups, and reconceptualizing planning history by using gender and race as categories of analysis. In a landmark essay, historian Joan Kelly argued that women's history has shaken the foundations of historical study by making problem-atic three basic concerns of historical thought – periodization, the categories of social analysis, and theories of social change (Kelly, 1984). One of the themes of feminist scholarship has been the issue of women's status; that is, the roles and positions women hold in society by comparison with those of men. In historical research, this means we look at ages or movements of great social change in terms of their liberation or repres-sion of women's potential. Once we do this, the period, or set of events, may take on a wholly different meaning from the normally accepted one.

If we apply Fourier's famous dictum – that the emancipation of women is an index of the general emancipation of an age – our notions of so-called progressive developments, such as classical Athenian civilization, the Renaissance, and the French Revolution, undergo a startling re-evaluation.

(Kelly, 1984: 5)

Kelly's own work on the question 'Was there a Renaissance for women?' provides the substantive evidence for her theoretical argument. With her question in mind, as to whether significant turning points in history have the same impact for women as they do for men, we can turn to planning histories and examine their periodizations from very different points of view. Instead of celebrating every milestone in the evolution of planning as a profession, we need to ask whether women (and other minorities) were part of this emerging profession, and what effect each milestone had on the lives of women living in cities. My own periodization of Australian planning history fell into three eras: an ideas phase (late nineteenth century through to World War I); a legislative phase (between the two world wars and immediately after World War II); and an implementation phase, primarily post-World War II (Sandercock, 1990). Applying a feminist framework to this periodization, a number of questions arise. With respect to the early formative ideas, were women active in writing or propagating any of these ideas? Were women organizing around urban issues at this time? How did the ideas of the 'great men' or 'founding fathers' potentially affect the lives of women in cities? What are the male-female relationships implied in ideas about 'the good city' and good planning? If women played only a marginal role in the emerging *profession*, why was that the case, and is that the end of the story, or should we broaden our horizon to include women's work in housing reform, social work, the playgrounds movement, and community organizing? In the United States, we might want to focus on the split between the housing reform movement and the planning profession, analysing the role of gender in this split. Similar questions can be asked of the phases of legislation and implementation. Were women involved as actors in these processes? What were the consequences of particular pieces of legislation on women's lives in the city? Has any planning legislation ever tried to broaden the opportunities for women to participate in public life? What assumptions about relations (of equality or inequality) between the sexes are built into planning legislation?

Similarly with Kelly's second challenge – the categories of social analysis. If gender is a category as fundamental to our analysis of the social order as other classifications such as class, and if we regard the relations between the sexes as socially rather than naturally constituted, then this would lead a planning historian to ask, of any set of ideas or practices, 'What are the male-female relationships implied here?' For example, what roles are being assigned to women when we design houses and neighbourhoods and transportation systems?

Kelly's third challenge is based on the second. If the relation of the sexes is as necessary to an understanding of human history as the social relationship of classes, then a theory of social change that incorporates the relation of the sexes has to consider how general changes in production affect and shape production in the household and, thereby, the respective roles of men and women. This in turn requires us to address the relations between the domestic and the public orders, and to look to the organization of the productive forces of society to understand the domestic order to which women, historically, have been primarily consigned (although not all women, and not for all of history). Conversely, women's history also views women as agents and the family as a social and productive force, and asks us to analyse the positive aspects of women's lives within household and community, producing use values and providing the caring and attachment without which both individual and social life is the poorer. Theories of social change that are derived from gender-neutral approaches to history assume that when 'things' change for the better, those things are better for women too. A feminist approach to planning history needs to demonstrate that this has not always been the case, and is not always a reasonable assumption. Planners who want to create a better world for both men and women need a theory of social transformation which has at its heart a consideration of relations between the sexes, how those relations are shaped by and in the built environment, and how that built environment is socially produced in accordance with pre-existing notions of what constitutes appropriate relations between the sexes

The feminist work discussed above has as a starting point an understanding of gender as a social construction. There is a group of French feminists whose work begins from a rather different starting point, that of the body as a social construction. When this work is linked with that of Foucault on disciplining the self and on the social creation of 'docile bodies', an interesting new line of inquiry emerges around regimes of regulation and discourses about regulatory regimes. This comes together in the planning history field around discourses of bodies, cities, and social order.

BODIES, CITIES, AND SOCIAL ORDER

Paul Rabinow's *French Modern* (1989) was the first work to emerge from that intellectual milieu with a direct relevance to our understanding and re/presentation of planning. *French Modern* is a study of the construction of norms and the search for forms adequate to understand and regulate modern society. While planning is not the focus of his study, Rabinow describes how, beginning in the nineteenth century, the 'corrective sociology' of positivist social and natural sciences began to define and valorize norms – along the binaries healthy/pathological, normal/abnormal, productive/non-productive, and so on – and to provide these norms with architectural and urban forms. He explores the ways in which the rising professions and professional experts created disciplinary practices which served to control and regulate people in modern societies – essentially to regulate bodies in space. Curiously, Rabinow does not pick up on the gender and other implications of applying Foucault's work to planning practices. Such an inquiry would ask how planning, as a profession, has functioned as a regulatory regime, specifically in its discourse on and rules concerning the 'appropriate' (or 'normal') place of women, or gays, or people of colour in the city.

We find a tantalizing beginning to such a project in Elizabeth Wilson's study of cities and planning, *The Sphinx in the City* (1991), and in an essay in *New Left Review*.

With the intensification of the public-private divide in the industrial period, the presence of women on the streets and in public places of entertainment caused enormous anxiety, and was the occasion for any number of moral and regulatory discourses.

(Wilson, 1992: 90).

Wilson argues that during the nineteenth century there was an increasing preoccupation among urban social reformers, politicians, and writers, with the subject of urban disorder. One of the causes of this growing disorder was believed to be the presence of women in the new industrial towns. She further suggests that 'the androgynous woman, the lesbian, the prostitute, the childless woman . . . all aroused fears and created anxieties concerning the eroticization of life in the metropolis' (Wilson, 1992: 106). Prostitution served as 'a metaphor for the new regime of nineteenth century urbanism' (Wilson, 1992: 105), a regime in which women – their bodies, their sexuality – were suddenly on the streets, potentially both tempting and threatening male order, male self-discipline, and the male disciplining of the city. She also argues that the emerging planning profession was preoccupied with controlling menacing sexualities in the city, thereby posing planners as early enemies of homosexual lifestyles. These ideas demand further historical research and re-reading of classic planning texts and plans in order to reveal such agendas.

On this theme, George Chauncey's *Gay New York: Gender, Urban Culture, and the Making of the Modern Gay World, 1890–1940* is an important work for planning historians. Chauncey argues that the thinking about the city that ultimately coalesced into urban planning theory identified 'sexual deviants' as one of the causes of social disorganization:

Some theorists in the first generation of American urban sociologists, who echoed many of the concerns of the reformers with whom they often worked, expressed similar anxieties about the enhanced possibilities for the development of a secret homosexual life that urban conditions created. Urbanization, they warned, resulted in the breakdown of family and social ties that kept an individual's behavior under control in smaller, more tightly organized and regulated towns. The resulting 'personal disorganization', the sociologist Walter Reckless wrote in 1926, led to the release of 'impulses and desires . . . from the socially approved channels', and could result 'not merely in prostitution, but also in perversion'.

(Chauncey, 1994: 132).

Chauncey's research places gays and lesbians at the centre of this debate over the threats to urban order. He argues that the attraction of the city was not merely the anonymity (which Elizabeth Wilson claims was central to the use of the city by women), but 'an organized, multilayered, and self-conscious gay subculture, with its own meeting places, language, folklore, and moral codes. What sociologists and reformers called the social disorganization of the city might more properly be regarded as a social reorganization' (Chauncey, quoted in Kenney, 1995: 79). Kenney's work provides a crucial link between the research of gay and lesbian historians and the issues that ought to be of interest to planning historians. She looks at three aspects of systematic discrimination against gays and lesbians: harassment in public places, housing regulations like exclusionary zoning laws, and public accommodation statutes, which govern access to the whole range of public spaces from streets to commercial establishments (Kenney, 1995). Her study of the processes of place-making and place-claiming in the gay community in Los Angeles, *Mapping Gay L.A.* (2001), reinforces Chauncey's argument that what is happening here is a social reorganization, a new process of community-building.

Working on late nineteenth-century Paris, critical urban scholar Barbara Hooper ploughs some of these same thematic fields. Grounded in feminist theory as well as the theories of Foucault, Henri Lefebvre, and Michel de Certeau, Hooper's analysis begins with and is centred in the body, specifically the female body. She outlines how and why the female body/woman has been subjected to an ordering in social space, through the hegemonic discourses and disciplinary practices of the social and natural sciences, from medicine to psychiatry to urban pathology, public hygiene and, of course, planning. Focusing on nineteenth-century Paris, on the texts of planners, public hygienists, sanitation engineers, and city fathers, Hooper shows how female/female body became synonymous with that which disorders, threatens, undoes the work of Man, the work of Reason, the idea of the Plan. Built into the origins of modern planning, she argues, is the nineteenth-century reassertion of sexual difference, and a whole set of cultural representations regarding male/mind and female/body, and the dominant/subordinate relations between them. Hooper's essay takes us into the streets of nineteenth-century Paris as well as into its planning mentality and planning texts, and shows us the relationship between all three: it is 'a story of bodies, cities, and social order, and more particularly of female bodies as a threat to male/social order'. Modern planning at its inception, she argues, was the idea of a plan, a scientific and rational plan, conquering the disorder of cities – the poverty and misery that were the effects of industrial capitalism. Focusing on modern planning's conceptual practices, Hooper explores how planning, in the moment of inventing itself as master, as knower, as producer of order in disorderly cities, took on the baggage of the dominant cultural tradition – a patriarchal tradition – and hence came to function not simply as the emancipatory practice it theorized, but as a participant in new forms of social control directed at women. She 'reads' the plans for 'the modern city' of Baron von Haussmann and his contemporaries, and of Le Corbusier, as 'poems of male desire', fantasies of control, written against the fears and upheavals of the nineteenth century that the female body comes to represent (Hooper, 1998; 2002).

The next two examples of insurgent planning histories are concerned with action, change, and empowerment. 'If modernist planning relies on and builds up the state, then its necessary counter-agent is a mode of planning which addresses the formations of insurgent citizenship', argues anthropologist James Holston (1998: 47), who urges planning theorists and historians to study the grass-roots mobilizations and everyday practices which subvert state agendas. The research of Clyde Woods and of Theodore Jojola answers this call.

RECOVERIES (1): THE BLUES EPISTEMOLOGY

Clyde Woods' account of the failed effort at regional economic development planning embodied in the short life history of the Lower Mississippi Delta Development Commission (LMDDC) forges a new historiography of regional planning (Woods, 1998). His project is the recovery of the memory, voices, and visions of the African American community of the Delta. Drawing on Foucault's archaeological/genealogical method, he 'excavates' a repressed African American tradition of resistance to the hegemonic definitions of planning and development in the Delta. Woods makes visible the existence of a regional epistemology grounded in African American experience – what he calls the 'Blues epistemology' – that, he argues, embodies an alternative theory of social, economic, and cultural development and change. Woods describes how the Blues operated to instill pride in a people facing daily denigration, as well as channelling folk wisdom, descriptions of life and labour, and critiques of bosses and sheriffs, planters, and the plantation regime. He argues that the Blues operated as a self-referential system of social explanation, as an epistemology. This new epistemology proceeded from the assumption that the indigenously developed folk culture, its orature, its ethics, its tradition of social explanation, and its prescriptions for social action, were the basic representational grid of working-class African American consciousness. Woods also explains why those voices, that tradition, were systematically marginalized in the interests of a hegemonic modernization of which planning was and is a complicit partner.

Within the oral and written record of these 'arrested agendas and movements' rests the regionally indigenous knowledge upon which to construct new relationships and new regional structures of equality and democracy. Woods is concerned as much with an empowering vision of the future for the region as he is with the region's past. Representing the region's past, however, is the first step in imagining a better future. Reacting to the appalling consequences of the modernization project for the African American population of the Mississippi Delta, Woods' insurgent historiography embodies an activist social imagination that draws on what already exists in the history of African American resistance to hegemonic definitions of planning and development in the Delta.

RECOVERIES (2): THE ALL-INDIAN PUEBLO COUNCIL

There could be no more glaring absence from the pages of the planning history of the United States than that of its original inhabitants, Native Americans, who were forcibly removed from their lands in order for most American cities to be built and farms to be established. But, once we have acknowledged that tribal communities have been victims of modernization and urbanization, have we reached a swift end to their inclusion in the planning narrative – an appearance on stage only briefly, as victims?

The most important contribution to an understanding of this hitherto invisible part of planning history is the work of Native American scholar and activist Theodore Jojola (1998). In his essay 'Indigenous Planning: Clans, Intertribal Confederations, and the History of the All Indian Pueblo Council', Jojola acknowledges that tribal communities have been victims of modernization, but the story he tells about this is twofold. He argues that tribal communities themselves have a history and planning traditions that have been rendered invisible by virtue of not being seen as part of the dominant narrative of modernization and nation-building. And he outlines a story of hundreds of years of resistance and survival despite overwhelming odds, a story of selective interaction and adaptation. He argues that this survival was possible precisely because of indigenous planning traditions, specifically the role of clans in community development and the tradition of consensus-seeking among intertribal confederations. Together, these constitute traditions of community and regional planning with a much longer history than their parallels in mainstream Euro-American planning. While Jojola's essay focuses on the history of these traditions among the Pueblo Indian nations of the Southwest, he notes that there are variations on these same models throughout what is known as Native America.

Planning as a tradition among Native Americans was not imposed by Euro-Americans. The hegemonic nation-building project that pre-occupied mainstream American historians of the nineteenth and early twentieth centuries (see Appleby, Hunt and Jacob, 1994) involved, by definition, a denial that Native Americans already constituted a nation with its own government, philosophy, and economics. Jojola examines nineteenth-and early twentieth-century historical and anthropological scholarship and notes its role as a tool enabling policy-makers to dismiss tribal leadership and deny the ability of tribes to plan for themselves. The paternalistic public policy approach towards Native American communities – policies of forced cultural assimilation developed by the Bureau of Indian Affairs in the 1800s and remaining in place until the 1960s – emerged as a result of this earlier scholarship and its allegedly scientific conclusions about the inferiority of Native Americans.

In contrast to that scholarship, Jojola describes how, at the time of European contact, there were planning traditions within Native American society, traditions characterized by distinctive world views, with clans serving as the basic social unit for mobilizing communities. Jojola likens the clan to the neighbourhood unit in planning theory. And when clans of various cultural communities came together to form regionally based groups, these groups – or tribal confederations – became the means by which Native Americans organized their own political community. Jojola equates this with a regional planning model, arguing that the confederations established an interdependent economic system that, in turn, was tied to managing and sustaining a shared ecosystem. One of the surviving tribal confederations is the All Indian Pueblo Council of the Southwest. Jojola describes the unified actions of the Pueblos in resisting first Spanish intrusion and exploitation; continuing regional resistance after the 1821 transfer of Spanish authority to the Mexican government; and again, after the American territorial government was established in New Mexico. With the induction of New Mexico into statehood in 1912 the Pueblos continued to mobilize against the unjust practices of local authorities.

Jojola's long march through the centuries can in fact be described as a success story – albeit with tragic overtones. In the long view, in spite of decimation, assimilation, and alienation from their lands, tribal communities have survived and are being revitalized, and the indigenous planning traditions that have made this survival possible are being reasserted. In keeping with the notion of the past as future – with history-writing directed towards present and future policy concerns – Jojola outlines the expanded policy role of the All Indian Pueblo Council today in matters of community and regional development and national policy, and advocates the formation and revitalization of other confederations which existed at the time of first European contact.

CONTESTING THE SPACES OF HISTORIC REPRESENTATION

Traditional planning histories have presented planning as the voice of reason in modern society, as the carrier of the Enlightenment mission of material progress through scientific rationality. The insurgent planning histories discussed above both implicitly and explicitly challenge the accuracy of this representation of planning. The 'rewritings' of Thomas, Woods, Jojola, Chauncey and Kenney represent 'subaltern consciousness' (of blacks, tribal communities, gays and lesbians) as a rationality of its own, which has been subjected to erasure by those in power. Each has captured/recovered subaltern consciousness through mixtures of oral history, political economy, cognitive mapping, critical theory, and textual analysis. And each underscores ways in which, through resistance and acquiescence, the subaltern confronts the world and may transform it.

The variety of insurgent planning histories outlined here all challenge the mainstream approach of planning history as synonymous with the history of the profession. They also, implicitly, challenge the very idea of 'the' history of planning, emphasizing instead plural histories of planning practices and plural readings of planning texts, according to the theoretical lens in use. Nevertheless some common themes do emerge in these new planning histories. The theme of planning as an ordering tool, as a kind of 'spatial police', first surfaced in the 1970s in Marxist accounts of urban planning, but has taken a new turn under the influence of postmodern attention to discursive practices and regulatory regimes. Earlier Marxist writings tended to argue that all planning must be interpreted as social control, as a disciplinary practice essential to the maintenance of the modern social order. More recent writings make no such totalizing claim. On the contrary, they are ever alert to the resistances that arise in the face of these disciplinary or controlling practices. The theme recurs, of marginalized groups contesting urban and regional spaces, which includes contesting the spaces of representation (as in the historical preservation and public history practices that Dubrow and Hayden write about), as well as the spaces of historical narratives themselves. The theme of bodies, cities, and social order offers a radically different way of conceptualizing and understanding planning's intentions and practices. And a range of scholars are now challenging the notion of 'rational planning in the public interest' by deconstructing the class, gender, race and ethnic origins, biases, and effects of the planning profession.

There is no single theoretical framework that informs this new work, nor is there a dominant theme. The goal is not to produce a new, unified, postmodern or feminist or postcolonial interpretation of planning history, the new 'official story'. I began by criticizing the inadequacies of mainstream or modernist planning histories, what they have rendered invisible, their *noir* side. Beyond this deconstruction, I have outlined new ways of thinking about and doing planning history, drawing on the works of scholars of the past decade. In part, this involves a reconceptualization of the subject – of mainstream definitions of planning and the role of planners as well as disputing dominant definitions of who is and is not a planner. We still need to see planning as, in part, a state-directed activity, a branch of city-building, but this need not be seen as an exclusively top-down, expert-driven process. There have always been oppositional movements within and outside mainstream planning, from the City Social tradition dominated by women urban reformers to the community-building traditions documented by Woods, Jojola, Kenney, Fitzgerald and Howard, and Thomas for African American, Native American, and gay and lesbian communities, as well as other white working-class and ethnic communities. Stories of resistance to 'planning by the state' are as important a part of the historical narrative as are the more familiar heroic stories of master plans and master planners, of planning legislation and state planning agencies. There is a tradition of community resistance (from people whose life space is at stake in the urban and regional development process), and of community planning, which needs to be incorporated as a counterpoint to the modernist narrative.

All of these forms of rewriting of American planning history could be equally well applied to other national planning cultures. Oren Yiftachel has been doing a stellar job for the past decade in critiquing the history of Israeli planning practices as discriminatory (Yiftachel, 1992; 1996; 2001). In post-apartheid South Africa, scholars have been engaged in documenting the ways in which the planning system was central to the implementation of racial segregation (Mabin and Smit, 1997; Narsoo, 2001), as well as to how contemporary planning practices that seek to restructure the apartheid city are also shaped by the past (Watson, 2002). Australian scholar Sue Jackson has broken new ground with her study of planning's colonial (as opposed to modernist) history. Her case studies of the role of planning in the northern towns of Darwin and Broome expose a story of domination over indigenous socio-spatial relations by using the environmental and racial discourses of settler colonialism. In her narrative, planning is a spatial technology of cultural dominance, repressing and/or marginalizing indigenous peoples' perspectives and concepts of place. She makes a persuasive case as to why contemporary Australian planning must begin to address the special nature of aboriginal relationship to place, and to develop a procedural equity rather than the current emphasis on management plans. She also shows how apparently well-meaning planning legislation such as the Heritage Act, in the context of Broome, is yet another means of containing and disempowering aboriginal society, and yet also illustrates how aboriginal groups have used such legislation in an insurgent way, as their own *de facto* planning tool (Jackson, 1998).

What this chapter has demonstrated is that planning by the state is, and always has been, only one part of the story. Today, not all professionally trained planners work in state agencies. Increasingly, planners work for diverse local communities, in a new dialogic relationship that goes far beyond advocacy. Planning as a profession has spread its wings to include environmental policy, historic preservation, community development, anti-poverty planning, and so on. There are many strands of planning, loosely held together through a common education and a professional culture that includes the teaching of some version of planning history. But is the subject presented in its full richness and diversity, its *noir* and insurgent as well as its triumphal versions? The diversifying of the profession over the past three decades – the influx of women, people of colour, new immigrants, activist gays and lesbians – has brought to the forefront the need to re-present planning history as part of a contemporary project of rethinking planning's future. *We have moved from planning history – the official story – to planning's contested and multiple histories.*

3

WHO KNOWS? EXPLORING PLANNING'S KNOWLEDGES

Country is underneath us all the time, but it's all covered up and we in our minds are all covered up. So when we walk in the land, we can't see anything for a while. We got all our possessions with us, and through these things we look at the land. Do you feel the sand you walk on? Are you aware of where your feet step? Are you aware of the trees you just passed, the birds that just landed? How much do you see? That has to shift and as soon as it does, we get a shift in mind which drops down to feeling. Then we wake up to feeling, what we call le-an here, and we become more alive, we start feeling, we become more sensitive. You start to read the country. Then all of a sudden there's an opening down there. Before there was only a wall, but now that tree has meaning, now that rock has meaning and all of a sudden that thing takes you. You just follow. . . . See, you are that land, and the land is you. . . . You wake up, and you see a lot of things and the country starts living for you. Everything is based on that feeling *le-an*, seeing through that feeling.

(Sinatra and Murphy, 1999)

'How much do you see?' asks Frans, a white man from Holland who has been living in the remote north-western region of Australia for the past two decades. Frans has been learning the importance and meaning of land from an Aboriginal perspective. His teacher is Paddy, an Aboriginal elder who is the custodian of the Lurujarri (coastal dunes) Dreaming Trail. The Lurujarri Dreaming Trail, an eighty-mile coastal strip near the town of Broome, is part of the great song cycle of the continent according to Aboriginal cosmology. Thinking politically, Paddy has taught Frans tribal knowledge of the land to enable him to act as spokesperson and mediator in Paddy's efforts to protect the living landscape. Paddy teaching Frans was the first step in creating cross-cultural appreciation of the meaning of the land, as a way of protecting it. Paddy invites people to walk with his family members along the Lurujarri Trail so they can appreciate the importance of local beliefs by experiencing this cultural and spiritual landscape. Together, Paddy and Frans' teachings provide an opportunity for people to see the beauty of the landscape – not in the western sense of a Kodacolor-registered beautiful landscape, but through understanding the power that land has to sustain life. It is Paddy's hope that the people who walk the trail will return home to become caretakers of their own 'country'.[1]

None of what Paddy teaches is written down. Aboriginal law/lore and cosmology are passed down through story-telling traditions, through song and dance and ceremony. Maintained within this oral tradition are the laws of how to live in harmony with everything that makes up the living country. Frans talks about 'a shift in mind, which drops down to feeling', what the local people call 'le-an'. 'I mean, you're trained one way or other and you actually look through that upbringing at the land. You project through your training process the reading in the land. And all of a sudden it doesn't fit anything . . .' Frans is talking about a shift in cognitive reality, discovering new ways of knowing. 'Everything is based on that feeling *le-an*, seeing through that feeling'.

It may appear odd to place a discussion of Aboriginal perceptions of land in the far north west of Australia at the beginning of a chapter on knowledge in the planning profession. It is intended to appear so. The intent is to ask what is missing from accounts of knowledge in planning, knowledge of cities and regions, that deny themselves a rich variety of ways of seeing/knowing, by privileging only one way – the epistemology of the Enlightenment. In fact, the Lurujarri Dreaming Trail is not so remote from the concerns of planners as this opening seems to suggest. The Trail begins near the fishing port and town of Broome. Aboriginal people make up 40 per cent of the population of the Shire of Broome and yet, in the 1993 Broome Planning Strategy there is almost no demographic or social, let alone cultural, information about the Aboriginal population (Jackson, 1998). In and around Broome there is land that is in the hands of Aboriginal custodians, and recent Native Title legislation makes it possible for Aboriginal groups to make further land claims. How can a Planning Strategy claim to be speaking for 'the community' when it systematically ignores 40 per cent of that community, and when it operates in a professional language that is the equivalent of a foreign language to the Aboriginal community?

WHO KNOWS? WHY EPISTEMOLOGY MATTERS

The story of Paddy and Frans, of black and white walking a Dreaming Trail together, is a graphic way into the subject of epistemology in planning. Why is or should epistemology be important to planners? Why should we care about the philosophy of knowledge? A short answer: legitimacy and authority. The questions at the heart of a planning epistemology are: What do I know? How do I know that I know? What are my sources of knowledge? How is knowledge produced in planning? How and when do I know what I know? How secure am I in my knowledge? What level of uncertainty or ambiguity can I tolerate? What forms of knowledge offer me most security? How adequate is my knowledge for the purpose at hand? How can I improve the knowledge base of my (and others') actions? What rights does my knowledge confer on me as a planner? What responsibilities do I assume for the application of what I claim to know? What is valid knowledge in planning? Who decides that? What is the relationship between knowledge and power? And who possesses knowledge that is relevant to planning? If these are the questions, the answers to them must surely constitute the very heart, or core, of planning.

How do we know what we know? How do we arrive at truth (itself a debated concept, as I shall discuss later), or certainty, or some adequate foundation for action? There have been at least half a dozen answers since the time of the ancient Greeks: from Greek rationalism to mysticism, empiricism to dialectical materialism, pragmatism to theoretical anarchism. Plato and Aristotle certainly didn't agree on an answer. Aristotle distinguished three kinds of knowledge: *episteme*, scientific or theoretical knowledge; *techne*, technical applications of theory; and *phronesis*, judgement or practical wisdom, which allowed a significant role for intuition, imagination, and emotion. For rational deliberation and choice in personal and public life, Aristotle advocated *phronesis*. For Plato, on the other hand, the idea that rational deliberation might draw on, even be guided by these elements (emotion, imagination, intuition), was a conceptual impossibility, since he defined the rational in opposition to these 'irrational' parts of the soul. Plato insisted that emotion and appetite (desire) were corrupting influences, and that the intellect needs 'to go off by itself' in order to make practical deliberations (Nussbaum, 1990: 76). Plato rejected sensuous cognition as part of his general rejection of the bodily. Imagination was rejected as being wedded to particularity and the recognition of incommensurables, and therefore a threat to the impartial assessment of facts and probabilities.[2]

Mysticism, through the ages, by contrast, has suggested that that which is most worth knowing is achievable through contemplation and meditation, and communicable only through poetic image and metaphor. Despite the virulent attacks on mysticism since the so-called Scientific Revolution beginning with Isaac Newton in the late seventeenth century, and continuing during the Enlightenment of the eighteenth century, mysticism appears in many arenas today, from New Age environmentalism and deep ecology to the descriptions by some Nobel Prize winning scientists of their actual methods of work. Albert Einstein, for example, wrote that 'only intuition, resting on sympathetic understanding, can lead to discovery; the daily effort comes from no deliberate intention or program, but straight from the heart'. And geneticist Barbara McClintock argued that 'reason is not by itself adequate to describe the vast complexity, indeed mystery, of living forms' (Keller, 1983: 199). Perhaps this is also the 'seeing through feeling', the *le-an* of Aboriginal culture.

With the scientific revolution of the seventeenth century ushering in what has come to be called the Age of Reason, the scientific method of empiricism became the dominant way of knowing. Observation, hypothesis, experiment; the search for mathematically based laws of nature; and a sharp distinction between reason and emotion: these became the defining characteristics of the empirical method which has dominated western approaches to truth/knowledge since the Enlightenment, and out of which developed the social sciences in the nineteenth century, earnestly trying to replicate the methods of the paradigmatic physical sciences. Apart from the voices of the romantic poets (Byron, Wordsworth), who embraced a pre-Enlightenment mysticism and reverence for nature that was in stark contrast to the Age of Reason's confidence in conquering and dominating nature, the most important sources of opposition to Enlightenment empiricism in the nineteenth century were the critiques of Karl Marx and Friedrich Engels.

Marx made the radical argument that all knowledge is a reflection of specific material conditions, and that the so-called objective scientific model of the Age of Reason was in fact the knowledge that served the emerging bourgeoisie whose industrial wealth was created by the technical applications of the scientific revolution. Marx dared to argue that knowledge is class-based and reflects class interests. Bourgeois social science was, in his words, mere ideology. He proposed to replace this ideology with a 'truly' scientific method, which he called dialectical materialism. Based on German philosopher Hegel's dialectics, Marx and Engels developed a method in which thought proceeds by contradiction and reconciliation of contradiction, to a new synthesis. Marxist social science was intended to expose the ideological foundations of 'bourgeois' social science, and to establish universal (dialectical) laws of society, nature, and thought. These dialectical laws, according to Engels, revealed that both nature and society are in a continuous process of evolutionary, though conflict-laden, development. Interestingly, Marxist doctrine is clearly based on the same Enlightenment territory of belief in objectivity and reason, only claiming that its method actually possesses those characteristics, while 'bourgeois' social science does not.

The New World had been very receptive to Enlightenment thought in the eighteenth and nineteenth centuries. By the late nineteenth century America was producing its own responses to empiricism (that is, to observation-based scientific method). The philosophy of pragmatism was very much an American invention of this era. Seeking action-relevant knowledge, philosophers like John Dewey criticized what they called the 'spectator theory of knowledge', arguing that the aim of knowledge was to make a difference in the world. What was important, therefore, was to assess the value of ideas by their outcomes, rather than by their (ideal) intentions. Dewey's writings gave an emphasis to social experimentation, to the reciprocity of theory and praxis, knowledge and action, facts and values. Out of this philosophical tradition came an epistemology of practice that we might call 'learning by doing', or social learning – a tradition that has developed a strong following in the planning literature (Friedmann, 1987). But in the West, the most dominant epistemology since the seventeenth century has been based on empiricism, the verification of the physical world through scientific observation. It is customary to refer to this as the epistemology of the Enlightenment, and it is this epistemology that has underpinned the history of planning thought.

PLANNING'S ENLIGHTENMENT EPISTEMOLOGY

Modernist planning is a child of the Enlightenment, that period stretching from the late seventeenth to the late eighteenth century (roughly from the time of the English revolution to that of the French revolution) which began with scientific breakthroughs in our understanding of nature and of our place in the heliocentric universe and ended not only with the technical applications of those scientific breakthroughs transforming the entire system of production (the industrial revolution) but also with challenges to the entire social and political order represented by the absolute power of Church and monarchy, and a feudal class structure. In his 1784 essay 'What is Enlightenment?' the German philosopher Immanuel Kant described it as that point in history when humanity put its

own reason to use, without subjecting itself to any authority, particularly ecclesiastical authority. 'It is humanity's passage to adult status.'

Historians today use the word 'Enlightenment' also as an adjective, as in 'the Enlightenment tradition', denoting a specific attitude of mind that gradually gained ascendancy among European intellectuals and bourgeoisie during this hundred-year period. We might characterize this attitude of mind as dedication to human reason, science, and education as the best means of building a stable society of free men on earth. Enlightenment thinkers were hostile to tradition, opposed to any authority based on custom and faith alone, and some (particularly the French *philosophes*) were anti-clerical as well. This was an era that was intoxicated with the idea of progress through reason, of perfecting the good life on earth guided solely by the light of reason, which would free *men's* minds from the bonds of superstition and ignorance. Liberty, equality, and fraternity were its slogans. In epistemology, the claim was that the world could be known objectively. The practice and logic of the physical sciences involved hypothesis-testing through experiment and careful measurement. Rigorously applying this 'scientific method' would result in the discovery of universal laws about the world of material facts.

Feminists have critically described 'the ascent of mathematical man' (Wertheim, 1995) and the rise and privileging of 'the science of measurement'. In his novel *Hard Times* Charles Dickens gives us, in Mr Gradgrind, a scathing portrait of the obsession with fact-finding and calculative power, a man always 'ready to weigh and measure each parcel of human nature, and tell you exactly what it comes to' (Nussbaum, 1990: 77). By the time Dickens was writing, in the middle of the nineteenth century, the social sciences were well on their way to defining themselves by virtue of their capacity to imitate the methods of the physical sciences, and it is here that we must locate the impulse to plan, in the Enlightenment view that reason, leading to knowledge, is the most powerful basis for acting in the world in order to change it. As Auguste Comte (the 'father' of sociology) argued, society itself would be governed by scientific principles, which would ensure the rationality of decisions.

While the history of planning thought contains many streams (Friedmann, 1987), all of them come from the same headwaters of Enlightenment epistemology, flowing through the social sciences, to produce what I called in Chapter 1 the 'heroic model' of modernist planning. The six pillars of this heroic model, enumerated there, can be re-stated succinctly here as rationality; comprehensiveness; scientific method; faith in state-directed futures; faith in planners' ability to know what is good for people generally, 'the public interest'; and political neutrality. As planning emerged as a profession in the years after World War II, it consolidated itself around a social science core that emphasized its claims to rationality and objectivity. In such classics as Harvey Perloff's *Education for Planning: City, State and Regional* (1957) or Andreas Faludi's *Critical Rationalism and Planning Methodology* (1986), the ideal planner appears as rational, detached, a-political; a servant of a benign state; confident in *his* own expertise, and in *his* ability to develop 'general principles applicable not in one situation alone, but, with modifications, in any similar one' (Perloff, 1957: 140), confident, that is, in the universality of planning principles.

Planning involves the careful elaboration and integration of a series of projected actions to attain the desired goals. Planning thus centers on the making of decisions and scheduled effectuation of policies. It takes form in a number of closely integrated steps, from the analysis of problems, the setting of broad objectives and the survey of available resources, to the establishment of specific operating targets; and through various succeeding stages until the results can be checked against the targets established and needed adjustments proposed.

(Perloff, 1957: 142)

Here speaks the voice of reason, in a detached, dispassionate tone. According to Perloff, planning is a kind of decision-technology, the science of society. In other words, planning was captured by a particular view of knowledge that privileges technical rationality and instrumental problem-solving ability over an array of what I will argue are equally important alternatives, such as value rationality. But before I set out these alternatives, I want to listen to some recent voices that have been raised in opposition to what Herbert Marcuse, in a book of the same title, called so succinctly '*one dimensional man*' – the man of technical reason, Rational Man.

FRIEDMANN'S MUTUAL LEARNING

Critiques of Enlightenment epistemology have been swelling over the past two decades. Within planning, there are at least three internal critiques that must be acknowledged as chipping away at the heroic model of Rational Man that the profession has aspired to. In *Retracking America* (1973), John Friedmann diagnosed a dual crisis in post-industrial society: a crisis of values and a crisis of knowing. Describing the latter, he talked of the growing polarity between experts and actors (or planners and people), with experts confident in their science-based, professional knowledge. Actors, on the other hand, possess a great deal of experiential knowledge that is not acknowledged as having any validity in the planning process. Further, experts tend to formulate problems in a language that actors often don't understand, thereby widening the gap. In Friedmann's view, neither camp has all the answers necessary for problem-solving, and the way forward is to bring the two together in a process of *mutual learning*. To bridge this gap between experts and client-actors, Friedmann urged the adoption of a *transactive style* of planning which would place more emphasis on inter-personal relationships and skills. He described the new world of transactive planning as revolving around the life of dialogue, with its emphasis on human worth and reciprocity. He wrote of accepting the authenticity of the other person; of a necessary fusion of thinking, moral judgement, feeling, and empathy; of recognition of the importance of the non-verbal; and the acceptance of conflict as inevitable and something that must be dealt with rather than denied.

SCHÖN'S REFLECTIVE PRACTITIONER

Ten years later, in *The Reflective Practitioner* (1983), Donald Schön also identified a 'crisis of confidence in professional knowledge', a crisis which he attributed in part to the way in which universities as institutions are committed to a particular epistemology, 'a view of knowledge that fosters selective inattention to practical competence and professional artistry' (Schön, 1983: vii). He contrasted the 'hard knowledge of science and scholar-ship' with the 'soft knowledge of artistry' and set out to inquire into the epistemology of practice, based on a close examination of what some practitioners actually do. Practi-tioners, he argued, usually know more than they can say, possessing a complex 'know-ledge-in-practice', most of which remains unarticulated. Schön's book then takes apart the 'dominant epistemology of practice', the model of technical rationality, a model of instrumental problem-solving made rigorous by the application of scientific theory and technique. This model, which is embedded in the institutional context of professional life, emerged in the nineteenth century with the rise of science and technology as the social movement aimed at applying the achievements of science and technology to the well-being of humankind. With positivism then in the ascendant in the social sciences, technical rationality became 'the positivist epistemology of practice' (Schön, 1983: 40).

For Schön, the main problem with this model is that it obscures or denies the differ-ence between problem-solving and problem-setting. For problem-solving, technical rationality is often the most appropriate model, but before a problem can be solved *it has to be defined*. Problem-setting is the process by which we define the decision that is to be made, the ends to be achieved, and the relevant or appropriate means. In order to convert a problematic situation to a problem, Schön explained, a practitioner must do a certain kind of work. He must make sense of an uncertain situation that initially makes no sense. For example, when a planner considers what road to build, s/he faces a complex and ill-defined situation in which geographic, social, political, topological, and financial issues are all mixed. Deciding what road to build, where, is so much harder than deciding how best to build it. It is the difference between *phronesis* and *techne*. And it is this sort of situation that is central to planning practice. Problem-setting, which is a necessary condi-tion for technical problem-solving, is not itself a technical problem. When we set the problem, we impose upon it a coherence that allows us to say what is wrong and what needs changing. 'Problem-setting is a process in which, interactively, we name the things to which we will attend and frame the context in which we'll attend to them' (Schön, 1983: 40).

The persistence today of the idea of technical rationality is obvious in the hunger of students for technique. Perhaps one of the most difficult tasks of planning educators is to teach the limits of technical rationality, to demonstrate that the scope of technical expert-ise is limited by situations of great uncertainty, instability, uniqueness, and conflict. According to Schön, this means that the only real claim to expertise that a professional/planner can make is the claim to be well-prepared to *reflect in action*. 'Professionals are best seen as participants in a larger societal conversation' (Schön, 1983: 353). If we think about how the problem to be solved and the policies to be adopted are constructed through these larger conversations – through the media, institutions, public debate – then we come to realize that descriptions of reality are themselves socially constructed. The reflective planner participates in these societal conversations; and in so doing, helps to construct the problem to be solved. Schön's work makes a very strong statement about the efficacy of technical and quantitative analyses. They are tools, no more and no less, frequently valuable, but incomplete without the richer study of human ends that they themselves cannot perform.

FORESTER'S TALKING AND LISTENING

The notion of a societal conversation leads us to the work of John Forester and others (Healey, 1992; Innes, 1995) who have been attracted to the work of the contemporary German social philosopher and political theorist Jürgen Habermas. Forester has spent a lot of time observing planners *in situ*, and talking with them about what it is that they are really doing. He concludes that planning is, more than anything, an interactive, communicative activity. As an emerging paradigm (Innes, 1995), the idea of planning as communicative action turns its back on the model of technical rationality and systematic analysis in favour of a more qualitative and interpretive mode of inquiry, seeking to understand the unique and the contextual rather than arriving at general rules for practice. These 'communicative' thinkers are also attracted to the story-telling mode, and to seeking insights from such stories about practice (Peattie, 1987; Throgmorton, 1991; 1996; Mandelbaum, 1991). Forester's *Planning in the Face of Power* (1989) and *The Deliberative Practitioner* (1999) have become the 'classic' texts in this emerging field. Surely influenced by Schön's lead, Forester defines the planner's key activities as focusing and shaping attention, talking and listening. Drawing on Habermas' work, particularly *The Theory of Communicative Action* (1984) and his concept of communicative rationality, Forester and his colleagues who are shaping this new paradigm are proposing a new method of knowing. One element is self-reflection, designed to identify one's own rationalizations and uncover what is hidden in the self. A second is that emancipatory knowledge comes from discourse and dialectic. A third way of knowing comes through praxis, through action in the world, through experience and practical know-how (Innes, 1995: 186). Finally, Forester emphasizes the political nature of all planning activity, in which relations of power are always involved and systemic inequalities influence outcomes. 'To be rational, be political', he advises (Forester, 1989: 25). Be aware of systemic inequalities and work to redress them. Pay attention to imbalances of information, to lack of representation. Make sure all the major points of view are heard, and not only those of the most articulate or powerful.

Interestingly, the combined works of Friedmann, Schön, and Forester, which constitute a clear challenge to the hitherto hegemonic Enlightenment epistemology, can also be seen as drawing on a much older tradition, that of Aristotelian thinking about practical wisdom. This link has been made consciously in the recent work of Danish scholar Bent Flyvbjerg (2001), who proposes a synthesis of Aristotle, Nietzsche and Foucault that he calls 'progressive *phronesis*' and 'the science of the concrete'. What is particularly important about Flyvbjerg's reworking of Aristotle's original conception of *phronesis* is that he foregrounds the issues of power, values, and conflict.[3] Flyvbjerg has produced a deep epistemological critique of the social sciences, arguing that their strength is not in attempting to imitate the natural sciences in explanatory and predictive theory, but rather in recognizing that their *forte* is the 'reflexive analysis of values and interests, which is the prerequisite for an enlightened political, economic, and cultural development in any society' (Flyvbjerg, 2001: 3).

CRITIQUES OF ENLIGHTENMENT EPISTEMOLOGY

Since there is now an array of individual challenges from within planning to its foundational epistemology, it may be appropriate to summarize some of the recent systematic
critiques of that Enlightenment epistemology – feminist, postmodern and postcolonial –
before drawing all these arguments together and outlining a possible *post-Enlightenment*
epistemology for planning. But before launching into these recent critiques, it is
important to note their 'prehistories' – in the intellectual traditions of the sociology of
knowledge (Mannheim, 1949), the Frankfurt School's critical theory (Adorno and
Horkheimer, 1982), in the history and philosophy of science (Kuhn, 1961, Capra, 1975),
and in hermeneutics (Gadamer, 1976).[4] Each of these earlier traditions remains
influential today, and each has helped shape contemporary feminist, postmodern and
postcolonial critiques of Enlightenment epistemology, which I now review.

FEMINIST CRITIQUES

An epistemology is both a theory of knowledge and a justificatory strategy (Harding,
1987). It frames questions such as who can be a knower, (can women, can non-experts?);
what tests beliefs must pass in order to be validated as knowledge (tests from observation, experiment, calculation, only? Or tests based on experience, perception, imagination?); what kinds of things can be known (can subjective truths count as knowledge?);
the nature of objectivity (does it require the absence of a point of view?); the appropriate
relationship between the researcher and her subject/s (must, can, the researcher be
detached, dispassionate?); and what should be the purpose of the pursuit of knowledge?

From the early 1970s, feminists' interest in epistemology was provoked by the apparent exclusion of women from the epistemology that has dominated the social sciences
since their emergence in the nineteenth century – that of positivism. Feminists argue that
positivist epistemology excludes women as 'knowers' or agents of knowledge and
excludes women's life experiences as valid foci of study; that the voice of science is a
masculine one; and that history has been written only from the point of view of men of
the dominant class and race. Since the late 1970s feminists have been proposing alternative theories of knowledge that legitimate women's claims as knowers (Harding and
Hintikka, 1983; Cook and Fonow, 1986; Jaggar and Bordo, 1989; Nielsen, 1989), and raise
the possibility of 'women's ways of knowing' (Belenky *et al.*, 1986). Most of the earlier
feminist work began by wanting to make a better science by 'adding women' to traditional analyses and by acknowledging that women had been historically excluded from
the institutions where knowledge is produced and validated, particularly with respect to
scientific knowledge (Keller, 1985; Harding, 1986; Wertheim, 1995).

Subsequently, feminists began to challenge the privileging of scientific and technical
knowledge at the expense of other ways of knowing, such as knowledge based on experience, intuition, and imagination, and to outline a distinctively feminist epistemology,
elements of which include the notions of 'connected knowing' (Belenky *et al.*, 1986),

passionate knowledge, 'maternal thinking' (Ruddick, 1989), the importance of dialogue and the validity of emotions in the pursuit of knowledge and understanding (Collins, 1990). Although the idea of a 'connected knowing' (the head and the heart, reason and emotion) suggests an attempt to transcend the dualism at the heart of positivist epistemology, the very idea of a *feminist* epistemology reinforces all those Enlightenment dualisms, from male/female to rational/irrational, mind/body, culture/nature. This is a particular problem in the eco-feminist literature, which first accepts these dualisms, and then tries to reverse the value placed on them. In other words, eco-feminists agree with Enlightenment arguments that identify women with (mother) nature, suggesting that women's superiority lies in their innate peace-loving and nurturing qualities (compared with man the aggressor and destroyer). This essentialist position concerning women's nature has come under much scrutiny (Spelman, 1988). Indeed, the danger in discussing 'the feminist epistemological project', and the problem inherent in much of the feminist literature of the mid-1970s to mid-1980s, was precisely the tendency to imply that there is a feminist social science, a feminist epistemology, a feminist research method. Disagreement is now widespread on these questions. Challenges to the very notion of a feminist epistemology have come from three directions: from women of colour, from non-western feminists, and from postmodern feminist philosophy. These will be further discussed in the next sections on postcolonial and postmodern critiques. Before we move on to these critiques however, it is important to summarize broad areas of feminist agreement with respect to theories of knowledge.

Feminists insist on the importance of discussing the politics of theory and method and the origins and implications of our theoretical hierarchies. We insist on paying attention to the political content of knowledge creation, to the ways in which knowledges are institutionalized, and to who benefits from the production of which knowledges. We argue that knowledge is not, has never been, gender-neutral and that knowledge in planning, for example, is loaded with assumptions about the appropriate relations (of subordination and domination) between the sexes, as well as with assumptions about who is a legitimate knower. We argue that knowledge is, above all, a social construction and as such will always be an unfinished business. Still, differences between modernist feminists and postmodern feminism with regard to theories of knowledge remain significant.

POSTMODERN CRITIQUES

The most familiar names in the postmodern pantheon, Lyotard, Derrida, Foucault, have each mounted formidable attacks on Enlightenment epistemology, which have in turn come under scrutiny from feminists and people of colour writing from what has come to be called a postcolonial perspective. Postmodern critiques begin with an attack on the very idea of a possible theory of knowledge (or justice or beauty), arguing that the pursuit of such theories rests upon the modernist conception of a transcendent reason, a reason able to separate itself not only from historical time and place but also from the body. 'There is no Reason; only reasons' (Lyotard, 1984, in Yeatman, 1994). The critique of the Enlightenment concept of rationality and its unitary definition of truth forms the basis of postmodern thought. The postmoderns claim that the Enlightenment privileged rational discourse by identifying it as the sole avenue to truth, and by defining that discourse in terms of its abstraction from social context. Postmodernism rejects this privileging of rational discourse, arguing that there cannot be one such privileged discourse.

Postmodern thinkers also reject the Enlightenment position that unless knowledge has an absolute ground, an unshakeable foundation (Reason, Nature, God) it cannot qualify as truth. In opposition to this tradition, they advocate what Richard Rorty has called 'a continuing conversation rather than discovering truth' (Rorty, 1979: 373). For Lyotard, Derrida, and Foucault, grand narratives of legitimation (meta-narratives) are no longer credible for they are all based on unitary definitions of truth. Whether the meta-narrative be that of the Enlightenment's story of the progress and triumph of reason, or the Marxian drama of class conflict culminating in proletarian revolution; the liberal/capitalist story of material progress through the hidden hand of the market, or the Freudian plots of father-son rivalry, mother-son love – all commit the epistemological sin of assuming one overarching truth. For the postmoderns, these meta-narratives are imprisoning, totalizing discourses, and they are intimately linked to structures of power.

Foucault explored the ways in which particular discourses create their own definitions of truth. In drawing attention to the more sinister connections between knowledge and power, Foucault exposed a dark side of Enlightenment thought which has necessarily transformed our understanding of the role of institutionalized knowledges. Foucault provided a critique of the way modern societies control and discipline their populations by sanctioning the knowledge claims and practices of the human sciences – medicine, psychiatry, psychology, criminology, sociology. His analysis makes us critical of the pre-sumed rationality of our discourses and practices, taking us behind the façade of univer-sality and objectivity to reveal the operation of modern techniques of domination – of which the modern, self-examining, self-policing, self-disciplining, 'normal' individual is a product. He asks us to look carefully at how the familiar objects of our everyday experience, from the self and our bodies to our social institutions and scientific norms, are 'objects produced in historically variable relations of power' – that is, neither 'nat-ural' nor 'scientific'. In Foucault's analysis, modern power is, above all, disciplinary. Its goal is normalization and the production of docile and useful bodies. The particular form modern power takes is centreless, it is capillary. Rather than located in the state, or in capital, power is a moving substratum of force relations, local and unstable. And the agents of this distinctively modern form of normalizing or disciplinary power include social workers, teachers, doctors, social scientists, and ordinary citizens who internalize the categories and values of the dominant regime of power.

Foucault's analysis of the role of the professions in power regimes should surely be extended to the planning profession.[5] If the rise of the professions created the possibility for new forms of domination, then each new profession carries within it the possibility and techniques for controlling others.[6] I have already noted in Chapter 2 how Foucault's work provides a new basis for exploration and interpretation of planning's history, an unveiling of its disciplinary and oppressive aspects. But there is also a liberatory side of Foucault's thinking which is potentially useful to planners. For if power is anchored in the micro-practices of everyday life, then that is also where oppositional politics needs to begin, with a deconstruction of the power relationships built into everyday practices, and a reconstructed, political planning. Before we leave Foucault, there is a caution in his writing about 'the paradox of rationality', and an ambivalence in his thinking about the Enlightenment, that I would like to adopt. 'If it is extremely dangerous to say that Reason is the enemy that should be eliminated, it is just as dangerous to say that any critical questioning of this rationality risks sending us into irrationality' (Foucault in Rabinow, 1984: 43). Here Foucault echoes Pascal's (seventeenth-century) insight that there are two equally significant dangers: one is to shut reason out, the other is to let nothing else in. Foucault was careful not to dismiss the Enlightenment but rather to see it as a historical production and as such to understand the limits it imposes on us as well as the possibility of going beyond them (Foucault in Rabinow, 1984: 50).

The preceding discussion of postmodern thinking has deliberately focused on the names most commonly associated with the discourse. But, as noted at the outset, these writers have been challenged both by feminists and by those who do not accept the privileging of western thought and thinkers. Feminists have pointed to the gender-blindness of the writers just discussed (significantly, all male), and have extended their analyses to incorporate a gender perspective into the critique of Enlightenment epistemology. From Locke to Rousseau, Hegel to Freud, from Newton to Boyle, the Enlightenment message about the inferiority of women was clear. John Locke asserted 'Woman cannot know; therefore she must believe'. Rousseau proclaimed that 'never has a people perished from excess of wine; all perish from the disorder of women'. Freud argued in *Civilization and its Discontents* (Chapter 4) that women are hostile to and in opposition to civilization. And German philosopher Hegel wrote that the community 'creates its enemy for itself within its own gates' in 'womankind in general' (Pateman, 1989: 17).

Feminists remain divided about the appropriate response to this historically based gendering of knowledge. Modernist feminists argue that we should accept the Enlightenment definition of rationality, but open it up to the inclusion of women, thereby completing the Enlightenment project of liberation through knowledge. Women are every bit as rational as men, so this argument goes. Other feminists, particularly those associated with eco-feminism (Merchant, 1980; Shiva, 1988), are prepared to accept the rational/irrational dichotomy as an accurate reflection of the 'true nature' of men and women, but argue for revalorizing the feminine side of the dichotomy, asserting its superiority. Postmodern feminists, myself included, attack rationality in its Enlightenment form, based on scientific reason and belief in objectivity, and reject the dichotomy rational/irrational of modernist thought. They also reject the universalism and essentialism implicit in the positing of an a-historical feminine nature (Nicholson, 1990). In particular, women of colour, lesbians, and non-western women have disputed the assumption that the category 'women' is or can be a unifying category capable of transcending differences in class, race, ethnicity, and sexual preference. They remind us that feminist theory has for the most part been written by white, western, middle-class, straight women, unconscious of their own position and special interests as members of a dominant culture (Collins, 1990; Anzaldúa, 1990; hooks, 1984; 1989; Narayan, 1989). Indeed, the issue of difference has preoccupied feminists for several decades, and is at the heart of postmodern feminist theorizing. The point here is not to deny the epistemological issues that divide feminists, but to clarify them.

Summarizing the epistemological orientation of postmodern feminist thought then, we can list the following characteristics: a deconstructive approach to the modernist theoretical traditions we have inherited; the disruptive assertion of 'minority' voices in the face of universalist theorizing; a refusal of the logic of the binary constructions that divide (as in 'either reason or emotion') in favour of an inclusive logic (as in 'both reason and emotion'); a conception of knowledge as historically contingent and possessing an embodied subjectivity (rejecting the mind/body dualism that is inscribed in modern social science); a critique of the gendered production of knowledge; a recognition of the power relations embedded in being a knower/theorist; and an acknowledgement of the determinative influence of language as a 'material, active, production system' (Pateman, 1988; Yeatmann, 1994).

POSTCOLONIAL CRITIQUES

Postmodernism is a hotly contested theoretical zone. Nevertheless, most commentators agree that it represents a crisis of authority for the western knowing subject, posed by the refusal to stay silenced on the part of those whom this subject had cast as Other: natives, colonials, women, and all who are placed in a client relationship to expert, professional authority (Yeatman, 1994: 27). By insisting on their own voice and status as subjects, these former objects of modern western knowledge have disrupted the dominant relations of knowledge and power which have existed since the Enlightenment's privileging of scientific and technical knowledge and since the imperialist activities of the western powers had imposed a relationship of domination/subordination based on the material superiority of western science and technology. From the standpoint of those who are contesting their status as Other, the project of seeking acceptance and assimilation within hegemonic discourse is no longer acceptable. It has been replaced by a politics of difference, informed by a post-foundationalist epistemology.

The postcolonial critique of Enlightenment epistemology begins with an epistemological politics of representation in which two strategic questions are posed: whose representations of reality prevail? And who has the authority to represent reality? (Or, who must be silenced for these representations to prevail? Whose voice is deprived of authority so that they may prevail?) 'This is a politics of representation which insists on the material effects of discursive power ... and which refuses legitimacy to the consensual community of rational scientists which both Karl Popper and Jürgen Habermas invoke in their respective conceptions of science and rational discourse' (Yeatman, 1994: 31).

Postcolonial discourse is clearly attempting to open up contested epistemological spaces, as bell hooks explains in a much-quoted passage. 'Spaces can be real and imagined. Spaces can tell stories and unfold histories . . . The appropriation and use of space are political acts' (hooks, 1990: 152). And Barbara Christian identifies in the Black narrative tradition a unique form of theoretical resistance to power:

> our theorizing . . . is often in narrative forms, in the stories we create, in riddles and proverbs, in play with language . . . And women, at least the women I grew up around, continuously specu-lated about the nature of life through pithy language that unmasked the power relations of their world.
>
> (Christian, 1988: 68)

Clyde Woods has made a similar argument with respect to the importance of the Blues in African American culture and its history of resistance. He identifies a 'Blues epistemol-ogy' – a system of social explanation that has informed daily life, social institutions, and social movements, affirming the value of the culture and its ability to deal with chaos and repression. 'The essential motive behind the best blues songs is the acquisition of insight, wisdom' (Larry Neal, in Woods, 1998: 84).

The works of Edward Said, Homi Bhabha, Guyatri Spivak, Trinh Minh-ha, Chinua Achebe, and Ngugi wa Thiong'o, along with Christian, Woods, Anzaldúa and hooks, are challenging not only Enlightenment epistemology but eurocentrism itself, insofar as western thought has worked as a colonizer of other cultures and sought to impose its own rationality and language. 'The bullet was the means of physical subjugation. Lan-guage was the means of the spiritual subjugation' (Thiong'o, 1986). The voices of postco-lonial critics offer and defend new/old ways of knowing, including the right to speak one's own language.

*

If we accept what is common to all of the above critiques – that all knowledge is embodied, historically situated, shaped by language, and embedded in power relations, institutionalized or not – then the very idea of the expert planner able to arrive at an understanding of 'the public interest' through rational deliberation will have to be revised in favour of a notion of planning for multiple publics, based on an epistemology of multiplicity. It is towards that new epistemology for planning that we are moving in the final sections of this chapter.

EPISTEMOLOGICAL POLITICS

There's nothing more political than epistemological struggles. From the debates about how best to arrive at truth, to all of the critiques of Enlightenment epistemology, the wars of words and philosophies have enormous practical consequences. They are debates about what counts as knowledge and who counts as a knower. Wittgenstein's observation, in *On Certainty*, that 'knowledge is in the end based on acknowledgement' (Wittgenstein, 1971: 378) captures a central theme of this chapter. All knowledge is a

social construction, and as such requires the validation of a community of knowers. But socio-political processes are at work in constituting that community (actually, multiple communities), and personal and political struggles take place around both the process and the price of admission. As feminist philosopher Lorraine Code has argued, the capacity to gain acknowledgement as a knower is gender-related in ways that Wittgenstein never envisaged. Like any other knower, a female knowledge claimant has to claim acknowledgement from other participants in a field, or process, or institution. But before she can begin to seek this acknowledgement, a woman has to free herself from stereotyped conceptions of her 'underclass' epistemic status, her cognitive incapacity, and her ever-threatening irrationality (Code, 1991: 215). And she has to achieve this freedom not only in the eyes of other people (the relevant community of knowers), who have historically denied her capacity by refusing to listen to or to value what she had to say, but also in her own eyes, trained as they may be to looking through stereotypical spectacles which tell her that neither her experiences nor her deliberative capacities are trustworthy sources of knowledge. For women to be released from these prisons of insecurity and lack of epistemic confidence, spaces have to be created where a woman's knowledge can be judged sufficiently authoritative to deserve acknowledgement, and these spaces need to be responsive to differences between and among women. The creation of such spaces must be a collective effort.

There is no more effective way to create epistemic dependence than systematically to withhold acknowledgement; no more effective way of maintaining structures of epistemic privilege and vulnerability than evincing a persistent distrust in someone's claims to cognitive authority; no surer demonstration of a refusal to know what a person's experiences are than observing her 'objectively' without taking her first person reports seriously.

(Code, 1991: 218)

While Code's work is an inquiry into the gender-related dimensions of knowledge construction, (reflected in the title, *What Can She Know?*), her concept of 'underclass epistemic status' is an evocative one, and clearly applicable to other groups of knowledge claimants, as we have seen in the postcolonial critique of western or eurocentric thought. What can planners learn from the feminist, postcolonial, postmodern critiques reported above?

As the previous pages have shown, there are serious problems with the model of knowing that planners have adopted as their reigning epistemology. These problems stem, first, from the limited applicability of scientific method to the study of human society in general, and to planning in particular (Flyvbjerg, 2001). Problems in planning have been described by Rittel and Webber (1973) as 'wicked', by Friedmann as the challenge of mutual learning (1973), and by Schön as the task of distinguishing between problem-setting and problem-solving (1983), where technical rationality is appropriate only for the latter. Second, there is the problem of what is excluded in the epistemic privileging of the scientific method at the expense of the many other ways of knowing that might be drawn on in practice (and that will be elaborated below). And third, there are problems with the exclusionary definition of legitimate knowers explicit in this scientific model, which only validates professional experts. How then might we revise our dominant epistemology of planning to better reflect these new understandings of planning?

TOWARDS AN EPISTEMOLOGY OF MULTIPLICITY FOR PLANNING PRACTICE

The hunger of students for skills, about which Donald Schön has written so well, is reflected in the pride of place given to courses on quantitative methods in most planning programmes (Friedmann, 1996). These courses reinforce the centrality of Enlightenment epistemology in planning education at the expense of equally important alternatives – experiential, intuitive, and local knowledges; knowledges based on practices of talking, listening, seeing, contemplating, sharing; and knowledges expressed in visual and other symbolic, ritual, and artistic ways. *Without discarding these scientific and technical ways of knowing*, we need to acknowledge, as well, the many other ways of knowing that exist; to understand their importance to culturally diverse populations; and to discern which ways of knowing are most useful in what circumstances. Such an *epistemology of multiplicity* for planning would consist of at least six different ways of knowing, in addition to what is usually taught in planning schools: knowing through dialogue; from experience; through seeking out local knowledge of the specific and concrete; through learning to read symbolic, non-verbal evidence; through contemplation; and through action-planning.

KNOWING THROUGH DIALOGUE

Earlier in this chapter I touched on the emergence of a new paradigm of communicative action, advocated by John Forester, Judith Innes, Larry Susskind and others in the US, and Patsy Healey in the UK. Best elaborated by Forester (1989; 1999), and Healey (1997), this paradigm defines planners' key activity as focusing and shaping attention, and their most important skills as talking and listening. In a wonderful chapter on 'Listening', which he describes as 'the social policy of everyday life', Forester begins with the acknowledgement that in planning practice, reason and emotion, fact and feeling, are usually tightly entwined, and anger and fear are always close at hand because people have large stakes, emotional and financial, in the built environment. In many situations, planners are dealing as much with people's passions as with their own earnest technical predictions. But how to deal with passion? 'Planners must not only be able to hear words; they also must be able to listen to others carefully and critically. Such careful listening requires sensitivity, self-possession, and judgement.' Forester talks about the 'work of listening', not only in planning but in everyday life as well, noting that how we respond, or fail to do so, makes up the politics of our everyday lives.

> We can hear words, but miss what is meant. We can hear what is intended, but miss what is important. We can hear what is important, but neglect the person speaking. As we listen, though, we can learn and nurture relationships as well. Listening is an act of being attentive, a way of being in a moral world. We can make a difference by listening or failing to do so, and we can be held responsible as a result.
>
> (Forester, 1989: 108)

To listen well also means to be able to ask good questions about deeper interests, about what others care about, hope for, and fear. Listening is a deeply hermeneutic activity.

When we listen well, we integrate hermeneutics and critical theory, phenomenology and the critique of ideology, and put them into practice together. Listening necessarily addresses questions of possible actions, of 'what can be done?' If planners do not listen carefully to members of the public, they lose any reputation for responsiveness or fairness. They send signals to the community that what they (the community) have to say is not really important, or valid. 'Listening well, we can act to nurture dialogue and criticism, to make genuine presence possible, to question and explore all that we may yet do and yet become' (Forester, 1989: 118).

In thinking about listening, the question arises to whom and to what should we listen? The advocates of the communicative action paradigm would answer the first part of the question – to whom should we listen – with: the relevant stakeholders. Identifying the relevant stakeholders is itself a deeply political question, which can only be answered in the particulars of a situation, but clearly implies something like 'all those affected', and not only those affected financially but also those affected emotionally, like about-to-be-displaced tenants. To be even more explicit regarding the ever-present power relations in planning, we should make an effort to listen to those who are least powerful. And to what should we listen? Beyond the obvious structured situations of formal dialogue between planners and communities of interest, I suggest that we need to tune in to oral traditions, such as storytelling (see Chapter 8).

The work of planners in multicultural societies is taking place in situations of increasing cultural diversity in which some groups, historically and/or culturally, have relied exclusively or semi-exclusively on oral traditions. The most important, sometimes the only way of acquiring knowledge, for some groups, is through stories and the act of storytelling. African tribes, Australian Aboriginals, Native Americans and First Nations in North America are obvious examples. As these groups become a more acknowledged part of planning processes and decision-making, it would seem that planners must be able to listen to their stories if they really want to understand people's cares, hopes, and fears, and if they want to be able to learn from such peoples – to tap into local knowledges. To return to the story with which I opened this chapter, how can the planners for the community of Broome in the remote Northwest of Australia imagine that they are planning for the whole community, 40 per cent of whom are Aboriginal people, unless they listen to and understand the songlines of the local people? African American Zora Neale Hurston collected stories from poor black folks for her novel *Their Eyes Were Watching God* (1937), a classic tale of empowerment. Might not planners' attention to peoples' stories be equally empowering, in terms of validating their knowledge and moving forward to a situation of mutual learning through respect for that knowledge?

KNOWING FROM EXPERIENCE

Tacit knowledge can be defined as that which people know but cannot say. As the philosopher Michael Polanyi (1962) observed, people usually know more than they can say. When that is so in a planning situation, it must be the responsibility of the planner to try to tap into people's tacit knowing. Particularly when they are working with disempowered communities who have always received messages about their ignorance and/or inferiority, planners need to begin the process of communication by helping people to articulate what they already know. This can be as simple as sitting at someone's kitchen table and saying 'Tell me about your street/village/neighbourhood'. A wealth of information and understanding is likely to tumble out, though not in a form that planners are used to digesting. In more structured participatory situations, planners can adopt the same approach. A social planning consultant who has been hired by a local council or planning agency to bring local residents into the discussion about a controversial development proposal might call a public meeting, to which 500 people show up. How such a meeting is run determines whether it is an empty public relations exercise or a genuine attempt to work with the community to find a solution. If the council or planning agency is genuine in its desire to reach a solution with the community rather than imposing one on them, then the meeting of 500 people needs to be broken up into small groups for meaningful discussion. The social planner needs to hire a team of facilitators, one for each table of small group discussion, and the first question such a facilitator might pose, to get dialogue going, could be 'Tell me about this community' (see Sarkissian and Perlgut, 1995). In this way, the planning process begins to tap into people's tacit knowledge.

Intuitive knowledge is harder to describe. It is a kind of informed guesswork. To intuit that a problem exists usually means that we are using our senses to interpret signs, in the environment, in people's behaviour, in a situation. The intuition comes not out of the blue, but precisely because we are immersed in something and are paying close attention to detail (like Barbara McClintock 'listening' to the ears of corn that were the subject of her research, as described in Keller, 1983, or like Aboriginal people knowing where to find water in an apparently desert landscape). Good intuitive skills are also an important part of good interpersonal skills, which are now being recognized as a vital part of a planner's repertoire.

Tacit and intuitive knowledge are each part of something larger that we describe as experiential knowing, a knowing that comes from living, from simply being, as well as from doing. Planners who have been around for a while are constantly drawing on their fund of experiential knowledge, often without consciously acknowledging that they are doing so. Besides drawing on their own experiential knowing, planners need to draw more consciously on the experiences of others. How better to learn about the social and urban impacts of, say, immigration policy, than to ask those who are living it, both immigrants and host communities. How better to design a playground than by working with children, a senior citizens' centre than by working with seniors. The very idea of an apprenticeship is an acknowledgement of the value – to an aspiring doctor, sculptor, planner, chef – of learning at the side of someone who has more experience. But in urging planners to be more receptive to experiential knowledge, I have in mind something much broader than professional experience. And that is the individual and collective experiential knowledge of those who dwell in the place in question – whether street, village, city or region, ethnic enclave or red-light district: those who possess local knowledge.

LEARNING FROM LOCAL KNOWLEDGE

Wisdom, as an African proverb has it, comes out of an ant heap. Practical wisdom, in Aristotelian thought, is concerned with the concrete, with particulars. To know a city is to know its streets, we might say. And who knows those streets better than those who live in them and use them? Who knows the needs of a village better than the villagers? A planner from Washington DC (or Paris or Geneva) flies into Quito, Ecuador, with a solution to 'underdevelopment' in her briefcase, a solution which is in 'the public interest' because it was generated by consultation with objective data files and through familiarity with economists' models of economic growth. Why be surprised if the solution is rejected by either the local politicians or the people of the villages, or both? Should planners be surprised if, despite substantial financial backing, the plan falters in implementation?

If it seems so obvious today that we need to draw on local knowledge in the planning process, whether the locale is south central Los Angeles or an Andean village, why then is it still the exception rather than the rule, the world over? In part, it is because planners believe that 'uncertified' people can't understand 'the complexities'. It is also because of the lingering belief – the all-too-pervasive influence of Enlightenment epistemology – that local knowledge is 'tainted' by self-interest: that is, by the passions, whether greed, love, attachment, anger, faith, power, prestige, beauty. I suggest that many planners, because of their positivist training, are afraid of the presence of these emotions in the community, do not know how to deal with their eruption in the midst of what is meant to be rational deliberation, and therefore choose to hide behind the apparent safety and alleged objectivity of data. We are a profession in a state of arrested emotional development.

LEARNING TO READ SYMBOLIC AND NON-VERBAL EVIDENCE

There are many forms in which knowledge can be expressed. I have already mentioned stories and storytelling as ways of knowing that might be explored by planners in particular cultural and class settings. We might also pay attention to music, painting, poetry, and theatre. We might think of music as including rap, folk songs, the blues, reggae, and more; of painting as including murals, graffiti, Aboriginal bark paintings, chalk drawings on pavements; of theatre as street demonstrations, performance art, rituals of all sorts.[7] Once we pay attention to these symbolic forms of expression, and learn how to 'read' them, we can learn from them about what's on people's minds, their hopes and anxieties. So, tuning in, getting a better understanding of particular groups (like youth) or marginalized peoples (Aboriginal, Native American) is one reason for paying attention to symbolic forms. Another is that we may be able to use such alternative ways of communicating in the planning process, as part of community consultation, or as a tool of community organizing. Two examples follow.

In the Watts neighbourhood of Los Angeles, African American performance artist James Woods uses chalk drawings on a pavement as part of his community organizing and educating work. He gathers people together, young and old, supplies chalk, occupies public space, and asks people to draw what's on their mind concerning a particular topic. Woods' approach is part of a broader interest in the way in which the arts can be used as part of community organizing and place-making.

In the township of Hastings on Westernport Bay, 70 kilometers south east of Melbourne (Australia), industrial development, recreational boating, tourism and real estate investment were, by the 1980s, beginning to threaten an area of immense ecological value, including a landscape of mudflats, salt marsh, and white mangroves. Dredging, swamp draining, the human waste created by large settlements on the Bay, and the industrial waste from steel mills, gas and oil refineries that were the area's large employers, were devastating the delicate environment. Residents became concerned, and arguments raged with industry and a pro-development council about the future of the area. A group called the Westernport and Peninsula Protection Council (WPPC) was formed and decided to raise local awareness by entering a float in the annual Hastings parade. Using his theatre and puppetry skills, one of the local residents, Ian Cuming, constructed an elaborate display – The Seagrass Story – which pointed to the unexplained disappearance from the bay of large tracts of seagrass, the basis of the food chain. The sensational appearance of this float in the parade precipitated a three-year campaign that involved many parts of the community (Winikoff, 1995: 69).

This community participated in workshops on biological research, oral history, puppetry, costume-making, acting and music. The result was the Seagrass Project, a three-year-long environmental theatre project which developed annual dramatizations of the story of the Bay in all its environmental and industrial complexity, and which brought together councillors, artists, scientists, business people, conservationists and residents. The theatre performances, which were held at twilight on a park adjacent to the bay that had formerly been a garbage tip, attracted huge audiences. The Seagrass Project helped people to see the problem from a different perspective, helped them to connect emotionally to a particular environment, and to come together in a non-confrontational way to explore solutions to a complex set of problems.

LEARNING THROUGH CONTEMPLATIVE OR APPRECIATIVE KNOWLEDGE

In the Enlightenment tradition, the truth of the world as it emerges from scientific inquiries is validated by becoming the basis for the mastery of the world. Learning the secrets of nature, we learn to fly, to harness the sun's energy, to transmit signals over vast distances. The social validation of knowledge through mastery of the world puts the emphasis on manipulative knowledge. But knowledge can also serve another purpose: the construction of satisfying and meaningful images of the world. Such knowledge, which we pursue primarily for the world-view it opens up, may be called appreciative knowledge. Contemplation, and the creation of symbolic forms expressing that contemplation, continue to be pursued as ways of knowing about the world, but because they are not immediately useful (what is the use value of a painting, or of the story of an Aboriginal songline?), they are not validated or respected socially.

In Native American and other indigenous cultures, knowledge was not acquired through anything remotely resembling the scientific method, or even the question and answer mode. Rather, knowing was founded on suggestion, example, divining, drawing out, showing, and storytelling. The 'product' of such knowledge is that these cultures have a very different attitude towards nature and their place within it. Native Americans think in terms of the Seventh Generation. Australian Aboriginals see themselves as custodians of the land, which they are merely passing through. They do not 'see' any qualitative difference, any separation, between nature and themselves. 'We all make up the Living Country', says Frans, who has learnt this from the Aboriginal elder Paddy (Sinatra and Murphy, 1999). 'See, you are that land, and the land is you.'

This kind of appreciative, contemplative knowledge is very much at odds with the instrumental knowledge of the Enlightenment tradition. That instrumental knowledge has contributed to what Max Weber called the 'disenchantment of the world', a feeling of profound alienation. Perhaps, if we are interested in re-enchanting the world, in re-enchanting our life spaces in cities and regions rather than having to escape from them in order to 'experience nature' or spirituality, then the way forward is to re-valorize contemplative knowledge and to follow where it takes us.

LEARNING BY DOING, OR, ACTION-PLANNING

Acting in the world, and continuously and critically reflecting on that action, is the only workable way of knowing according to John Dewey and the philosophy of pragmatism, and a number of other sources that constitute this 'social learning tradition' (Friedmann, 1987). From Jane Addams' founding of the activist Settlement House movement to Miles Horton and the Highlander School's approach to popular education, the argument is that our knowledge comes from our practice, and returns to it. The social learning approach has, historically, been strongest in the world of community organizing, particularly among practitioners whose goal is community empowerment. Those ideas have in turn infiltrated into planning, through concepts of 'action planning' (Hamdi and Goethert, 1997), and through the community-based approaches practiced by King (1981), Leavitt (1994), Leavitt and Saegert (1990), Heskin (1991), and Reardon (2003), in which the planner works with, and from the perspective of, the poor and the disempowered rather than from the perspective of state-directed, or expert-centred planning practices. As opposed to the advocacy model, in which professionals work *on behalf of* poor communities, in the empowerment model (see Chapters 6 and 7) the role of the professional planner is to enable communities to do things for themselves.

*

In this chapter I have asked what constitutes valid knowledge in planning, and who counts (that is, who is recognized) as a legitimate knower. I have examined mainstream planning's answer to these questions by exploring the Enlightenment epistemology on which planning has been founded. That epistemology has been shown to have serious weaknesses, as reflected in the range of critiques discussed. I have argued that we need to revise our dominant epistemology, to better reflect these new understandings of knowledge. And, finally, I have proposed an *epistemology of multiplicity*, which recognizes at least six different ways of knowing. In principle, there should be no hierarchy between the ways of knowing that I have outlined. They are all potentially valuable. A good planner will be sensitive to them all, without *a priori* privileging any particular one. And part of the skill of the good planner will be her perception of when to use which way, or ways, of knowing, and to see them all as context-dependent. This is the artistry of planning.[8]

PART II

LOOKING FORWARD: MONGREL CITIES AND THE 21ST-CENTURY MULTICULTURAL PROJECT

4

MONGREL CITIES

How can we live together?

The biggest impetus to fragmentation, violence, and anarchy today does not emerge from political engagement with the paradox of difference. It emerges from doctrines and movements that suppress it. Specifically it arises from totalistic identities engaged in implacable struggles against those differences that threaten their hegemony or exclusivity. Such culture wars do not reflect *too much* diversity, difference, or variety: they express contending demands to control the exclusive form the nation, state, or community must assume.

(Connolly, 1995: xxi, my emphasis)

How can we stroppy strangers live together without doing each other too much violence?
(Donald, 1999: 147)

INTRODUCTION

Arriving and departing travellers at Vancouver International Airport are greeted by a huge bronze sculpture of a boatload of strange, mythical creatures. This 20-foot long, 11-foot wide and 12-foot high masterpiece, *The Spirit of Haida Gwaii*, is by the late Bill Reid, a member of the Haida Gwaii First Nations band from the Pacific Northwest. The canoe has 13 passengers, spirits or myth creatures from Haida mythology.[1] The bear mother, who is part human, and the bear father sit facing each other at the bow with their two cubs between them. The beaver is paddling menacingly amidships, and behind him is the mysterious intercultural dogfish woman. Shy mouse woman is tucked in the stern. A ferociously playful wolf sinks his fangs into the eagle's wing, and the eagle is attacking the bear's paw. A frog (who symbollizes the ability to cross boundaries between worlds) is partially in, partially out of the canoe. An ancient reluctant conscript paddles stoically. In the centre, holding a speaker's staff in his right hand, stands the chief, whose identity (according to the sculptor) is deliberately uncertain. The legendary raven (master of tricks, transformations, and multiple identities) steers the motley crew. *The Spirit of Haida Gwaii* is a symbol of the 'strange multiplicity' of cultural diversity that existed millennia ago and wants to be again (Tully, 1995: 18).

Amongst other things, this extraordinary work of art speaks of a spirit of mutual recognition and accommodation; a sense of being at home in the multiplicity yet at the same time playfully estranged by it; and the notion of an unending dialogue that is not always harmonious. For the political philosopher James Tully, the wonderfulness of the piece lies in 'the ability to see one's own ways as strange and unfamiliar, to stray from and take up a critical attitude toward them and so open cultures to question, reinterpretation, negotiation, transformation, and non-identity' (Tully, 1995: 206). The near extermination of the Haida by European imperial expansion is typical of how Aboriginal peoples have fared wherever Europeans settled. The positioning of the sculpture at Vancouver International Airport, and an identical piece at the Canadian Embassy in Washington, DC, gives a poignant presence on both coasts of North America to a people who are still struggling today for recognition and restitution. *The Spirit of Haida Gwaii* stands as a symbol of Aboriginal peoples' survival and resurgence, and also as a more ecumenical symbol for the mutual recognition and affirmation of all cultures that respect other cultures and the earth.

For me, this sculpture is also a powerful metaphor of contemporary humanity and of the contemporary urban condition, in which people hitherto unused to living side by side are thrust together in the mongrel cities of the 21st century. Most societies today are demographically multicultural, and more are likely to become so in the foreseeable future. The central question of this book, then, is how to come to terms with this historical predicament: how can we manage our co-existence in the shared spaces of the multicultural cities of the 21st century. The practical question is what challenges does this present to citizens, to city governments, and to the city-building professions. This chapter explores some theoretical dimensions of the question. The next chapter looks more closely at one particularly insidious enemy of co-existence: fear of strangers. Chapter 6 asks specifically what kind of a challenge difference presents to cities, city planning and urban governance, and provides examples of and experiments with successful accommodation of difference, concerning the integration of immigrants.

My goal in this chapter is to rethink multiculturalism as a form of democratic politics and as a perspective on human society and thereby to elaborate the components of a revivified 21st-century multicultural project. I do this in three stages. First I discuss four different imaginings of how we might live together in all of our differences: Richard Sennett's vision of a diverse civic culture based on meaningful intercultural interaction; James Donald's more limited notion of co-presence, or indifference to difference; the British government's recent answer, of 'community cohesion' through a shared identity; and Ash Amin's emphasis on local negotiations of difference in 'the city's micro-publics of banal multicultures' (Amin, 2002: 13). Through these different imaginings I explore what it means to be 'at home' in an increasingly globalized world; what a sense of belonging might be based on in a multicultural society; what it takes to combat racism and learn to live with difference; and how to encourage more intercultural encounters and exchanges.

In order to act within mongrel cities, we must understand 'difference' and how it becomes significant in identity politics, in claims regarding multiculturalism, and in spatial conflicts as well as cooperative endeavours. In the second section, I seek to deepen our psychological and political understanding of the concept of difference and through this to explain why a politics of difference is related to basic questions of identity and belonging and therefore cannot be wished away. Dealing with the paradoxical politics of difference is, I argue, a necessary condition of peaceful co-existence in multicultural cities and is best addressed through an agonistic view of democratic politics, 'fragile and temporary resolutions springing from the vibrant clash between empowered publics' (Amin, 2002: 1) rather than the search for a permanent consensus.

In the third section of this chapter I develop a multicultural perspective for 21st-century cities that embraces the cultural embeddedness of all human beings; the inescapability but also desirability of cultural diversity and intercultural exchange; the right to the city, which is part of the right to difference; political community rather than ethno-(or any other sub-)cultural identity as the basis for a sense of belonging in multicultural societies; and social recognition as well as a just share of economic and political power for all cultures as a necessary basis for a stable, vibrant, and dynamic multicultural democracy.

HOW MIGHT WE LIVE TOGETHER: FOUR IMAGININGS

RICHARD SENNETT: TOGETHERNESS IN DIFFERENCE

In *Flesh and Stone* (1994: 358) Sennett laments that the apparent diversity of Greenwich Village in New York is actually only the diversity of the gaze, rather than a scene of discourse and interaction. He worries that the multiple cultures that inhabit the city are not fused into common purposes, and wonders whether 'difference inevitably provokes mutual withdrawal'. He assumes (and fears) that if the latter is true, then 'a multicultural city cannot have a common civic culture' (*ibid.*). For Sennett, Greenwich Village poses a particular question of how a diverse civic culture might become something people feel in their bones. He deplores the ethnic separatism of old multicultural New York and not only looks but longs for evidence of citizens' understanding that they share a common destiny. This becomes a hauntingly reiterated question: nothing less than a moral challenge, the challenge of living together not simply in tolerant indifference to each other, but in active engagement. For Sennett, then, there is a normative imperative in the multicultural city to engage in meaningful intercultural interaction.

Why does Sennett assume that sharing a common destiny in the city necessitates more than a willingness to live with difference in the manner of respectful distance? Why should it demand active engagement? He doesn't address these questions, nor does he ask what it would take, sociologically and institutionally, to make such intercultural dialogue and exchange possible, or more likely to happen. But other authors, more recently, have begun to ask, and give tentative answers to, these very questions (Parekh, 2000; Amin, 2002). In terms of political philosophy, one might answer that in multicultural societies, composed of many different cultures each of which has different values and practices, and not all of which are entirely comprehensible or acceptable to each other, conflicts are inevitable. In the absence of a practice of intercultural dialogue, conflicts are insoluble except by the imposition of one culture's views on another. A society of cultural enclaves and *de facto* separatism is one in which different cultures do not know how to talk to each other, are not interested in each other's well-being, and assume that they have nothing to learn and nothing to gain from interaction. This becomes a problem for urban governance and for city planning in cities where contact between different cultures is increasingly part of everyday urban life, in spite of the efforts of some groups to avoid 'cultural contamination' or ethnic mixture by fleeing to gated communities or so-called ethnic enclaves. A pragmatic argument then, is that intercultural contact and interaction is a necessary condition for being able to address the inevitable conflicts that will arise in multicultural societies. Another way of looking at the question of why intercultural encounters might be a good thing would start with the acknowledgement that different cultures represent different systems of meaning and versions of the good life. But each culture realizes only a limited range of human capacities and emotions and grasps only a part of the totality of human existence: it therefore 'needs others to understand itself better, expand its intellectual and moral horizon, stretch its imagination and guard it against the obvious temptation to absolutize itself' (Parekh, 2000: 336–7). I suspect that this latter argument is what Sennett might have had in mind.

JAMES DONALD: AN ETHICAL INDIFFERENCE

In *Imagining the Modern City* (1999), Donald takes a less moralistic, less prescriptive, more pragmatic approach to the question of how we might live together. He is critical of the two most popular contemporary urban imaginings: the traditionalism of the New Urbanism (with its ideal of community firmly rooted in the past) and the cosmopolitanism of Richard Rogers, advisor to Tony Blair and author of a policy document advocating an urban renaissance, a revitalized and re-enchanted city (Urban Task Force, 1999). What's missing from Rogers' vision, according to Donald, is 'any real sense of the city not only as a space of community or pleasurable encounters or self-creation, but also as the site of aggression, violence, and paranoia' (Donald, 1999: 135). Is it possible, he asks, to imagine change that acknowledges difference without falling into phobic utopianism, communitarian nostalgia, or the disavowal of urban paranoia.

Shadowing Iris Young (1990), Donald sets up a normative ideal of city life that acknowledges not only the necessary desire for the security of home, but also the inevitability of migration, change and conflict, and thus an 'ethical need for an openness to unassimilated otherness' (Donald, 1999: 145). He argues that it is not possible to domesticate all traces of alterity and difference. 'The problem with community is that usually its advocates are referring to some phantom of the past, projected onto some future utopia at the cost of disavowing the unhomely reality of living in the present' (*ibid.*). If we start from the reality of living in the present with strangers, then we might ask, what kind of commonality might exist or be brought into being? Donald's answer is 'broad social participation in the never completed process of making meanings and creating values . . . an always emerging, negotiated common culture' (Donald, 1999: 151). This process requires time and forbearance, not instant fixes. This is community redefined neither as identity nor as place but as a productive process of social interaction, apparently resolving the long-standing problem of the dark side of community (which has always troubled Sennett), the drawing of boundaries between those who belong and those who don't. Donald argues that we don't need to share cultural traditions with our neighbours in order to live alongside them, but we do need to be able to talk to them, while also accepting that they are and may remain strangers (as will we).[2]

This is the pragmatic urbanity that can make the violence of living together manageable. Then, urban politics would mean strangers working out how to live together. This is an appropriately political answer to Sennett's question of how multicultural societies might arrive at some workable notion of a common destiny. But when it comes to a thicker description of this 'openness to unassimilable difference', the mundane, pragmatic skills of living in the city, sharing urban turf, neither Donald nor Sennett have much to say. Donald suggests 'reading the signs in the street; adapting to different ways of life right on your doorstep; learning tolerance and responsibility – or at least, as Simmel taught us, indifference – towards others and otherness; showing respect, or self-preservation, in not intruding on other people's space; picking up new rules when you migrate to a foreign city' (*ibid.*: 167). Donald seems to be contradicting himself here in retreating to a position of co-presence and indifference, having earlier advocated something more like an agonistic politics of broad social participation in the *never completed process* of making meanings and an *always emerging* (never congealed), *negotiated common culture.* Surely this participation and negotiation in the interests of peaceful co-existence require something like daily habits of perhaps quite banal intercultural interaction in order to establish a basis for dialogue, which is difficult, if not impossible, without some pre-existing trust. I will turn to Ash Amin for a discussion of how and where this daily interaction and negotiation of ethnic (and other) differences might be encouraged. But before that, I ask what British politicians and their advisors concluded about living together when they reflected on the aftermath of the race riots in three British cities in 2001.

THE BRITISH HOME OFFICE: 'PUBLIC ORDER AND COMMUNITY COHESION'

Riots sparked by interracial or interethnic conflict are not new to British cities since the first wave of postwar migration ferried former colonial subjects into the heartland of the erstwhile empire, confronting locals with the realities of decolonization and creating an uneasy and unresolved postcolonial stew (Chapter 1). But the magnitude of damage and disturbance in Bradford, Oldham, and Burnley in the spring and summer of 2001 posed a perceived crisis of public order and prompted the Blair government to set up an inquiry inside the Home Office to address possible policy responses.[3] The inter-departmental Ministerial Group on Public Order and Community Cohesion was asked to report to the Home Secretary on what Government could do to minimize the risk of further disorder, and to help build stronger, more cohesive communities. Independent review teams had also been set up in each city after the disturbances, and the Ministerial Group drew on the reports of those teams, as well as the findings of the Commission for Racial Equality's research into segregation in the North West of England, and the Policy Innovation Unit's study of ethnic minority access to the labour market. The outcome was *Building Cohesive Communities: A Report of the Ministerial Group on Public Order and Community Cohesion* (Home Office, 2001).

In searching for underlying causes, the Ministerial Group described these towns and their communities as 'deeply fractured' and segregated, but was unsure why and how this had come about. Nevertheless, the report notes a number of commonalities between the three cities, and the specific neighbourhoods (wards) in which the rioting erupted: all had average incomes amongst the lowest in the country; all wards affected were amongst 'the 20 per cent most deprived in the country', and some were among the most deprived 1 per cent; the participants were mostly young men, 'both white and ethnic minority'; extremist groups were active in these areas; and disturbances occurred in areas which had become fractured on racial, generational, cultural, and religious lines and where there was little dialogue, or much contact, between the various groups across these social divides (Home Office, 2001: 8). Drawing on the other sources noted above, the Ministerial Group identified the following 'key issues': the lack of a strong civic identity or shared social values to unite diverse communities; the fragmentation and polarization of communities; disengagement of young people from the local decision-making process, and an increasingly territorial mentality in asserting different racial, cultural and religious identities in response to real or perceived attacks; high levels of unemployment; 'weakness and disparities in police response to community issues, particularly racial incidents'; and 'irresponsible coverage of race stories' by the local media (*ibid.*: 11). In less bureaucratic and less euphemistic language, these issues could be summarized as poverty, exclusion, racism (institutionalized as well as interpersonal), and segregation.

There are a number of remarkable things about this report. It acknowledges the complex mix of causes of the riots: economic, social, and cultural. Real material deprivation, as reflected in poor housing and high levels of unemployment, is compounded by low levels of education and poor recreational facilities. But equally important are 'the intrinsically difficult and controversial issues of social identity and values on which cohesion depends' (*ibid.*: 34). Accordingly the recommendations include not only a range of spending programmes designed to target deprived areas, but also the call for a widespread debate about identity, shared values, and common citizenship as part of the process of building what the report calls 'cohesive communities'. There is concern that 'we cannot claim to be a truly multicultural society if the various communities within it live . . . a series of parallel lives which do not touch at any point' (*ibid.*: 13). There is the finding that most young people 'want to grow up in a mixed and inclusive society', and that there has been too little reaching out to young people, and particularly to women. There is even explicit recognition that 'there is no single dominant and unchanging culture into which all must assimilate . . . Citizenship means finding a common place for diverse cultures and beliefs, consistent with our core values' (*ibid.*: 20). The report intends that national government should take the lead in this debate about citizenship, civic identity, and shared values, but it also hopes that local government will recognize the need for this dialogue to take place at a local level. While the financial resources of the national government were to be mobilized in a series of programmes for neighbourhood regeneration, steps would also be taken to appoint facilitators 'to foster dialogue within and between fractured communities'.

How do you turn fractured communities into cohesive ones? How do you create a 'common sense of belonging regardless of race, culture or faith'? What underlying values about identity and nation are assumed, taken for granted, as opposed to open for debate? The report leaves me queasy on these matters. It has erased history. There is no colonial past stalking its pages. There is no postcolonial hangover of racism among the 'white community' in these towns. The clarity of the report's thinking about policy instruments for addressing deprivation is matched by an opacity of thinking about the crucial symbolic issues of identity and belonging. There is a tautological definition of community cohesion as a 'shared sense of belonging based on common goals and core social values, respect for difference, and acceptance of the reciprocal rights and obligations of community members working together for the common good' (*ibid.*: 18). But if that shared sense of belonging is absent, and 'none of this can be imposed by government' (*ibid.*), how then will it be conjured into being? Through community facilitators? No, the government will take the lead in articulating a vision (*ibid.*). So whose vision is it, after all?

If we turn to David Blunkett, the Home Secretary in the Blair government, for guidance, we are plunged back into the problem of history and of unspoken assumptions about whose country it is and who does and does not belong. 'We have norms of acceptability and those who come into our home – for that is what it is – should accept those norms' (Blunkett, quoted in Alibhai-Brown, 2001). The hybrid realities of a changing nation and culture have been swept under the carpet in the Home Secretary's statement. He seems to define the problem of living together as a problem of 'them' adjusting to 'us', being gracious guests in 'our home'. The strength of the Home Office report was its attention to the macro issues of the political economy: the lack of employment, the quality of housing among both poor white and ethnic minority communities. Its lacunae are the historical/symbolic and the micro-sociological issues of living together. The micro-sociological issues require a much closer look at what actually happens in multicultural cities and neighbourhoods, what kinds of interactions take place, what ways people are finding, or not, of co-existing. This brings me to the fourth example of imagining ways of living together in 21st-century mongrel cities, the Report on *Ethnicity and the Multicultural City* by University of Durham geographer Ash Amin, commissioned by another arm of the British government, the Department of Transport, Local Government and the Regions.

ASH AMIN: A POLITICS OF LOCAL LIVEABILITY

Amin's *Ethnicity and the Multicultural City. Living with Diversity* (2002) is a self-described 'think piece' that uses the 2001 riots as a springboard 'to discuss what it takes to combat racism, live with difference and encourage mixture in a multicultural and multiethnic society' (Amin, 2002: 2). This paper is partly an extension and partly a critique of the three previous imaginings of peaceful co-existence (although it specifically addresses only the third). It goes deeper and draws on different sources from the Home Office document. The political economy approach of the Home Office analysis of the riots never once mentions globalization, or the colonial past. That is Amin's starting point. The dominant ethnic groups present in Bradford, Burnley and Oldham are Pakistani and Bangladeshi, of both recent and longer-term migrations. What this reflects is the twin and interdependent forces of postcolonialism and globalization. As several scholars have pointed out (Sassen, 1996; Rocco, 2000), the contemporary phenomena of immigration and ethnicity are constitutive of globalization and are reconfiguring the spaces of and social relations in cities in new ways. Cultures from all over the world are being de- and re-territorialized in global cities, whose neighbourhoods accordingly become 'globalized localities' (Albrow, 1997: 51). The spaces created by the complex and multidimensional processes of globalization have become strategic sites for the formation of transnational identities and communities, as well as for new hybrid identities and complicated experiences and redefinitions of notions of 'home'. As Sassen has argued:

What we still narrate in the language of immigration and ethnicity . . . is actually a series of processes having to do with the globalization of economic activity, of cultural activity, of identity formation. Too often immigration and ethnicity are constituted as otherness. Understanding them as a set of processes whereby global elements are localized, international labor markets are constituted, and cultures from all over the world are de- and re-territorialized, puts them right there at the center along with the internationalization of capital, as a fundamental aspect of globalization.

(Sassen, 1996: 218)

This is the context for Amin's interpretative essay on the civil disturbances, which he sees as having both material and symbolic dimensions. He draws on ethnographic research to deepen understanding of both dimensions, as well as to assist in his argument for a focus on the everyday urban, 'the daily negotiation of ethnic difference'. Ethnographic research in the UK on areas of significant racial antagonism has identified two types of neighbourhood. The first are old white working-class areas in which successive waves of non-white immigration have been accompanied by continuing socio-economic deprivation and cultural and/or physical isolation 'between white residents lamenting the loss of a golden ethnically undisturbed past, and non-whites claiming a right of place'. The second are 'white flight' suburbs and estates that have become the refuge of an upwardly mobile working-class and a fearful middle class disturbed by what they see as the replacement of a 'homely white nation' by foreign cultural contamination. Here, white supremacist values are activated to terrorize the few immigrants who try to settle there. The riots of 2001 displayed the processes at work in the first type of neighbourhood, but also the white fear and antagonism typical of the second type (Amin, 2002: 2).

What is important to understand is that the cultural dynamics in these two types of neighbourhood are very different from those in other ethnically mixed cities and neighbourhoods where greater social and physical mobility, a local history of compromises, and a supportive local institutional infrastructure have come to support cohabitation. For example, in the Tooting neighbourhood of South London, Martin Albrow's research inquired about the strength of 'locality' and 'community' among a wide range of local inhabitants, from those born there to recent arrivals, and among all the most prominent ethnic groups. His analysis reveals that locality has much less salience for individuals and for social relations than older research paradigms invested in 'community' allow. His study reveals a very liquid sense of identity and belonging. His interviewees' stories suggest the possibility that

Individuals with very different lifestyles and social networks can live in close proximity without untoward interference with each other. There is an old community for some, for others there is a new site for community which draws its culture from India. For some, Tooting is a setting for peer group leisure activity, for others it provides a place to sleep and access to London. It can be a spectacle for some, for others the anticipation of a better, more multicultural community.

(Albrow, 1997: 51)

In this middle income locality there is nothing like the traditional concept of community based on a shared local culture. Albrow describes a situation of 'minimum levels of tolerable co-existence' and civil inattention and avoidance strategies that prevent friction between people living different lifestyles. The locality is criss-crossed by networks of social relations whose scope and extent range from neighbouring houses and a few weeks' acquaintance to religious and kin relations spanning generations and continents.

This study gives us an important insight into the changing social relations within globalized localities. Where is community here? It may be nowhere, says Albrow, and this new situation therefore needs a new vocabulary. How meaningful is the newly promoted (by the Home Office) notion of community cohesion, when people's affective ties are not necessarily related to the local place where they live? Where is the deconstruction, and reconstruction, of what 'community' might mean in the globalized localities of mongrel cities? 'Globalization makes co-present enclaves of diverse origins one possible social configuration characterizing a new Europe' (Albrow, 1997: 54).

While Albrow's research seems to support the urban imaginings of James Donald, discussed earlier, in terms of the feasibility of an attitude of tolerant indifference and co-presence, the difference between Tooting and the northern mill towns that are the subject of Amin's reflection is significant. In those one-industry towns, when the mills declined, white and non-white workers alike were unemployed. The largest employers soon became the public services, but discrimination kept most of these jobs for whites. Non-whites pooled resources and opened shops, takeaways, minicab businesses. There was intense competition for low-paid and precarious work. Economic uncertainty and related social deprivation has been a constant for over 20 years and 'a pathology of social rejection . . . reinforces family and communalist bonds' (Amin, 2002: 4). Ethnic resentment has bred on this socio-economic deprivation and sense of desperation. It is in such areas that social cohesion and cultural interchange have failed.

What conclusions does Amin draw from this? For one thing, he argues against several currently popular policy fixes. One such fix is based on the belief that cultural and physical isolation lies at the heart of the disturbances, so the way forward must lie in greater ethnic mixing in housing at the neighbourhood scale. The Home Office, in its response to the riots, made such recommendations that future housing schemes should be ethnically mixed, and others have suggested that existing estates should create mini-villages and develop better public spaces so that interaction can take place between ethnic groups. Another popular policy fix in the urban literature, and rooted in republican urban theory, looks to the powers of visibility and encounter between strangers in the open or public spaces of the city. The freedom to associate and mingle in cafés, parks, streets, shopping malls, and squares (a feature of Richard Rogers' recipe for urban renaissance) has been linked to the development of an urban civic culture based on the freedom and pleasure of lingering, the serendipity of the chance encounter, and the public awareness that these are shared spaces.[4] The depressing reality, Amin counters, is that far from being spaces where diversity is being negotiated, these spaces tend either to be territorialized by particular groups (whites, youth, skateboarders, Asian families . . .) or they are spaces of transit, with very little contact between strangers. 'The city's public spaces are not natural servants of multicultural engagement' (Amin, 2002: 11).[5]

If ethnic mixture through housing cannot be engineered, and public space is not the site of meaningful multicultural encounter, how can fear and intolerance be challenged, how might residents begin to negotiate and come to terms with difference in the city? Amin's answer is important and will be supported by my examples from Frankfurt, Rotterdam, Vancouver, and other cities in Chapter 6. The contact spaces of housing estates and public places fall short of nurturing inter-ethnic understanding, he argues, 'because they are not spaces of interdependence and habitual engagement' (ibid.: 12). He goes on to suggest that the sites for coming to terms with ethnic (and surely other) differences are the 'micro-publics' where dialogue and prosaic negotiations are compulsory, in sites such as the workplace, schools, colleges, youth centres, sports clubs, community centres, neighbourhood houses, and the micro-publics of 'banal transgression' (such as colleges of further education), in which people from different cultural backgrounds are thrown together in new settings which disrupt familiar patterns and create the possibility of initiating new attachments. Other sites of banal transgression include community gardens, child-care facilities, community centres, neighbourhood watch schemes, youth projects, and regeneration of derelict spaces. I provide just such an example in Chapter 7, the Community Fire Station in the Handsworth neighbourhood of Birmingham, where white Britons are working alongside Asian and Afro-Caribbean Britons in a variety of projects for neighbourhood regeneration and improvement. In Chapter 6, I will discuss the Collingwood Neighborhood House in Vancouver as another example of a successful site of intercultural interaction. Part of what happens in such everyday contacts is the overcoming of feelings of strangeness in the simple process of sharing tasks and comparing ways of doing things. But such initiatives will not automatically becomes sites of social inclusion. They also need organizational and discursive strategies that are designed to build voice, to foster a sense of common benefit, to develop confidence among disempowered groups, and to arbitrate when disputes arise. The essential point is that 'changes in attitude and behaviour spring from lived experiences' (Amin, 2002: 15).

The key policy implication from Amin's work, then, is that the project of living with diversity needs to be worked at 'in the city's micro-publics of banal multicultures' (ibid.: 13). Local intercultural policy initiatives might include hiring youths bent on writing graffiti to create urban murals, establishing 'self-schools' that use alternative methods to reintegrate youths who have dropped out of school, and bringing live music to hospitals, to help break down ethnic and cultural barriers. What seems misguided, in terms of addressing ethnic tension, is the Home Office's emphasis on 'community cohesion', defined as shared values and a shared sense of place. It is clear from Albrow's work, as well as that of Amin, that in today's globalized localities there is no shared sense of place and that this is not the best 'glue' for understanding and co-existence within multi-

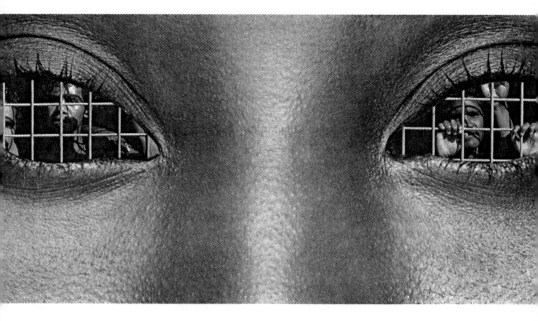

cultural neighbourhoods. Ethnographic research on urban youth cultures referred to by Amin confirms the existence of a strong sense of place among white and non-white ethnic groups, but it is a sense of place based on turf claims and defended in exclusionary ways. The distinctive feature of mixed neighbourhoods is that they are 'communities without community, each marked by multiple and hybrid affiliations of varying geographical reach' (Amin, 2002: 16). They are not primarily place-based communities, and this surely blunts any policy approach based on assumptions of (or intentions of creating) an integrated community of mutuality and common interest (the social networks and social capital approach of American literature based on communitarian values).

There are clear limits then to how far 'community cohesion' can become the basis of living with difference. Amin suggests a different vocabulary of local accommodation to difference – 'a vocabulary of rights of presence, bridging difference, getting along' (*ibid.*: 17). To adopt the language of Henri Lefebvre, this could be expressed as the right to difference, and the right to the city. The achievement of these rights depends on a politics of active local citizenship, an agonistic politics (as sketched by Donald) of broad social participation in the never completed process of making meanings, and an always emerging, negotiated common culture. But it also depends on a *multicultural political culture*, that is, one with effective antiracism policies, with strong legal, institutional and informal sanctions against racial and cultural hatred, a public culture that no longer treats immigrants as 'guests', and a truly inclusive political system at all levels of governance. This is the subject of the third section of this chapter. In the next section I take up the issue of difference and identity in relation to national belonging and question the adequacy of framing the issues of a multicultural society through the language of race and minority ethnicity. One remaining dimension of the civil disturbances in Britain in 2001 is this aspect of identity and belonging, and this spills over into the next section.

THINKING THROUGH IDENTITY/DIFFERENCE

We have norms of acceptability and those who come into our home – for that is what it is – should accept those norms.

(David Blunkett, quoted in Alibhai-Brown, 2001)

. . . seven years ago I finally decided this place was my place, and that was because I had a daughter whose father was of these islands. This did not make me any less black, Asian or Muslim – those identities are in my blood, thick and forever. But it made me kick more vigorously at those stern, steely gates that keep people of colour outside the heart of the nation then blame them for fighting each other in the multicultural wastelands into which the establishment has pushed them. A number of us broke through. The going was (and still is) incredibly hard but we are in now and, bit by bit, the very essence of Britishness is being transformed.

(Alibhai-Brown, 2001)

The above remarks of David Blunkett were made in December of 2001, after Britain's experience of a spring and summer of 'race riots' in three northern cities. It was a time of questioning of the previous half-century of immigration, the race relations problems that had emerged, and the policy response of multiculturalism. At the heart of this questioning was a perturbation over what it meant/means to be British. Notions of identity were being unsettled. The response of Blunkett, the Home Secretary in the Blair government, was a rather crude reassertion of us-and-them thinking. His words epitomize a long-standing but much-contested view that immigrants are guests in the home of the host nation and must behave the way their hosts want them to behave: adopt the norms of 'Britishness', or get out. Implicit in this view is that there is only one correct way to be British and that it is the responsibility of newcomers to learn how to fit in with it. Yasmin Alibhai-Brown, herself an immigrant of three decades' standing, contests this pure and static notion of national identity, counterposing it with a notion of a more inclusive, dynamic and evolving identity which can accommodate the new hybrid realities of a changing culture. She urges 'a national conversation about our collective identity' (Alibhai-Brown, 2000: 10).

At stake here, and across European (or any of the large number of globalizing) cities today, are contested notions of identity and understandings of difference, and conflicting ways of belonging and feeling at home in the world. The Home Secretary expresses the view that there is a historic Britishness that must be protected from impurity. (Sections of the Austrian, Danish, French and Dutch populations have been making similar noises in 2002.) In this view, what it means to be British, to be 'at home' in Britain, is being threatened by immigrants who bring a different cultural baggage with them. Interestingly, the (fragile) notion of identity at the heart of this view is one that is both afraid of and yet dependent on difference. Let's think about how this works.

When a person's self-identity is insecure or fragile, doubts about that identity (and how it relates to national identity may be part of the insecurity) are posed and resolved by the constitution of an Other against which that identity may define itself, and assert its superiority. In order to feel 'at home' in the nation and in the wider world, this fragile sense of identity seeks to subdue or erase from consciousness (or worse) that which is strange, those who are 'not like us'. Attempts to protect the purity and certainty of a hegemonic identity – Britishness, Danishness, and so on – by defining certain differences as independent sites of evil, or disloyalty, or disorder, have a long history.[6] There are diverse political tactics through which doubts about self-identity are posed and resolved, but the general strategy is the establishing of a *system of identity and difference* which is given legal sanctions, which defines who belongs and who does not. Over long periods of time, these systems of identity and difference become congealed as cultural norms and beliefs, entrenching themselves as the hegemonic status quo. Evil infiltrates the public domain, Connolly (1991) argues, when attempts are made to secure the surety of self- and national identity – and the powers and privileges that accompany it – with spatial and social and economic policies that demand conformity with a previously scripted identity, while defining the outsider as an outsider (a polluter of pure identities) in perpetuity.

There is a paradox in the relationship between identity and difference. The quest for a pure and unchanging *identity* (an undiluted Britishness, or Brummie-ness, or Danishness . . .) is at once framed by and yet seeks to eliminate difference; it seeks the conformity, disappearance, or invisibility of the Other. That is the paradox of identity. But what of *difference* and *its* political strategies? Surely difference, too, is constituted by its Other – as woman is in patriarchal societies, or to be gay and lesbian in heterosexual societies, or to be Black in white societies – and so is constituted by the hegemonic identity which it resists and seeks to change. Difference, defined as that which is outside, in opposition to the congealed norms of any society, is constituted by/against hegemonic identity. Identity and difference then are an intertwined and always historically specific system of dialectical relations, fundamental to which is inclusion (belonging) and its opposite, exclusion (not belonging). Here then is a double paradox. Some notion of identity is, arguably, indispensable to life itself (Connolly, 1991), and some sense of culturally based identity would seem to be inescapable, in that all human beings are culturally embedded (Parekh, 2000: 336).[7] But while the politics of pure identity seeks to eliminate the Other, the politics of difference[8] seeks recognition and inclusion.

A more robust sense of identity, as outlined by Yasmin Alibhai-Brown or Salman Rushdie, must be able to embrace cultural autonomy and, at the same time, work to strengthen intercultural solidarity. If one dimension of such a cultural pluralism is a concern with reconciling old and new identities by accepting the inevitability of 'hybridity', or 'mongrelization', then another is the commitment to actively contest what is to be valued across diverse cultures. Thus Alibhai-Brown feels 'under no obligation to bring my daughter and son up to drink themselves to death in a pub for a laugh', nor does she want to see young Asian and Muslim women imprisoned in 'high-pressure ghettoes . . . in the name of "culture" ', a culture that forces obedience to patriarchal authority and arranged marriages (Alibhai-Brown, 2001). Negotiating new identities then becomes central to daily social and spatial practices, as newcomers assert their rights to the city, to make a home for themselves, to occupy and transform space.[9]

What now seems insidious in terms of debates about belonging in relation to the nation is the way in which the identities of minorities have been essentialized on the grounds of culture and ethnicity. The ethnicization and racialization of the identities of non-white or non-Anglo people in western liberal democracies, even the most officially multicultural among them (Canada and Australia), has had the effect of bracketing them as minorities, as people whose claims can only ever be minor within a national culture and frame of national belonging defined by others and their majority histories, usually read as histories of white belonging and white supremacy (Amin, 2002: 21; Hage, 1998). But the claims of the Asian youths in Britain's northern mill towns, just as those of Black Britons or 'Lebanese Australians' or 'Chinese Canadians', are claims for more than minority recognition and minority rights. Theirs is a claim for the mainstream (or perhaps it is a claim for 'the end of mainstream' (Dang, 2002)), for a metaphorical shift from the margins to the centre, both in terms of the right to visibility and the right to reshape that mainstream. It is nothing less than a claim to full citizenship and a public naming of what has hitherto prevented that full citizenship – the assumption that to be British, Canadian, Australian, Dutch, and so on, is to be white, and part of white culture. As long as that assumption remains intact, the status of minority ethnic groups in all the western democracies will remain of a different order to that of whites, always under question, always at the mercy of the 'tolerance' of the dominant culture, a tolerance built on an unequal power relationship (Hage, 1998).

The crucial implication of this discussion is that in order to enable all citizens, regardless of 'race' or ethnicity or any other cultural criteria, to become equal members of the nation and contribute to an *evolving national identity*, 'the ethnic moorings of national belonging need to be exposed and replaced by criteria that have nothing to do with whiteness' (Amin, 2002: 22). Or as Gilroy (2000: 328) puts it, 'the racial ontology of sovereign territory' needs to be recognized and contested. This requires an imagination of the nation as something other than a racial or ethnic territorial space, perhaps an imagination that conceives the nation as a space of travelling cultures and peoples with varying degrees and geographies of attachment. Such a move must insist that race and ethnicity are taken out of the definition of national identity and national belonging 'and replaced by ideals of citizenship, democracy and political community' (Amin, 2002: 23). This brings me to the rethinking of 20th-century notions of multiculturalism (based on ethno-cultural recognition), which is the subject of the final section of this chapter.

MULTICULTURALISM: PART OF THE SOLUTION OR PART OF THE PROBLEM?

'Multiculturalism is a boring word. It is grey and small and domestic. It does not include Europeans, it does not include internationalism. It is like an old cardigan knitted out of different coloured scraps of wool.'

(Young Asian man, quoted in Alibhai-Brown, 2000)

'I think this kind of thing is for sad old people.'

(Young Black man, quoted in Alibhai-Brown, *ibid.*)

I am sick of being told that I must be loyal to all that Britain is and was (including its destructive historical role) but that at the same time I must never forget that I am only a guest (unwanted and merely to be tolerated), with such a fragile existence that the bag must always be half-packed. Every time a political leader speaks in this way – and they have done so since 1948 – they take away our right and desire to belong.

(Alibhai-Brown, 2001)

If multiculturalism is my self-declared social project for the mongrel cities of the 21st century, then surely it's time to declare my hand, to explain what I mean by the term and engage with its detractors. I'd like to start with the young Black and Asian men in the above quotations. For them, multiculturalism is passé, yesterday's fashion, too limiting in the range of identities it permits. British feminist Yasmin Alibhai-Brown enlists these young men to her cause, which is to argue that what might once have been a good idea has reached the end of its shelf life, is no longer relevant, in fact is downright divisive. Confessing that she was 'once a priestess of this philosophy', Alibhai-Brown's case, in her pamphlet *After Multiculturalism* (2000), is that too much power and money have been given to Black and Asian 'community', encouraging the perpetuation of ethnic enclaves that 'imprison the young and women in the name of "culture" '. Teenagers who have grown up with multiculturalism, she argues, are impatient with the whole ideology.

'They reject the traditional categories which multiculturalism tries to shoehorn them into . . . their identities are changing in unpredictable ways'. This ideology is also guilty of creating resentment among poor whites, a conclusion reached by the Home Office's inquiry into community cohesion after the summer race riots, with which Alibhai-Brown agrees. She wants a 'new shared sense of Britishness . . . a strong diverse British identity' (Alibhai-Brown, 2000).

Alibhai-Brown is not in fact talking about *the* 'ideology of multiculturalism' but about a specific version of it, which took root in Britain in the 1960s, proposed as a progressive response to the arrival of immigrants from Britain's former colonies with very different cultural backgrounds from traditional Anglo-Saxon and Anglo-Celtic Britons. As a *fact*, multiculturalism describes the increasing cultural diversity of societies in late modernity. Empirically, many societies and many cities could be described today as multicultural. But very few countries have embraced and institutionalized an *ideology* of multiculturalism. Australia and Canada have done so since the late 1960s, as have Singapore and Malaysia, while during the same period the USA has lived through its 'multicultural wars', still uneasy with the whole notion, preferring the traditional 'melting pot' metaphor and its associated politics of assimilation. France has been most adamant that there is no place for this political recognition of difference in their republic. The Dutch and the Danish have been, at least until 2002, the most open to multicultural policy claims. Each of these countries has a different definition of multiculturalism, different sets of public policies to deal with/respond to cultural difference, and correspondingly different definitions of citizenship (see Chapter 6).

As an *ideology*, then, multiculturalism has a multiplicity of meanings. What is common in the sociological content of the term in the West – but never spoken of – is that it was formulated as a framework, a set of policies, for the national accommodation of non-white immigration. It was a liberal response that skirted the reality of the already racialized constitution of these societies and masked the existence of institutionalized racism.[10] The histories of multicultural policies are in fact much more complex and contested than this, and I can't really do justice to the genealogy of the term without a much more contextualized discussion of each country, which is not my purpose here. So instead, drawing on the distinguished British cultural studies scholar Stuart Hall, I will simply summarize the *range* of meanings that have been given to multiculturalism as ideology, and some of the dangers embedded in it. I then argue that since it is impractical to do away with the term, it is important to be precise about how we might want to use it.

Hall (2000) theorizes the multicultural question as both a global and local terrain of political contestation with crucial implications for the West. It is contested by the conservative Right, in defence of the purity and cultural integrity of the nation. It is contested by liberals, who claim that the 'cult of ethnicity', the notion of 'group rights', and the pursuit of 'difference' threaten the universalism and neutrality of the liberal state. Multiculturalism is also contested by 'modernizers of various political persuasions'. For them, the triumph of the (alleged) universalism of western civilization over the particularisms of ethnic, religious, and racial belonging established in the Enlightenment marked an entirely worthy transition from tradition to modernity that is, and should be, irreversible. Some postmodern versions of *cosmopolitanism* oppose multiculturalism as imposing a too narrow, or closed, sense of identity. Some radicals argue that multi-culturalism divides along ethnic lines what should be a united front of race and class against injustice and exploitation. Others point to commercialized, boutique, or con-sumerist multiculturalism as celebrating difference without making a difference (Hall, 2000: 211).

Clearly, multiculturalism is not a single doctrine and does not represent an already achieved state of affairs. It describes a variety of political strategies and processes that are everywhere incomplete. Just as there are different multicultural societies, so there are different multiculturalisms.

Conservative multiculturalism insists on the assimilation of difference into the traditions and customs of the majority. Liberal multiculturalism seeks to integrate the different cultural groups as fast as possible into the 'mainstream' provided by a universal individual citizen-ship . . . Pluralist multiculturalism formally enfranchises the differences between groups along cultural lines and accords different group rights to different communities within a more . . . communitarian political order. Commercial multiculturalism assumes that if the diversity of individuals from different communities is recognized in the marketplace, then the problems of cultural difference will be dissolved through private consumption, without any need for a redistribution of power and resources. Corporate multiculturalism (public or private) seeks to 'manage' minority cultural differences in the interests of the centre. Critical or 'revolutionary' multiculturalism foregrounds power, privilege, the hierarchy of oppressions and the move-ments of resistance . . . And so on.

(Hall, 2000: 210)

Can a concept that has so many valences and such diverse and contradictory enemies possibly have any further use value? Alternatively, is its contested status precisely its value, an indication that a radical pluralist ethos is alive and well? My position is that we are inevitably implicated in the politics of multiculturalism, given the importance of the demographic and socio-cultural forces discussed in Chapter 1 (international migrations; a contested postcoloniality; the resurgence of indigenous peoples; and the rise of mobil-ized civil society). Therefore we need to find a way to publicly manifest the significance of cultural diversity, and to debate the value of various identities/differences; that is, to ask which differences exist, but should not, and which do not exist, but should.[11] Far from banishing the concept to political purgatory (as the Australian Prime Minister John Howard has done since 1996), or inventing a new term, we need to give it as rich a substance as possible, a substance that expands political possibilities and identities rather than purifying or closing them down. This leads me to define a *multicultural perspective*, (rather than a programme), as a political and philosophical basis for thinking about how to deal with the challenge of difference in multicultural cities.

My multicultural perspective for the 21st century[12] is composed of the following premises:

- The cultural embeddedness of humans is inescapable. We grow up in a culturally structured world, are deeply shaped by it, and necessarily view the world from within a specific culture. We are capable of critically evaluating our own culture's beliefs and practices, and of understanding and appreciating as well as criticizing those of other cultures. But some form of cultural identity and belonging seems unavoidable.

- 'Culture' cannot be understood as static, eternally given, essentialist. It is always evolving, dynamic and hybrid of necessity. All cultures, even allegedly conservative or traditional ones, contain multiple differences within themselves that are continually being re-negotiated.

- Cultural diversity as a positive and intercultural dialogue is a necessary element of culturally diverse societies. No culture is perfect or can be perfected, but all cultures have something to learn from and contribute to others. Cultures grow through the everyday practices of social interaction.

- The political contestation of multiculturalism is inevitable. Among other things, it is symptomatic of an unresolved postcolonial condition in the West, an unfinished decolonization project.

- At the core of multiculturalism as a daily political practice are two rights: the right to difference and the right to the city. The right to difference means recognizing the legitimacy and specific needs of minority or subaltern cultures. The right to the city is the right to presence, to occupy public space, and to participate as an equal in public affairs.

- The 'right to difference' at the heart of multiculturalism must be perpetually contested against other rights (for example, human rights) and redefined according to new formulations and considerations.

- The notion of the perpetual contestation of multiculturalism implies an agonistic democratic politics that demands active citizenship and daily negotiations of difference in all of the banal sites of intercultural interaction.

- A sense of belonging in a multicultural society cannot be based on race, religion, or ethnicity but needs to be based on a shared commitment to political community. Such a commitment requires an empowered citizenry.

- Reducing fear and intolerance can only be achieved by addressing the material as well as cultural dimensions of 'recognition'. This means addressing the prevailing inequalities of political and economic power as well as developing new stories about and symbols of national and local identity and belonging.

There are (at least) two public goods embedded in a version of multiculturalism based on these understandings. One is the critical freedom to question in thought, and challenge in practice, one's inherited cultural ways. The other is the recognition of the widely shared aspiration to belong to a culture and a place, and so to be at home in the world. This sense of belonging would be lost if one's culture were excluded, or if it was imposed on everyone. But there can also be a sense of belonging that comes from being associated with other cultures, gaining in strength and compassion from accommodation among and interrelations with others, and it is important to recognize and nurture those spaces of accommodation and intermingling. This version of multiculturalism accepts the indispensability of group identity to human life (and therefore to politics), precisely because it is inseparable from belonging. But this acceptance needs to be complicated by an insistence, a vigorous struggle against the idea that one's own group identity has a claim to intrinsic truth. If we can acknowledge a drive within ourselves, and within all of our particular cultures, to naturalize the identities given to us, we can simultaneously be vigilant about the danger implicit in this drive, which is the almost irresistible desire to impose one's identity, one's way of life, one's very definition of normality and of good-ness, on others. Thus we arrive at a lived conception of identity/difference that recognizes itself as historically contingent and inherently relational; and a cultivation of a care for difference through strategies of critical detachment from the identities that constitute us (Connolly, 1991; Tully, 1995). In this multicultural imagination, the twin goods of belonging and of freedom can be made to support rather than oppose each other.

From a multicultural perspective, the good society does not commit itself to a particu-lar vision of the good life and then ask how much diversity it can tolerate within the limits set by this vision. To do so would be to foreclose future societal development. Rather, a multicultural perspective advocates accepting the reality and desirability of cultural diversity and then structuring political life accordingly. At the very least, this political life must be dialogically and agonistically constituted. But the dialogue requires certain institutional preconditions, such as freedom of speech, participatory public spaces, empowered citizens, agreed procedures and basic ethical norms, and the active policing of discriminatory practices. It also calls for 'such essential political virtues as mutual respect and concern, tolerance, self-restraint, willingness to enter into unfamiliar worlds of thought, love of diversity, a mind open to new ideas and a heart open to others' needs, and the ability to persuade and live with unresolved differences' (Parekh, 2000: 340).

A notion of the common good is vital to any political society. From a multicultural perspective, this common good must be generated not by transcending or ignoring cultural and other differences (the liberal position), but through their interplay in a dialogical, agonistic political life. Finally, a sense of belonging, which is important in any society, cannot be ethnic or based on shared cultural, ethnic or other characteristics. A multicultural society is too diverse for that. A sense of belonging must ultimately be political, based on a shared commitment to a political community (Parekh, 2000: 341; Amin, 2002: 23). This commitment 'does not involve sharing common substantive goals, for its members might deeply disagree about these, nor a common view of its history which they may read differently, nor a particular economic or social system . . . commit-ment to the political community involves commitment to its continuing existence and well-being . . . and implies that one cares enough not to harm its interests and under-mine its integrity' (Parekh 2000: 341–2).

Since commitment, or belonging, must be reciprocal, citizens will not feel these things unless their political community is also committed to them and makes them feel that they belong. Here's the rub, then. A multicultural political community 'cannot expect its members to develop a sense of belonging to it unless it equally values and cherishes them in all their diversity, and reflects this in its structure, policies, conduct of public affairs, self-understanding and self-definition' (Parekh, 2000: 342). It would be safe to say that no existing (self-described) multicultural society can yet claim to have achieved this state of affairs, for reasons that have already been elaborated: political and economic inequalities accompanied by an unresolved postcolonial condition that we may as well name as racism. But in recent years these issues have been identified, increasingly documented, and are becoming the focus of political activity in many countries. The 21st century is indisputably the century of multicultural cities and societies. It will also be the century of struggle for multiculturalism, and against fundamentalism, which is a belief in cultural (or religious) purity. The following chapters turn to how this struggle plays itself out in cities and neighbourhoods, and what citizens, city governments, and the city building professions can do to advance the project of multiculturalism.

*

The understanding of identity/difference developed in this chapter is important for the next, which discusses fear in contemporary cities, specifically fear of outsiders, strangers, foreigners, and how that fear is linked to notions of home and nation, and to 'nation as home', metaphorically. There are numerous practical questions to be addressed in developing practices that are responsive to various kinds of difference, and that task is taken up in Chapter 6, where I examine positive stories from Frankfurt and Berlin to Rotterdam, Chicago, Sydney and Vancouver. Through these stories I provide some practical answers to the question posed by this chapter, how we stroppy strangers might live together without doing each other too much violence.

5

HOME, NATION, AND STRANGER

Fear in the city

'They've come all the way from I don't know where, and they've stolen my dreams.'
(Self-described university drop-out, Sydney, quoted in Hage, 1998: 218)

Strangely, the foreigner lives within us: he is the hidden face of our identity, the space that wrecks our abode, the time in which understanding and affinity founder.
(Kristeva, 1991: 1)

'THERE IS NO PLACE LIKE HOME'

Vienna, 2000.
It is Christmas season in Vienna. Cars sweeping towards Karlsplatz, one of the city's main traffic hubs, are greeted with an unusual Christmas message, a wall of big new billboards. The 'ads' take the form of alternating purple and yellow, blue and orange, and black and white rectangles, but they are not part of a new Benetton or Gap campaign. They are art works, commissioned by the Museum in Progress, a contemporary art museum with a difference, one that exhibits in public spaces. The billboard artist is Ken Lum, a Vancouver photographer whose Chinese grandfather had emigrated to Canada to work on the railroads.

Lum's first image is of an angry man with a raised fist. He looms from behind some trees at the corner of the site and the caption above him shouts: 'Go back to where you come from! Why don't you go home?' A dark-skinned girl with a sad face follows him in the next rectangle. 'I don't want to go home, mommy,' she says, 'I don't want to go home.' Next, a woman who hisses: 'I'm sick of your views about immigrants. This is our home too!' An Asian man rages, 'You call this a home? This ain't no goddam home.' Then another woman, Muslim presumably, from her headscarf, confesses, 'I'm never made to feel at home here.' The series of six rectangles ends with a bright-eyed young tourist: 'Wow', she says, 'I really like it here. I don't think I ever want to go home!' (Rhodes, 2001: V3).

In this very public space, Lum had crystallized the new 21st-century Vienna, reluctant mongrel city, Jörg Haider's Vienna, a cosmopolitan, multicultural city troubled by the politics of right-wing reaction against immigration and the realities of a changing urban and social fabric. Lum's project, which was in place for several months, was called 'There is no place like home'. He had been invited by the Museum in Progress to conceive of such a project shortly after the newly elected Austrian government had decided to include Haider's far-right Freedom Party as a coalition partner.[1] The cultural community in Vienna wanted to signal that not all Austrians were delighted with this political turn. Lum's art has been preoccupied for some time with the nature of a multicultural society. Multiculturalism's vision of an integrated world serves as his political inspiration and also provides a conceptual model of a possible new form for his art, which is both hybrid and dialectical. In Vienna his billboards confronted residents with a series of questions about the meaning of home and nation, and whether those meanings can accommodate and welcome migrants. This question is at the heart of this chapter, which explores the nature of fear in contemporary multicultural, multiethnic cities, specifically the fear of strangers/outsiders, and the connection between that fear and certain notions of home and identity.

As I noted in Chapter 1, there has been a reaction across European nations for the past decade against the increasing presence and concentration of migrants in some cities and neighbourhoods, and this reaction gathered political strength in the first couple of years of the new century. In Chapter 4, I quoted the British Home Secretary, David Blunkett, in a public statement that chastised immigrants for not being gracious enough guests in the home of the British nation. His metaphor of the nation as 'home' is central to the exploration I want to pursue in this chapter, linking it to the earlier discussion about the nature of identity/difference. I argue that it is important to look harder at the nature of fear in contemporary cities in order to arrive at more effective and less discriminatory policies for managing our co-existence in the shared spaces of streets and neighbour- hoods, spaces that are increasingly characterized by a social heterogeneity. The costs of fear (of outsiders) in a democracy are several and serious. They may include the suspen- sion of civil rights because people fear terrorists; the building of literal as well as meta- phorical walls around 'our' spaces to keep out those who are 'not like us', thus exacerbat- ing social polarization; and a dramatic decline in the quality of the urban public realm as people retreat to their privatized and fortified spaces. Fears have consequences, and the descriptive core of this chapter focuses on four examples of contemporary city fears and some of their consequences.

But I begin by exploring a distinguished line of sociological and social psychological inquiry about fear in the city as it relates to the figure of the stranger, the outsider. In particular, I want to forge links between this historical line of inquiry, Pierre Bourdieu's concept of *habitus*, and a discussion of the homely imaginary of nationalist practices by the Lebanese-Australian anthropologist Ghassan Hage. I argue that there is a political economy of city fears (whether these fears are real or imagined), and an unavoidable question is whose fears get legitimized and translated into policy responses, and whose fears get silenced or marginalized. The final section reflects on the potency of discourses of fear, and the threat that these pose to the sustainability of cities of difference, to a democratic civic culture and the vibrancy of the urban public realm – that is, to the very possibility of *cosmopolis*.

Planning and urban management discourses are, and always have been, saturated with fear. The history of planning could be rewritten as the attempt to manage fear in the city:

generically, fear of disorder and fear of dis/ease, but specifically fear of those bodies thought to produce that disorder or dis/ease – at different historical moments and places these have included women, the working-classes, immigrants, gays, youth, and so on. At least four generic kinds of 'solution' have been promoted for the past hundred years: one is policing, that is, more law and order; a second is spatial containment and segregation, keeping certain bodies out of certain areas; a third is moral reform, the attempt to produce certain kinds of citizens and subjectivities, good Londoners, good New Yorkers, by providing parks and playgrounds, settlement houses, community centres, and other 'civilizing' urban facilities. A fourth, more recent, approach is assimilation through social policies such as national language requirements and civics classes, to make 'the Other' into 'one of us'.[2] These approaches, which seek to banish fear by either banishing or transforming those seen as inducing fear, have surely exhausted themselves in their futility. In the next chapter, I shift to a discussion of what might be better ways of dealing with these fears of the stranger.[3]

CITIES, HABITUS, AND FEAR OF CHANGE

Lewis Mumford, in *The City in History* (1961), wrote of the need for cities to be more than 'containers' guaranteeing the coherence and continuity of urban culture over time. He warned of the danger of a too-stabilized community, arguing that urban experience is also about mobility and mixture, encounters and challenges. The city multiplies the opportunities for psychological shock and stimulus. Cultural intermixture, he argued, is what makes the city a civilized place to live. For this reason, 'the stranger, the outsider, the traveller, the trader, the refugee, the slave, yes, even the invading enemy, have had a special part in urban development at every stage' (quoted in Robins, 1995: 48). In this aspect of his work, Mumford is part of a larger tradition of sociological writing which has been concerned with the civilizing potential of the stranger, beginning with Georg Simmel and continuing in Robert Park's interest in the movement and migration of peoples and the way this loosens local bonds and creates the freedoms of cities.

A new generation of urbanists has drawn on this tradition, celebrating the city as 'a coming together of strangers' (Young, 1990), and urban dwellers as people 'always in the presence of otherness' (Sennett, 1990: 123). But Mumford also took seriously the realities of human antagonism and aversion, the fear eating at the soul of the city, the city as a container of disruptive internal forces. He recognized fear and anxiety as the dark side of the stimulation and challenge associated with one's encounters with strangers. What happens when strangers become neighbours, when the Other moves in next door? What changes with the awareness that we might touch or be touched by a stranger on the street, or when 'the odor of North African barbecues offends noses that are used to other festivities' (Kristeva, 1991: 104)? The fears, anxieties, aversions thus aroused are, simultaneously, unspeakable, and yet have powerfully shaped urban political discourses and, consequently, the agendas that have been developed around immigration and urban management. We need to look harder at the nature of fear in the city, and the ways in which it is related to notions of home, homeliness, and belonging because, if such fears cannot be legislated out of existence, we will need different approaches to managing our co-existence in the shared spaces of neighbourhoods and cities (Sandercock, 2000a).

There was in the 1990s a burgeoning of literature about fear, the fear of strangers and foreigners, fear in the city (see Ellin, 1997; Beck, 1998). To the extent that this literature has infiltrated the planning field, it is pragmatic and design-based, appearing under the rubric of 'crime prevention through environmental design', or its predecessor, 'defensible space', both of which tackle what I would like to call the 'hardware' of crime prevention rather than the 'software' of fear in the city. I would like to come at the issue of fear in a very different way, recognizing, to begin with, that individual identity is often suffused with anxiety, and that these anxieties are projected onto the figure of the stranger, the alien, whose very presence seems to challenge and undermine the known social order. For Robert Park, for example, the fundamental cause of prejudice is the insecurity of relations with the stranger. We hate because we fear (Park, 1967: chapters 11 and 13). Sociologists from Park and Simmel in the early twentieth century to Ulrich Beck towards its end have emphasized this social psychological disturbance stimulated by the presence of strangers. Julia Kristeva's analysis, in *Strangers to Ourselves* (1991), develops an understanding of fear and its relation to the homely (that which is comfortable and familiar), to the socio-spatial ordering of life. In her opening paragraphs, Kristeva sets out her project:

Strangely, the foreigner lives within us: he is the hidden face of our identity, the space that wrecks our abode, the time in which understanding and affinity founder.

(Kristeva, 1991: 1)

Her choice of words is revealing – '*the space that wrecks our abode, the time in which understanding and affinity founder*' – resonating with the Bourdieu-ian sociology of *habitus*, invoking its destruction, the destruction of our socio-spatial and socio-temporal sense of place and identity. In everyday language, we might say that this is the destruction of all that is familiar and homely, all that we have grown up with and take for granted, including the socio-spatial knowledge of our neighbourhoods and indeed, the nation as a whole. *Habitus*, which is a disposition to act, is, for Bourdieu, always specific to a structurally defined field of social relations, but that 'field' also has its spatial dimension, the spaces of the city, as well as the social spaces in which one feels 'at home', where we experience both a positive sense of belonging and a sense of knowing where we belong in the social order – which is also a spatial ordering of the city (Bourdieu, 1977).

The small French town of Orange (population 29,000) in Provence provides a recent illustration of the dynamic I have just outlined. In 1996 voters elected a member of Le Pen's National Front Party as Mayor, and re-elected him five years later with a massive 60 per cent of the vote. The town's director of communications explained to a reporter that France was in 'terrible danger from unchecked immigration'. 'The country has been invaded. Daily life is ruined . . . It's not home anymore, and we are not protected by the state . . .' (Hilton, 2002: 43). Here we see the linking of home and nation and the claim that the national space has been invaded. Experientially, this is felt in daily life, which is 'ruined' as the homely space is disrupted by those 'others' who are identified as Arabs in the article. But there is extreme bitterness towards the national state, which is seen as having betrayed the locals by not protecting them from this 'invasion'.

The stranger, the outsider, threatens to bring chaos into the social order, from the imagined community of the nation to that of the familiar neighbourhood. Individual strangers are a discomforting presence. In numbers, they may come to be seen as a tide that will engulf us, provoking primitive fears of annihilation, of the dissolving of boundaries, the dissolution of identity. In the face of this unsettling, according to German sociologist Ulrich Beck, the desire for the logic of order and identity is reasserted. 'We' must secure our centrality and 'they', those who disrupt our homely space, must be pushed out from the centre. Difference is an attribute of 'them'. They are not 'like us' and therefore they are threatening. And yet, the very strangeness of strangers is not only frightening but also enticing (Beck, 1998: 130). Our ambivalence towards strangers expresses both fear and fascination, which is also desire (including erotic desire) fused into one, and is thus doubly unsettling.

Kristeva also talks about our love/hatred for the figure of the stranger. As a psychoanalyst, she unravels another layer, drawing on Freud's discussion of the homely and unhomely (*heimlich/unheimlich*). Since Freud's explorations into the unconscious, she argues, we have had to acknowledge that we are 'strangers to ourselves' and this very knowledge corrodes our sense of identity and security. The foreigner, the wanderer, the immigrant is a symptom. 'Psychologically he signifies the difficulty we have of living as an other and with others; politically he underscores the limits of nation-states and of the national political conscience that characterizes them and that we have all deeply interiorized to the point of considering it normal that there are foreigners, that is, people who do not have the same rights as we do' (Kristeva, 1991: 103). The strangeness of strangers is, in this understanding, both frightening and potentially liberating. We fear strangers because we fear that which is strange in ourselves, the foreign component in our psyche. And yet, a journey into the strangeness of the Other could lead to an acceptance of these hidden dimensions of the self. 'By recognizing him within ourselves, we are spared detesting him in himself' (Kristeva, 1991: 1).

Longings, yearning, the uncanny *vs.* belonging, security, the familiar. Un/settling. Must the stranger, who was the 'enemy' in primitive societies, be doomed to play out this part forever, or (as a still and perhaps forever utopian question) can we find ways of living with others without ostracizing but also without levelling? This is Kristeva's question. Her answer is that we can accept the foreigner if we can accept that which is foreign in ourselves, and we can do so by moving towards an 'ethics of respect for the irreconcilable' (Kristeva, 1991: 183). While I find her psychoanalytic exploration of the question of the stranger illuminating up to a point, I don't think her answer suffices. By remaining in the psychological realm she avoids dealing with the interdependencies of fears/aversions that, I will argue, are simultaneously material, communicative, and symbolic, and need to be dealt with on all three levels.

Strangers, fear, ambivalence. I want to take this exploration now in two directions. First into the work of Ghassan Hage, and his confronting book *White Nation* (1998), and then into a broader political economy of fear. In doing so, I want to suggest a different way of understanding the history of planning policies – as spatial practices of power deeply implicated in longings and belongings, as the attempt to manage fear in the city.

Hage retells the story from the movie *Falling Down*, in which Michael Douglas plays the role of a man (D-Fens) whose world is disintegrating. His primary experience of disintegration is the breakdown of his family. As the film follows his desperate attempt to rebuild his family, however, we see that to him the experience of breakdown extends also to the breakdown of the neighbourhood, the nation, and the American way of life. The film begins with D-Fens in his car, in a traffic jam, when a fly enters the vehicle. D-Fens snaps as he tries, unsuccessfully, to get rid of the fly, which provides a powerful metaphor for what follows: his attempt to regain control of his 'home space'. Throughout the movie the 'hero' moves within and across overlapping spaces, his car space, his family space, his neighbourhood space, his national space, as he encounters one 'fly' after another – feminists, fascists, bureaucratic mentalities, as well as a variety of ethnic and racial others, all of them uncontrollable 'flies' in his space of being, his 'home'.

Hage uses this film as an illustration of what he calls the 'mechanics of nationalist practices of exclusion', a way of categorizing otherness/ethnicity within a practice of domesticating the social environment in pursuit of a homely space. 'Because of the emotionally charged portrayal of the "hero", the film reminds us that the space of the home that the nationalist is trying to recover is not just a functional space, but also an affective one, a space where he is staging the very meaning of his life' (Hage, 1998: 76). Hage argues that in Australia both White racists and White multiculturalists share a conception of themselves as nationalists and as managers of the national space, a space which is structured around a White culture, and in which Aboriginal people and non-White 'ethnics' are merely objects to be moved or removed according to a White national will. Although his discussion is specifically about contemporary Australia, the argument has broader relevance, in view of the recent intensification of racist and xenophobic sentiments and practices in European countries.

What's interesting here is Hage's discussion of the *homely imaginary* of nationalist practices. I suggest that although 'national space' is an imaginary, it is an imaginary that is actually, literally, embodied in the local spaces of one's street, neighbourhood and city, where it is either reinforced or undermined. It is an imaginary which involves a sure knowledge (if one is British) that down the street there is, for example, an English butcher's shop, a Protestant or Catholic church, an English pub, and not a Halal butcher, Buddhist temple, or gay bar. When the locality begins to change, one's imaginary of national space is no longer congruent with one's actual experience of local space. And this produces insecurity (when security is equated with the absence of a threatening otherness). Through interviews, Hage talks to people (in Sydney) who are deeply unsettled by an immigrant presence in their neighbourhood, but specifically the presence of those whom he describes as 'Third World-Looking People (TWLP's)' like himself, a dark-skinned Lebanese. 'When the nationalist feels that he or she can no longer operate in, communicate in, or recognize the national space in which s/he operates, the nation [via locality] appears to be losing its homely character' (Hage, 1998: 40). Fears are generated. Loss is experienced. 'The Other', the stranger, is thought to be taking over, or as having already taken over. Resentment builds. One of Hage's interviewees, a young Australian born of Greek immigrant parents, and self-described university drop-out, said: 'They've come all the way from I don't know where, and they've stolen my dreams' (Hage, 1998: 218).

In his exploration of diaspora formation, Sayyid (2000) adds another dimension to our understanding of fear of strangers. The arrival in European cities of large numbers of migrants from, for example, Muslim countries is, he argues, perceived as a new diaspora in formation.

Unlike the nation with its (imagined) homogeneity and boundedness, diaspora suggests heterogeneity and porousness. If nations define home, then diasporas[4] interrupt the closure of nation. The existence of a diaspora (Jewish, Muslim, Chinese, Indian) prevents the closure of the nation, since a diaspora is by definition located within another nation. In other words, migrants who form tightly knit communities within a nation that is not their homeland may be perceived as a threat to the stability of the host nation. Questions of loyalty arise. Locals want to force the newcomers to conform, in order to enhance the security of their own identity, insofar as that identity is tied to the nation. Sayyid draws on Hannah Arendt's reflections on the relationship between identity and belonging for Jews in Europe after Nazism to point to the importance of a notion of home as a way in which 'the nation sutures the subject. It is the nation as home that acts as an arena for our everyday practices, practices that give focus and meaning. If identity is "a way of life", then the nation, by providing a home, is the stage upon which a particular way of life is enacted' (Sayyid, 2000: 42).

Sayyid's and Hage's analyses help us to understand that the national issue of migration becomes a struggle which is played out at the level of the locality in terms of an experience of threat and loss, and the desire to reassert control over one's territory, one's spatial *habitus*. The affective dimension is related to a deep sense of loss and displacement on the part of some residents who, instead of being able to incorporate and adapt to the social changes around them, perceive these changes as a threat to their accustomed way of life, and resist in whatever ways are available – whether through hate crimes or by lodging complaints through the planning system, by behaving offensively, by leaving the neighbourhood, or removing their children from neighbourhood schools.[5]

But where does this insight – into the connections between home and nation, strangers and identity – take us? The point I want to pick up on, in returning to the material city in the next section, is precisely the issue of social change and people's capacity to adapt to it. In the next section I argue that discourses of fear emerge in different cities and societies at particular historical moments and are linked to profound structural changes of a socio-cultural and spatial as well as economic kind. Fear, at this symbolic level, fear of psychological displacement, is every bit as important as those more tangible fears of economic displacement, of strangers arriving and stealing one's job. The two fears feed off each other in ways that are not necessarily susceptible to rational argument, and this has huge implications for how we might think about policy interventions (the subject of the next chapter).

URBAN POLITICAL ECONOMIES AND DISCOURSES OF FEAR

If urban political economy, in dealing with the material city, asks the question 'whose city?' – that is, who gets what and where in the distribution of urban goods, services, and locational advantages – then a political economy of urban fear might ask 'who's afraid of whom?' and where in the city is fear concentrated and acted out? In the following examples, from the United States, Brazil, South Africa, and Europe, I explore the links between emergent discourses of fear and changes to urban political economies and social structures.

THE AMERICAN URBAN CRISIS OF THE 1960S: FEAR OF THE GHETTO

In American cities since the mid-1960s, discourses of fear and of urban decline have been all-pervasive (Beauregard, 1993). The trigger was the inner-city rioting that spread across the country from the mid to late 1960s. Long-developing changes like postindustrial transformation become crises when a significant number of people take notice of them, and that usually happens when the consequences of gradual change are displayed all at once in what seems like a sudden, violent disruption. The term 'the urban crisis' usually describes this period of particularly violent social upheaval in inner cities from the mid-1960s to about 1970, and the sources of this urban crisis are generally attributed to the continuing postindustrial transformation of these inner cities: two decades of sustained Black migration to Northern inner cities, white and middle-class exodus to the suburbs, and the flight of capital and manufacturing jobs from urban to suburban neighbour-hoods. These structural changes formed the context for the upheavals surrounding the civil rights movement, rising expectations of urban Blacks in tension with social and physical conditions in the inner city, and the inadequate responses of the state to the continuing problems of racial conflict, poverty, inequities in housing and education, and increasing criminal violence.

As Beauregard puts it in *Voices of Decline*, a single theme emerged from and gave unity to the fevered discourse about urban decline. 'The theme was race, the problem was the concentration, misery, and rebellion of Negroes in central cities, and the reaction was one of fear and eventually panic' (Beauregard, 1993: 169). Thereafter, racial violence (as in the 'race riot') and racially coded violence (as in the figure of the 'mugger', who is always assumed to be either Black or Hispanic) became rubrics under which to reduce the complexity of urban transformation to sharply representable and narratable form. The widespread tendency to understand the relationship between whites and Blacks in the postindustrial city as primarily a problem of too little law and order in the ghetto led to what Sharon Zukin has called 'the institutionalization of fear' as a defining principle of urbanism during and after 'the urban crisis' in America (Zukin, 1996: 39).

The endless repetition and interpretation of images of 'urban disorder' – riots, mug-gings, police and National Guard responses – chart the sudden shock of Americans' encounter with the slower, duller, more obscure disorder of shifting economic and social arrangements. The racial logic that dominated the discourse gave Americans a way to think about, or not think about, historical processes like the emergence of postindustrial urbanism. One way to understand the urban crisis of the 1960s, Carlo Rotella suggests, is to regard it as the period in which Americans – especially Americans who steered clear of the (Black) inner city – were forced to confront that emergent urbanism (Rotella, 1998: 216). For my purposes, in reflecting on fear and the city, what is significant is the way this discourse of disorder and fear produced a particular politics and set of policy responses. Zukin calls this period a 'watershed in the institutionalization of urban fear'. Voters and policy elites could have chosen to approve policies to attack poverty, manage ethnic competition, integrate everyone into common public institutions. Instead they chose to buy protection, fueling the growth of the private security industry. Employment in this industry tripled from 1970 to 1990 and, as factory jobs disappeared, urban workers – especially minority group members – sought jobs in the security industry, while their white counterparts in small towns sought jobs in the increasing numbers of prisons being built in or on the edge of small-town America (particularly small-town California, some of whose economies are described (Barthels, 2003) as being 'prison-dependent').

Choosing the path of fear and fortification, the path of the closed city, is, I suggest, a downward spiral in which the less we know about and are exposed to strangers, the more afraid we are. The terrorist attacks on New York and Washington on September 11th have multiplied the fears of strangers, resulting in racial profiling of anyone who looks like they might be from the Middle East. Against this natural tendency to retreat behind walls and increase the security hardware, there is the 'challenge of the Open City, a city that is life affirming, that reaches out to others who are not necessarily like us, and that acknowledges our common humanity and the pleasures of a life lived among multipli/ cities' (Friedmann, 2002a: 237). We need to address the fears that hold us in their grip, and I will need to return to the 'project of the Open City' as one possible way of doing this.[6]

SÃO PAULO'S FORTIFIED ENCLAVES: FEAR OF THE POOR

Brazil has experienced an equally powerful set of structural changes in the past decade. Here I draw on the excellent work of Teresa Caldeira (1999) in documenting the emergence of fortified enclaves in São Paulo as part of a new urban segregation in this mega-city of 10 million inhabitants. Caldeira argues that the new pattern of spatial segregation of the 1990s is inseparable from three structural change processes. From the 1940s to the 1970s the middle and upper classes lived in central and well-equipped neighbourhoods, and the poor in the precarious hinterland where many squatted and, over the space of several decades, built their own housing. In the early 1980s, perhaps reflecting the waning control of the military regime, an out-of-control economy produced astronomical inflation and increasing unemployment, and escalating land prices on the periphery put it beyond the reach of a new generation of working-class households, who were ultimately forced back into the city, into *favelas* (shanty towns of self-built housing). In 1973 *favelas* housed 1 per cent of the city population; in 1993 it was 19.4 per cent, almost 2 million people.

Second, the consolidation of democratic government after almost two decades of military rule brought trade unions and social movements to the centre of politics, and led to increasing investment in infrastructure in peripheral neighbourhoods, and the regularization of land markets on the periphery. These, in turn, further pushed up land prices and pushed the poor out of the periphery and into the city's *favelas*, bringing them into close physical proximity with the middle and upper classes. Third, changes in the urban political economy characterized by an expansion of the service sector and a corresponding relative decline in the industrial sector saw the city of São Paulo for the first time lose its position as the number one industrial pole of the country (Caldeira, 1999: 116–17), and there were corresponding changes to the urban fabric, as the oldest areas of the city went through both deterioration and gentrification.

Along with these structural changes came an increase in violent crime, insecurity, and fear which saw citizens adopting new strategies of protection that, over time, are changing the city's physical landscape, patterns of residence and circulation, everyday trajectories, habits and gestures related to the use of streets and public transportation. Fear of crime has contributed to changes in all types of public interaction. A new aesthetics of security shapes all types of construction and imposes a new urban logic of surveillance and distance. São Paulo is becoming 'a city of walls', as physical barriers are constructed everywhere.[7] New enclaves of socially homogeneous housing for the middle and upper classes are emerging on the periphery, adjacent to and yet completely separate from self-constructed working-class neighbourhoods and *favelas*. The elites have abandoned the streets, no longer using them as spaces of sociability as has been the Brazilian custom, and they now seek, through a variety of design strategies, to prevent street life from entering their enclaves (Caldeira, 1999: 118–19).

Caldeira analyses the advertising for these new gated communities and describes how they elaborate the myth of 'a new concept of residence' shaped by images of security, isolation, homogeneity, and luxurious facilities and services. The advertisements invoke privileged islands to which one can return every day, in order to escape from the city and its deteriorated environment and to encounter an exclusive world of pleasure among peers. The image of the gated enclaves is opposed to the image of the city as a deteriorated world pervaded not only by noise and pollution, but, more important, by confusion and mixture – that is, social heterogeneity. The ads suggest the possibility of constructing a life of total calm and security. 'In a context of increased fear of crime in which the poor are often associated with criminality, the upper classes fear contact and contamination, but they continue to depend on their servants.' Their rising anxiety levels relate to concerns about the most effective way of controlling these servants, with whom they have such ambiguous relationships of dependency and avoidance, intimacy and distrust. 'Total security' is crucial to the 'new concept of residence.' Security and control are the conditions for keeping the others out, for assuring not only isolation, but also happiness, harmony, and even freedom (Caldeira, 1999: 120–22).

This contemporary urban re-segregation is complementary to the issue of urban violence but also reflective of Brazilian ways of negotiating deeper changes, from an industrial to a postindustrial urbanism, and from military to democratic rule. What is of particular interest is how the fear of crime is used, on the one hand, to legitimate

increasing measures of security and surveillance but, on the other hand, how the proliferation of everyday talk about crime becomes the context in which residents generate
stereotypes as they label different social groups as dangerous, as people to be feared and
avoided. These everyday discussions about crime, as Caldeira argues, create rigid symbolic differences as well as physical distances between social groups. Two issues emerge
here. One is the way in which advertising for the new gated communities plays on and
uses the discourse of fear of the city and the implied criminality of the poor, in order to
create an alternative to the city, a utopia of total calm and security (and yet a utopia
which is utterly dependent on the badly paid labours of the working-classes). The second
is the importance of everyday talk about crime, in generating a climate in which such a
rejection of the city becomes first thinkable, then necessary.

CAPETOWN: FEARS OF LOSING CONTROL

A similar trend can be observed in post-apartheid Capetown today. At the level of
national discourse in South Africa, integration is on everyone's lips. There is talk of a
new spatial framework at the level of the urban, of a new rationality for future planning,
which includes initiatives to integrate urban spaces, like parks, and to showcase different
cultures in an attempt to reduce fear.[8] But the dominant official discourse coming from
the predominantly white Capetown Council, and more specifically from its economic
development branch, is fear of inner urban decay.[9] Here, the endless repetition and
interpretation of images of 'urban disorder' – deterioration, pollution, filth, decay, waste,
illegal immigrants (from neighbouring African states), violence and crime, anarchism –
is a coded way of talking about the arrival and presence of non-whites in the inner city,
and particularly of groups considered to be marginal, the street vendors, the parking
attendants (referred to as 'parking terrorists'), the homeless. The Capetown Partnership,
an initially informal but now formalized alliance between the City Council and the
business sector, is the driving force behind this discourse of fear of inner urban decay.
They see the inner city as the economic heart of any world class city, which must now
compete with the greater safety of the suburban shopping mall. Capetown aspires to be a
world class city, yet it fears becoming an African city (and is the only major city in South
Africa which is refusing to adopt an African name).

These fears are an expression of white Capetown's ambivalence towards changes in
society since the African National Congress came to power in 1994. Their response is to
try to manage the fear by marginalizing and defining as a threat certain social groups,
such as the informal traders, the parking attendants, the illegal immigrants, and the
homeless, by controlling them, reducing their numbers, introducing codes of conduct
relating to their economic activities. The desire is to create a clean and safe city, with the
shopping mall as one model, and New York's Business Improvement Districts (BIDs) as
another. This approach, which seeks to restructure urban space into a sophisticated
consumption environment (with an eye on the tourist market), has a focus on security
and law enforcement, with 8.5 million Rand initially allocated for surveillance equipment, rather than focusing on addressing the social problems of the inner city. In other
words, official discourse transforms a generalized white anxiety about social change into

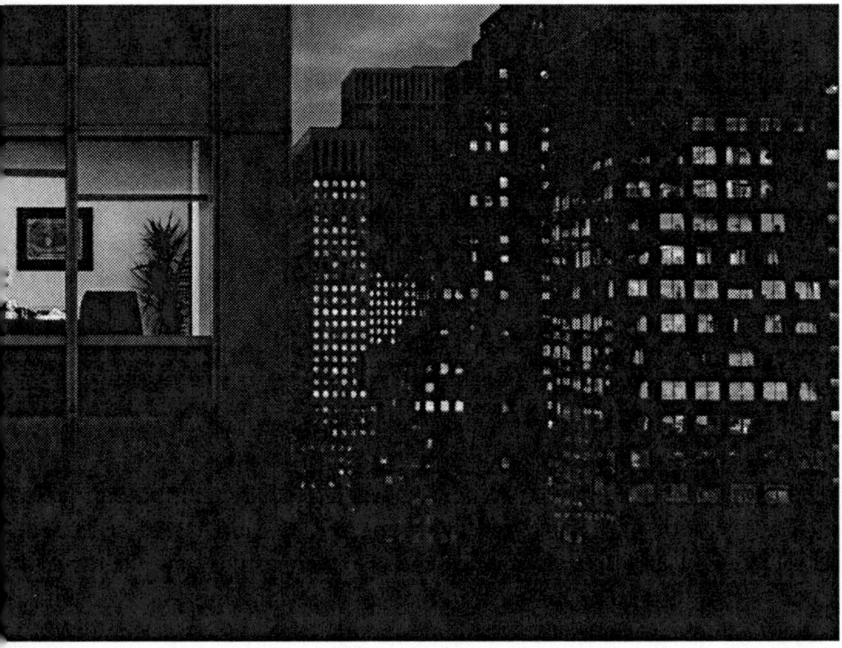

specific fears about the decay of the inner city, and responds with policies that institutionalize that fear by enhancing security and surveillance. Here is a case where a
discourse of fear *creates* a problem which, in turn, marks certain urban bodies as
undesirable and as the target of policy intervention, and in so doing, no doubt, goes
some way towards producing the undesirable subjectivities which it fears.

In all three examples discussed so far – São Paulo, Capetown, and American cities'
responses to the urban crisis of the 1960s – what is feared by the dominant culture is
what I will call 'the stranger within'. In American cities this is the repressed African
American population, as that population tries to assert its civil and human and urban
rights. In Capetown, in post-apartheid South Africa, the historically dominant white
population fears losing control – with all the material and also psychological advantages that implies – to the non-whites. And in São Paulo, the middle and upper classes
fear the poor, the squatters, whom they see as an invading force in urban space. In
each case the response has been to turn to new forms of spatial exclusion, such as
gated communities, and to increase the hardware of surveillance and other security
measures. The idea of co-existing in shared space with these 'strangers within' is not
considered realistic or desirable by the majority of the dominant culture. The result is
cities that are becoming increasingly fortress-like, closed rather than open cities. Now,
perhaps I have chosen deliberately apocalyptic examples to make my point. Surely,
pleasant 'civilized' cities like Copenhagen, Amsterdam, Vienna, do not have these
problems?

EUROPEAN CITIES: FEAR OF FOREIGNERS/MIGRANTS/OUTSIDERS

The age of migration that has affected European cities since the 1980s is another historical moment in which changes that began decades earlier (with the need for 'guest
workers', as well as with the obligation to accept members of former empires as immigrants) crystallize into fears that these guests are not going to leave, and these foreigners,
former colonial subjects, are taking over 'our cities' and threatening 'our way of life'. This
latter phrase, 'our way of life', has various meanings: from liberal democracy to economic prosperity to cultural homogeneity. Muslim immigrants are widely perceived as
threatening what is liberal in liberal democracies, specifically because of their patriarchal
practices and their opposition to homosexuality. This is a particular concern in countries
with a strong social liberal tradition in recent decades such as the Scandinavian countries
and the Netherlands. Moreover, in working-class neighbourhoods and towns, especially
those where there is high unemployment, immigrants are perceived as taking jobs away
from the traditional working-class, and also taking too much in the way of welfare
payments and subsidies. And among more conservative citizens, migrants from diverse
cultures are seen as bringing strange customs and lifeways that do not fit with their idea
of the identity of the nation, and of being 'at home' in that nation.

What has been alarming since the late 1990s is the way in which these fears about how
'our way of life' is being undermined are being mobilized by conservative politicians into
'coalitions of the fearful', coalitions that are winning seats in parliaments and have begun
to introduce legislation to restrict further immigration and to turn away refugees. One

notable feature of this new discourse of fear in Europe is the way in which immigration and criminality are merged (Gallego-Diaz, 2002; Bodie-Gendrot, 2000).[10] Another feature is the invocation of essences. The essence of Danishness (or Austrian-ness, or German-ness) is allegedly being threatened. A third feature is the metaphor of invasion. Those strangers are invading 'my' home, swamping 'our' ways of doing things with new and strange ways. In the final section I want to tease out the common themes in these four examples of fear in the city and their implications for the practices of planning and urban management.

CONCLUSIONS

I've provided two lines of inquiry into the question of fear in the city, one sociological/socio-psychological, the other political economic, and I now want to suggest that these are mutually reinforcing. I also want to suggest that the existence of fear in the city is not a simple reflection of social reality but is a complicated production of that 'reality' through the power of discourse (from everyday talk to advertising, to official documents about the city). The social psychological reading in the first section suggests that the capacity to be drawn into urban fearing lives within us all: that we are all vulnerable to being unsettled by the presence of strangers, in part because we are strangers to ourselves. The political economic reading developed in the second section suggests that such fears tend to be collectively mobilized as a response to historical moments of profound structural/social/cultural/demographic change. These moments or epochs produce urban transformations, re-shapings of the city that give rise to new contestations over whose city it is, who belongs where in the city, which groups are benefiting, which are being pushed out.

These contestations over the re-shaping of the city are in turn accompanied by and partially conducted through a discourse, actually by multiple and competing discourses. These discourses seek to define who and what is to be feared in the process of change, and, in so doing, to influence the management and direction of change in ways that privilege the rights of some at the expense of others, the sense of place of some at the expense of others, one group's homely imaginary at the expense of others. These discourses draw upon, even as they transcend, the material conditions that govern the realities and prospects of cities, and mediate among espoused values, future possibilities and current dilemmas. Discourses of fear function ideologically to shape our attention, to convey a comprehensible and compelling story of the fate of the city, and to provide reasons for how we should act in response to perceived problems (Beauregard, 1993: 8).

Discourses of fear are maps of a social reality perceived as problematic in moments when we are unsure what direction to take: whether to fight or flee, where and how to live, where to invest. The reality of fear in the city is always mediated by these discourses or representations of it. Portraying parts of cities as sites of physical and/or moral decay, of economic and/or social disorganization, as places to avoid, has intended or implicit policy consequences – clearance, clean-up, redevelopment. Portraying certain groups in the city as people to be feared, Blacks, gays, youths, the homeless, immigrant youths, Aborigines, Jews, and so on, also has intended policy consequences, from police sweeps, to increasing the hardware of surveillance, to defensive architectural and design practices. What is less explored, and therefore less clear, is that portraying certain groups as fear-inducing surely serves to some extent to produce the very behaviours that are dreaded, while also increasing the likelihood that such groups will be victimized (through hate crimes and/or official brutality) with relative impunity. Rising levels of police violence against people of colour in the USA, and against the poor in São Paulo attest to this, as do increasingly harsh policies directed at the homeless in New York or Johannesburg, or at 'youth' in many cities.[11]

Discourses of fear, then, have potency. One of the tasks of planners and urban intellectuals is to deconstruct these discourses, and to provide counter-discourses. Official urban discourses (those produced by City Councils, Departments of Planning, Police Departments, mainstream media) tend to legitimize and privilege the fears of the bourgeoisie, their fears of those Others who might invade or disrupt their homely spaces, their *habitus*. We rarely hear from those folks whom official discourse classifies as Other, about *their* fears: the fear, for example, of being hungry, homeless, jobless, of having no future in the city, of being unable to provide for one's children, the fear of not being accepted in a strange environment, the fear of police or citizen violence against them.[12]

Beyond the sheer power of discourse, the exploration of the political economy of fear demonstrates two things. One is that there is a material as well as psychological basis for fearing strangers. This is either a fear of being a victim of crime (break-ins, hi-jackings of cars by armed men ('car-jacking'), and so on), if you're well-to-do, or a fear of being economically displaced and further impoverished if you're already close to the bottom of the heap. And, as Marris (1996) has argued convincingly, it is the latter who have suffered most from globalization through the downward displacement of uncertainty by those in power. The second is that not all fears are treated with equal weight by the state. In my examples from São Paulo, Capetown, and US cities, it is the fears of the haves, rather than the have-nots, which have driven urban policies. If our goal is for cities of difference, mongrel cities, to be Open Cities, rather than walled fortresses, then policies will need to respond at material, communicative, and symbolic levels, dealing with material and psychological fears, and the misunderstandings they each generate.

If we accept that fear will always be with us, that it is on some emotional level an understandable reaction to changes in one's *habitus*, occasioned by the presence of strangers, then we do need to think about how to manage fear in the city. But surely we need to think about this in a very different way than we have in the past: different from the Capetown Council; different from the urban development industry in São Paulo or Johannesburg; and different from contemporary European demagoguery on the subject of migrants. Those approaches are transforming the city as a vital public realm. The consequences of the 'hardware' approach to managing fear include changes in the character of public space and of citizens' participation in public life. One of the most tangible threats to public culture, as Zukin has argued, comes from the politics (and discourses) of everyday fear (Zukin, 1996: 38). As urban public spaces have included more strangers, those who used public spaces before have abandoned them, leaving them to a generalized ethnic Other, a victim of the politics of fear. When public space is perceived as too dangerous to venture into, then the principle of open access, of a civic culture, is destroyed. Johannesburg may be on the verge of such destruction as a city, as is São Paulo. Is this the direction of European cities in coming decades, a retreat from public spaces and public institutions as citizens seek to inhabit spaces filled with people who are just like themselves, and to avoid the immigrant others?

Among the conditions necessary for a genuinely pluralist democracy, as I argued in Chapter 4, is that people acknowledge those from different social groups as co-citizens, that is, as people having similar rights. Cities that become increasingly enclaved are not environments that generate conditions conducive to an open and tolerant way of life. The new urban socio-spatial segregations increase the difficulty of engaging a variety of social groups in political life, in which common goals and solutions would have to be negotiated.[13] This enclaving of the city builds on particular discourses of fear that seek to cleanse and purify the city as a moral order, as well as to make the city safe for consumption, and so to protect the economic order. Rather than being swept under the carpet as undiscussable, or tackled as an issue of increasing urban fortification or outright exclusion, these fears need to be *communicated and negotiated* if we are to keep alive the idea of the city as a vital public sphere.[14] One step in this direction has been taken in the UK, where members of various faith communities are involved in trans-faith discussions in cities, like Birmingham, whose citizens span Christian, Muslim, Jewish, Hindu, and other faiths. They are very aware of the need to prevent religious differences from spilling over into sectarian aggression. These inter-faith efforts have done a lot since September 11th to promote an attitude of religious tolerance in their respective communities. In this way, alternative discourses are established which can undermine hegemonic conceptions of 'axes of evil' and the fear and violence on the streets that such conceptions engender. This is an example of organized civil society working to counter dominant discourses of fear and violence and thus engaging in the necessary project of 'managing fear' in the city.

The next chapter expands on this challenge of dealing with fear of strangers by tackling head-on the vexed issue of integrating immigrants. We will visit various cities on three continents in search of examples of daily practices as well as public policies supporting intercultural co-existence.

6

THERE IS NO HIDING PLACE

Integrating immigrants

'We've pretty much come to the end of a time when you can have a space that is 'yours only' –
just for people you want to be there . . . we've finished with that kind of isolating. There is no
hiding place. There is nowhere you can go and only be with people who are like you. It's over.
Give it up.

(Reagon, 1981: 357)

INTRODUCTION

This chapter sets out, in a very practical way, to address the question posed in Chapter 4:
how can we stroppy strangers live together without doing each other too much violence?
This question is a challenge to urban governance and to city dwellers, as well as to
planning theory and practice. I first ask what kind of a challenge it is, and then what
policies and processes and institutions exist or might need to be invented for dealing
with the problem as I understand it: the problem of co-existing in the shared spaces of
cities of difference. What might it mean to 'manage difference' in ways that could be
transformative rather than repressive? How can migrants be integrated into cities that are
unused to thinking of themselves as multicultural? Can 'white flight', and its European
equivalents, be counteracted? How might intersecting material and psychological fears
and needs be mediated? How might marginalized or excluded communities become
organized to make effective claims on the urban political economy? Are there paths to
cosmopolis, or only a one-way street leading to the City of Fear?

The great possibility of the mongrel cities of the 21st century is the dream of *cosmopolis*: cities in which there is acceptance of, connection with, and respect and space for 'the
stranger', the possibility of working together on matters of common destiny and forging
new hybrid cultures and urban projects and ways of living. The great danger is that
difference will further fracture, fragment, splinter the fragile urban social fabric as new
demands for rights to the city emerge: rights to a voice, to participation, and to co-
existence in the physical spaces of the built environment, which are then opposed by
those who feel too threatened by the disruption to their accustomed way of life. Mongrel
cities present challenges to city governments, to citizens, and to city planners, as well as to
traditional notions of citizenship. This chapter explores those challenges and looks at
how some cities have become involved, in positive ways, in addressing these challenges.
What kinds of planning, supported by what forms of urban governance and modes of

citizenship, are best able to accommodate difference and have a beneficial impact on exclusion and marginality?

In the first part of the chapter, I look at four ways in which difference challenges planning practices. In the second part, I note five possible types of response: through legislation and the courts; through the market; through dialogue; through social mobilization; and through a transformed planning education. In the third section, I turn to one specific form of the challenge of difference, that of integrating immigrants. I discuss recent efforts in Frankfurt and Rotterdam to actively construct new ways of living together by dealing with the emotional/symbolic as well as the material issues involved. And I contrast these European experiences with efforts in Australia and Canada (actually Sydney and Vancouver) to 'manage difference' at the local government level. In the fourth section, I ask what European cities might learn about integrating immigrants from the American city of Oak Park, in its 40-year effort as a diversity pioneer. Finally, I discuss models of citizenship that can address the everyday realities of life in immigrant cities.

THE CHALLENGE OF DIFFERENCE

Historically, exclusion and marginality have been the constant companions of difference. Think of generations of slaves, indigenous peoples, immigrants and other groups who have not belonged to or have chosen different paths from the dominant culture to which they were subordinate. I am under no illusions about the scope of this task. For in spite of all the talk, in planning, about working for the 'common good', the reality has all too often been otherwise. As a function of the state, planning is one of many social technologies of power available to ruling elites, and has primarily been used to support the power and privileges of dominant classes and cultures.[1] We have seen this in extreme form in colonial planning (see King, 1976; 1990; Rabinow, 1989); in planning under apartheid in South Africa (see Mabin and Smit, 1997); and in ethnocratic states today, such as Israel, where a dominant ethnicity imposes its power through the management of space (see Yiftachel, 1992; 1996; 2000; Fenster, 1999a; 1999b). In only slightly less subtle forms, this use of planning as a technology of power has produced residential segregation by race in the United States (Thomas and Ritzdorf, 1997; Martin and Warner, 2000) and the attempted exclusion of indigenous people from metropolitan areas and country towns in Australia (Jacobs, 1996; Jackson, 1998). Is it realistic to imagine planning practices that can reverse or address these historic and systemic inequalities? Where, institutionally, would such practices be located? In state planning agencies, or are they necessarily insurgent practices, located in civil society and social movements?

In addressing these questions we have to be mindful that planning, in western cities, takes place in a context of racialized liberal democracies and an as yet unresolved 'postcolonial' condition. Planners have not yet sufficiently analysed their own role in an everpresent yet invisible cultural politics of difference, a historic role that has reinforced the power of the dominant culture as well as the dominant class. Across Europe, North America, Australia, and New Zealand, that dominant culture has been ethnically white/ Caucasian and planning, as a technology of power, has been an implicitly racialized practice. Nor has planning in this postcolonial era been decolonized by accepting difference as a category of analysis in the city. If difference matters, in the ways that I have argued in previous chapters, and if we accept the claims of hitherto excluded groups to their rights to the city, then difference is on a collision course with planning, or vice versa. How to avoid the crash?

IN WHAT WAYS IS DIFFERENCE A CHALLENGE TO PLANNING?

In 1992, the Royal Town Planning Institute commissioned two British researchers to explore the sensitivity of the British planning system to the needs of black and ethnic minorities. After surveying over 100 local planning authorities, their report concluded that there was a great deal of ignorance about the existence and nature of racial/ethnic disadvantage in planning, and they recommended creating an institutional framework which would give greater priority to the issue (Krishnarayan and Thomas, 1993). This work perhaps inspired, certainly prefigured, a handful of similar studies in Australia (Watson and McGillivray, 1995: Sandercock and Kliger, 1998a; 1998b) and Canada (Qadeer, 1994; 1997; Wallace and Milroy, 1999; Dale, 1999; Ameyaw, 2000; Edgington and Hutton, 2002) that have drawn attention to a number of issues: from the overall failure of the planning system to respond to the increasing cultural diversity of the city, to the ways in which the values and norms of the dominant culture are reflected in plans, planning codes and bylaws, legislation, and heritage and urban design practices, to planners' inability to analyse issues from a multicultural perspective or to design participatory processes that bring (cultural, religious, and other) minorities into the planning process (Sandercock, 2000a).

Thomas and Krishnarayan have continued to do path-breaking work in this field of cultural diversity and planning, particularly in relation to the ways in which planning is influenced by and implicated in the racialization of social processes (Thomas and Krishnarayan, 1994; Thomas 1995a; 1995b; 1997). And work is now emerging from the USA (Burayidi, 2000) and Europe (Khakee, Somma and Thomas, 1999; Ratcliffe, 1999) of both a theoretical and empirical kind, documenting the circumstances and needs of indigenous and ethnic minorities, and critiquing urban policies and planning practices which either ignore these needs or actively contribute to the ongoing social exclusion of minorities. The work of some Israeli scholars should also be noted as pioneering both for drawing attention to the plight of minorities such as the Bedouin and Ethiopian Jews under the geo-politics of Israeli planning, and for delineating the conflicts between the discourses (and practices) of cultural difference and of human rights (Yiftachel, 1992; 1996; 2000; Fenster, 1999a; 1999b).

From the body of literature referred to above, it is possible to distil four different ways in which diversity challenges existing planning systems, policies and practices. *First*, these studies have shown that the values and norms of the dominant culture are usually embedded in legislative frameworks of planning, bylaws, and regulations. This should not be surprising, since this legal framework for planning evolved at a time when most societies were not yet multicultural, or at least imagined themselves as more homogeneous than they are now. The planning system thus unreflectively expressed the norms of the culturally dominant majority. It is disturbing, however, to recognize that these values are still driving decisions that, in turn, are legitimated and reinforced by the courts.

To take a recent case in the United States: a dispute between the Navajo tribe and the US Forest Service over proposed road construction and logging led to claims by the Navajo that this development would violate their rights of religious freedom, which had been established in the American Indian Religious Freedom Act of 1978. The case ended up in the Supreme Court, where the majority ruling handed down by Justice O'Connor was in favour of the Forest Service. The fundamental issue in dispute was the definition of what constitutes 'religious use' of the land. O'Connor's argument was that the land in question was not actively used for ritual purposes and did not contain a specific religious site. This finding, however, 'begs the central question in planning for a multicultural society: it imposed a form of Judeo-Christian standard of "exercising one's religion" on Native American cultures' (Meyer and Reaves, 2000: 94). What the Supreme Court's ruling did not allow for is that not all religious practices are bound in time and space as are the church-based belief systems of the dominant US culture. The ruling raises the broader question of how a secular society is able to recognize and accommodate a culturally different sense of the sacred.

There is an additional issue relating to legal frameworks and the right to difference. Planning's legal frameworks in the West have been embedded in a particular conception of democracy as a form of majority rule in a multiparty system, and a corresponding belief that the right to difference disappears once the majority has spoken. As one planner whom we interviewed in Melbourne expressed it: 'Local laws and regulations are framed for the majority of the community. If the minority can't fit in, then bad luck' (Sandercock and Kliger, 1998a). For the most part, planners have not questioned the modernist paradigm of 'one law for all', in spite of precedents in feminist planning literature, which have challenged the universalism of the legal framework of planning, a framework which has generally been regarded as neutral, or unbiased, with respect to age, gender, religion, and culture. Applying a critical lens to this framework reveals, however, that it is underpinned by all sorts of implicit assumptions – about what constitutes a 'normal household' (the nuclear family);[2] about an 'appropriate urban form' for such households (single family housing); about gender relations and their spatial expression (women occupying domestic space, men public space); about religious practices (ritual sites versus sacred landscapes); about preferred forms of recreation (cricket and football), and so on. These norms not only conceal gender and sexual preference biases. They also conceal cultural biases.

A *second* way in which the recognition of the right to difference presents a challenge to planning practice is that the norms and values of the dominant culture are not only embedded in the legislative framework of planning, but are also embodied in the attitudes, behaviour, and practices of actual flesh-and-blood planners. Burayidi (2000a) has suggested six ways in which 'cultural misunderstanding' might occur between planners (who belong for the most part to the dominant culture in the societies of Europe, North America and Australia) and cultural minorities:

(i) communication style (cultural differences affect the outcomes of the transactive and social learning processes in planning); (ii) attitude toward disclosure (cultural differences influence the types of information people are willing to share with planners); (iii) attitude toward conflict (this has implications for the role that the planner plays as mediator in community conflicts); (iv) approaches to accomplishing task (this may affect the way in which planners and other professionals undertake teamwork in planning projects); (v) styles of decision making (different cultural groups have different decision-making procedures); and (vi) approaches to knowing (this affects the procedural approach to planning).

(Burayidi, 2000a: 5)

Problems can arise not just from cultural misunderstandings such as these, however, but from more deep-seated beliefs in the superiority of one's own culture, or the belief that all immigrants should adapt to the mores of the 'host' culture – which is the dominant attitude in Europe today.

A *third* challenge revealed by research concerns situations in which the xenophobia and/or racism within communities and neighbourhoods finds its expression or outlet through the planning system, in the form of a planning dispute over, say, the location of a mosque or Hindu temple, the use of a suburban house as a Buddhist community centre, the conversion of an abandoned factory into a training facility for indigenous youth, or the retailing practices of Vietnamese traders (see Sandercock and Kliger, 1998a; 1998b). In such conflicts, it is not the planning system as such which is the problem, but rather the fact that the system becomes an outlet for the deep-seated fears, aversions, or anxieties of some residents. How might the planning system respond in constructive ways?

A *fourth* challenge arises when (western) planners come up against cultural practices that are incommensurable with their own perceptions, values, and practices. One way of interpreting the Supreme Court ruling described above would be to see it as an incommensurable issue of different perceptions of and attitudes towards the meaning of land between secular mainstream American society and Native American communities.[3] Another illustration of this dilemma is Tovi Fenster's sensitive account of planning new towns for Bedouins and housing for Ethiopian Jews in Israel. Fenster's post-occupancy research uncovered a deep distress amongst both the Muslim Bedouin women and the Ethiopian Jewish women as a result of the failure of the site plans and the housing design to deal with their culturally specific needs for spatial separation – the separation of women from certain men in the case of the Bedouin, and the separation of menstruating women in special huts away from their own family compound in the case of the Ethiopian Jews. The problem, as Fenster describes it, is far more complicated than that of a top-down planning process that failed to consult with those for whom the towns and housing were being planned. There is a double dilemma of control and power at work here: of the state over minorities, and of certain community members (men) over other community members (women) within the minority community itself.

Fenster's nuanced discussion of planning across the divide of incommensurable cultural values and practices raises a profound difficulty for planners working in cross-cultural situations. She herself is conflicted, as a feminist on the one hand, and as a planner committed to the acknowledgement of and respect for cultural difference on the other. Her way through this dilemma is two-fold; one step is to open up a dialogue within Bedouin and Ethiopian Jewish communities concerning the cultural construction of space and the associated lack of freedom of movement for women, and another is imagining more flexible design solutions which may be amenable to change over time, as inter-generational family values are likely to change. This is what she terms 'mapping the boundaries of social change' (Fenster, 1999a: 165).

RESPONSES TO DIFFERENCE

How can planners and the planning system respond to these multiple challenges? How is, and how might the right to difference be accommodated in our cities and neighbourhoods? As Wallace and Milroy have noted, neither the planning literature nor experiences in planning practice make it obvious how one *ought* to deal with difference in planning (Wallace and Milroy, 1999: 55). I suggest that there are five broad kinds of response. *First*, we might consider overhauling the planning system, either by revising legislation, or challenging it in the courts or appeal tribunals, testing whether it is consistent with, say, anti-discrimination legislation, or espoused multicultural policies. Wallace and Milroy drew this conclusion in their study of planning issues in Toronto and Southern Ontario, arguing that rather than the 'neutral' framework currently in place, difference needs to be taken as the point of departure. However, the (institutional and procedural) template for this kind of planning, as they note, has not yet been developed (Wallace and Milroy, 1999: 70). Furthermore, overhauling any legislation is a daunting task, and usually only occurs as a result of powerful lobbying which often takes at least a generation. (Think of feminist or civil rights reforms and how long and hard they were fought for.) This suggests that unless social movements are actively working on behalf of the rights of cultural minorities in and to the built environment, this kind of change is unlikely to come about in the short term. Nevertheless, the task of decolonizing planning will ultimately have to be addressed at this level.

A *second* type of broad response to the needs of different cultural groups is through market mechanisms, and here we can see a certain amount of progress in most cities. Most notably, stores open up to provide specialist goods and services (Halal and Kosher butchers, Asian and African markets for fruit and vegetables, Turkish video stores, Mexican bridal wear, Greek pastries, Chinese acupuncturists and herbalists). Shopping malls and whole precincts within a city spring to life providing, say, Vietnamese hairdressers, lawyers, tax accountants, shoe repairers, for predominantly Vietnamese (or Bengali or Korean . . .) enclaves of the city, whose members are unwilling as yet to venture beyond their own community for these common services.

Other kinds of small businesses emerge, for example in housing construction and renovation, to cater for culturally specific kinds of domestic spaces (Jewish builders who know how to do a kosher kitchen; Muslim builders who know about the orientation of bedroom and bathing spaces to Mecca, or about the gender-based spatial separations, or the spatial requirements for praying). The activities of 'immigrant place entrepreneurs' (Light, 2002) have been even more significant for the changing urban landscape of global cities. Ivan Light's research in Los Angeles and Kris Olds' in Vancouver demonstrate the significant roles of Korean and Chinese entrepreneurs in regional property development in Los Angeles, and of Chinese developers in Vancouver (Light, 2002; Olds, 2001). The immigrant land developers buy land cheaply, promote it in Chinese or Korean emigration basin areas, then sell it to co-ethnic immigrants at a profit. In the process these developers reduce the difficulties of immigration for their community, and are the primary forces in creating ethnic residential clustering (Light, 2002).

But what has this market response got to do with planning? In the case of small businesses, there will be requests for signage, or for a change in regulations concerning retail practices, to allow street vendors, or to allow street displays of wares. Planners and city governments can ease these neighbourhood transitions by facilitating such changes, or they can be obstructive (see Sandercock and Kliger, 1998a, for such a case). In the case of immigrant property developers, local planners and politicians may be involved in delicate negotiations about the use of and design guidelines for large sites, as well as mediating adjacent users' fears of the prospect of a large-scale immigrant presence. Planners' own values and attitudes matter in handling these potential and real conflicts. Mediation processes may be necessary when local conflicts arise. Sophistication about other cultures is increasingly necessary in handling such negotiations and mediations.

This market response, and planning accommodations to it, is all well and good for those who can afford to pay for such goods and services. But we only have to think of the appalling housing situations of certain cultural minorities (indigenous peoples almost everywhere), or of the poorest members of any immigrant group (Bengalis in London, Vietnamese in Melbourne, Sri Lankan Tamils in Toronto . . .), to recognize that the market does not, and never will, address all the needs arising from and problems relating to cultural diversity.

This was indeed the conclusion drawn from a recent cross-national comparative research project that investigated the socio-spatial exclusion of ethnic minorities in six European countries (Khakee, Somma and Thomas, 1999). The specifics of the research inquired into the impact of urban renewal or regeneration policies on immigrant communities, and concluded that whereas 'property-led renewal' has tended to displace ethnic minorities (by demolishing or upgrading inner city housing), state-led programmes have resulted in the ghetto-izing of immigrants in the worst housing in the worst neighbourhoods, and have failed to address associated issues of economic and political integration. The general pattern that emerges from these six national studies shows a strong concentration of immigrant minorities in the worst housing, in specific districts of large urban areas, either in inner-city high density housing or in peripheral districts. In all six countries (Sweden, Portugal, Italy, the Netherlands, France and Britain), discussions of immigration are framed by the conception of the 'immigrant as problem'. And, most disturbingly, each national case study notes the intensification of national and cultural forms of racism, an observation which has been reinforced by the political successes of anti-immigrant parties in Austria and Switzerland in 1999, the Netherlands and Denmark in 2002 (and in France much earlier), and the accompanying discourses, which both racialize and spatialize the immigration issue, portraying it as an invasion of national space by 'foreigners', those with different everyday practices, which manifest themselves most dramatically in the concrete spaces of streets, shops, schools, housing and neighbourhoods.

Thus far I have discussed two responses to the right to difference: through legislation and the courts, and through the market. There are three other (interdependent) possibilities, which will occupy the remainder of this chapter. One is the process-based response of establishing an intercultural dialogue that addresses fears and anxieties, as well as social needs and material conflicts. A second is the possibility of excluded groups mobilizing to fight for their rights to the city.[4] A third, (to be discussed in Chapters 8 and 9) is a profound reconsideration of the different qualities and skills that might be required if planners are to work in cross-cultural contexts. In the next section of this chapter I discuss several positive efforts by city governments and planners (in Frankfurt and Rotterdam, Sydney and Vancouver, and Oak Park, Chicago) to 'manage' difference with respect to integrating immigrants – efforts to think through the implications of multiculturalism not only symbolically, but street by street, neighbourhood by neighbourhood, neither ignoring the fears aroused by the presence of strangers, nor the fears experienced by the strangers themselves as they struggle to accommodate to a new environment and develop new attachments to a strange place.

WHEN STRANGERS BECOME NEIGHBOURS: INTEGRATING IMMIGRANTS

When immigrants with different histories, cultures, and needs arrive in global cities, their presence disrupts taken-for-granted categories of social life and urban space as they struggle to redefine the conditions for belonging in their new society. The need to construct communities seems to be a deep and universal feature of the human condition (Tully, 1995). In a world of globalizing cities, there are many ways of belonging to many kinds of community, which are not territorially defined or bounded (as I argued in Chapter 4). Nevertheless, place-identification and a sense of belonging to a place do not seem to have diminished in importance for most people. And that sense of belonging to a place is usually inseparable from the ties to the particular human community that inhabits the place.

Immigrants have a particularly strong need for community, for practical as well as emotional support, and past experience shows that they will almost always form their own communities over time, sometimes spatially concentrated (enclaves), sometimes spatially more dispersed. (This is particularly important for those refugees who come as single men or women, without possessions, with little knowledge of language, and no money.) A truly multicultural society not only encourages and supports community organizations *within* immigrant groups, but also works to incorporate immigrants into wider, cross-cultural activities and organizations. How is this second step achieved? How do societies establish civility, then conviviality, across difference? How do we (migrants and host society) generate an everyday capacity to live and work with, and alongside, those who are (perceived as) different?

The presence of migrants in the national imaginaries of some host countries, especially those countries that have not traditionally seen themselves as countries of immigration, is confined to a distant awareness of the migrant body as a source of cheap, and preferably temporary, labour. In these places there is, from the migrants' point of view, no social space that beckons them as a positive and permanent feature. They must endure a painful process of acquiring a new spatial and social sense of belonging, a new sense of home. From the hosts' point of view, there is an equally painful disruption of their own homely space, from the imaginary space of the nation to the very real spaces of neighbourhoods, the kinds of shops and churches, the smells coming from restaurants, the way people dress. All this can seem an affront to an established and comfortable way of life. Nostalgia for a disappearing community mixes with fear of and aversion towards the stranger, the outsider (see Chapter 5).

The stranger, on the other hand, the migrant, has left his/her home and taken up residence in someone else's 'home', where s/he encounters suspicion, disdain, indifference, even outright hostility. Migrants need to construct a new place that they, too, can call home, and there are several stages of home-building and place-making that migrants typically go through. Pascoe (1992) describes Italian migrants' place-making processes in Australia as involving three sets of strategies: naming, rituals, and institutions. Naming refers to giving homeland names to places in the new country. It also applies to business signs in homeland languages. Rituals refer to public events that affirm the belonging and cohesion of the group, such as the 'blessing of the fleet' that regularly takes place wherever Italians own fishing boats. Institutions include welfare associations, sporting and other clubs, churches, revolving credit associations, and so on, that both demonstrate the presence of a community and provide the services it needs.

A richer understanding of these strategies can provide some guidance in thinking about integration in Europe. To become a multicultural society requires more than a top-down policy declaration of multiculturalism from the Hague, Stockholm, or Berlin. I have emphasized thus far the importance of *feelings* (fears, anxieties, hopes, and so on) in the lived experience of migration, the feelings of the host society as well as the newcomers, because I want to stress that becoming a multicultural society/city is more than a matter of bureaucratic management,[5] or of citizenship legislation. *It also requires the active construction of new ways of living together, new forms of spatial and social belonging.*

It is a long-term process of building new communities, during which such fears and anxieties cannot be dismissed but need to be worked through.

This is easy to say, but difficult to do: difficult politically, while xenophobic feelings are on the rise in European and Australian cities; and difficult to implement, precisely because it means dealing with those feelings among the host society as well as with the more obvious material needs of immigrants, such as housing and jobs and schooling. I now turn to the experience of two European cities, each of which has tried to tackle fears as well as material needs, followed by the experiences within an Australian and a Canadian city in actually institutionalizing responses to these issues.

FRANKFURT

From 1989 to 1995 Frankfurt, under the Red-Green coalition city government, embarked on an ambitious social experiment to create a multicultural city in an anti-immigrant society, establishing AMKA, the Amt für Multikulturelle Angelegenheiten (the Municipal Department of Multicultural Affairs), in the Lord Mayor's office. AMKA's tasks were to work in collaboration with all the agencies of the state to promote the social integration of the city's 30 per cent foreign (non-German) population, and to work directly in the public sphere, to involve itself in a process of 'Zusammenwachsen' or 'growing together' of all ethnic groups into a peaceful multicultural society, respectful of difference (Friedmann and Lehrer, 1997). In AMKA's own estimation, the successful completion of this process could take as long as two or three generations, the result of a long period of mutual learning, mutual adjustment, and continuing (non-violent) conflict. Their political objectives included:

- reducing the German population's fear of 'the Other' and the number of violent acts against foreigners
- encouraging public discussion of migration and the limits of social tolerance
- working towards the active participation of newcomers in the public affairs of the city
- encouraging the cultural activities of each group of foreign residents
- offering in-service training for members of the municipal bureaucracy in intercultural communication
- forming a culture of everyday life in the context of immigration (Wolf-Almanasreh, 1993, quoted in Friedmann and Lehrer, 1997: 68–9).

AMKA worked towards these objectives on three main fronts: public hearings; the creation of a Municipal Advisory Council of Foreign residents; and strengthening the many voices of civil society among foreign residents. Over three years there were two hearings and a public forum. The first, *A Hearing on the Situation of Foreigners in Frankfurt*, took place in the Plenary Hall of the City Council, with all its symbolic resonance. 190 groups, organizations, and individuals were invited and almost all came, to hear and be heard. The message was that the new city government regarded them as an important part of the city and would work towards improving their circumstances. The second event, *A Hearing on the Situation of Migrant Women*, attracted 30 organizations and women from diverse cultures shared the fact of living in patriarchal regimes inside the relatively emancipated West German cultural environment to which they were exposed on a more or less daily basis. They raised numerous issues, including legal status, labour market participation, education, safe houses for young women wanting to leave the parental home, and sexual exploitation. The third hearing was conducted as a two-day forum on 'Living Together'. Lengthy preparations for this event included interviews with 50 Frankfurters on the subject of what Frankfurt thought and felt about its foreigners. The forum itself focused on *Suggestions and Demands for an Urban Policy Concerning Frankfurt's Population*, and 45 policy recommendations were produced, all of which reiterated AMKA's commitment to a philosophy of transformational dialogue (Friedmann and Lehrer, 1997: 70–71).

The second sphere of AMKA's work involved the creation of a Foreign Residents' Advisory Board, whose members were chosen by election, and had the right to attend city council meetings, and the opportunity to review and comment on the municipal budget proposal. The third sphere, strengthening civil society, involved a number of activities, including preparing a register of all organizations run by migrants, supporting multicultural events with financial and technical assistance, working with sports clubs, and providing allotment gardens for migrants.

The extraordinary ambition of AMKA and the Red-Green coalition of moving towards the practical utopia of a multicultural society came to an end in 1995 with the election of the Christian Democrats to City Council. It had been a very bold, innovative experiment on European soil, in a country in which the majority had shown little inclination to turn foreigners into Germans and to share citizens' rights with them. But experiments like these have a life beyond their own short span, as inspirational examples, which sometimes pave the way for broader changes. What was particularly significant about AMKA is worth summarizing:

- it dealt with multicultural citizenship at the *level of the city* and everyday life
- it was committed to a *long-term* perspective
- it promoted *mutual* learning
- it recognized and tried to address *fear of foreigners*, and the violence that often accompanies this fear
- it addressed the culture of the municipal bureaucracy (police, teachers, judges, planners)
- it saw its main role as educational, oriented to learning and communication

One political conclusion that might be drawn is that for a project of migrant integration at the level of the city, there needs to be multi-party support. Another might be that support from the national state is essential if conditions of becoming a citizen are to change. A third insight has to do with the micro-politics of integration. The public forums were incredibly important symbolic events, and may also have contributed to the empowerment or confidence-building of those migrant organizations and individuals who took part, but there is also micro-sociological work that needs to be done street by street, neighbourhood by neighbourhood, and across a range of institutions. This was the argument in Chapter 4, which stressed the importance of the daily negotiations of difference in the 'micro-publics' of the city.

ROTTERDAM

The importance of a micro-sociological approach to integration has been understood in Rotterdam and directed specifically at cultural institutions and practices. When Rotterdam was designated as Europe's City of Culture for 2001, the city decided on a number of programmes that would address the challenge of its increasing ethnic diversity (164 different nationalities form 45 per cent of the total population of 600,000). Under the umbrella of 'Erasmus 2001', and invoking the qualities of 'dialogue, tolerance, and forbearance that goes beyond indifference' for which Erasmus (1466–1536) himself was famous, the mission the city set for itself was 'to stimulate cohesion in a changing society', inspired from an arts and cultural perspective. The arts were posited as 'an improved way of dealing with the tensions that go with a society of differences'. The cultural programme included the establishment of a World Music faculty at the Rotterdam Conservatory; a reorganization of the public library to develop a culturally diverse programme offering; the multicultural Theater Zudplein (located in an ethnically diverse neighbourhood on the outskirts of the city), which attempts to connect with its culturally diverse environment; discovering and developing a municipal safety net for new multicultural artistic talent; expanding the range of cultural voices in the local broadcast media; and staging an exhibition with the theme of 'unpacking Europe', by inviting 20 non-European artists to present their interpretations of 'Europe'.

Social themes included building multicultural housing; asking the primary health care sector to examine its cultural sensitivity; exploring the possibility of a multicultural football club; investigating funeral customs across cultures; and researching the realities, as opposed to the myths, of safety and danger in ethnically mixed neighbourhoods.[6] Of course it is too soon to evaluate the effectiveness of these initiatives in Rotterdam, but they deserve attention because they were conceived in a new spirit of cultural exploration and sharing, in a spirit of welcoming the changes that are happening in the city as a result of immigration and building on them so as to nurture a comfortably hybrid city. For this reason, Rotterdam builds on Frankfurt as a lesson in the importance of openness, creativity, and risk – in the continuing experiment of *cosmopolis*.

SYDNEY

While European cities struggle to shift personal and institutional mindsets not used to thinking of themselves as countries of immigration, we might expect that New World cities such as those in Australia and Canada, nations necessarily founded on immigration, have come to grips with living with difference. In fact, this is far from true, for reasons discussed in previous chapters, and particularly related to their founding as racialized liberal democracies. Nevertheless, as officially multicultural societies, Australian and Canadian governments have been preoccupied with the challenge of accommodating (rather than assimilating) diversity for at least three decades. How far have they come? There is some very good research now available in Australia based on the first national survey of the responsiveness of local governments to cultural diversity.[7] I draw on this in the following brief summary of the efforts of one local municipality (Canterbury) in Sydney. But first some context.

Until the latter third of the twentieth century Australia had a restrictive immigration policy that was known colloquially as the White Australia Policy, meaning that if you weren't of European/Caucasian lineage you weren't likely to be allowed to settle. That policy unravelled in the late 1960s, and was replaced by an official endorsement of multiculturalism in 1973, with the publication of *A Multicultural Society for the Future* (Grassby, 1973). Over the next decade, national government documents advocated a model of cultural pluralism based on principles of social cohesion, cultural identity, equality of opportunity, and full participation in Australian society. Various federal government programmes and agencies over the past three decades have been devoted to overseeing the development and implementation of a national multicultural philosophy. For the most part, state and local governments have lagged behind the federal level in their enthusiasm for implementing this new society. Nevertheless, in the most populous state, New South Wales (NSW), legislation is in place to encourage local government to act responsively to its diverse citizenry. The *Charter of Principles for a Culturally Diverse Society* (Ethnic Affairs Commission NSW, 1993) has been incorporated into local government legislation and requires local councils to respond (across all departments and services) to cultural diversity. This was done in 1998 with an amendment to the Local Government Act requiring councils to develop a detailed social plan addressing issues related to indigenous communities and migrants from non-English-speaking backgrounds. Such institutional pressures have, in principle, compelled councils to confront the need for reform. In practice, as the research shows, a systematic response to the needs of diverse groups is a long way off. 'Some councils were surprisingly ignorant of the nature of their local diversity, and had failed to identify and abandon discriminatory and iniquitous practices in the provision of services and facilities' (Thompson, 2003).

Still, there are some remarkable cases where change has been institutionalized, one of which is in the municipality of Canterbury, 17 km south west of downtown Sydney, with a population of 132,360 and a growth in the non-English-speaking born population from 28 per cent in 1981 to 45 per cent in 1996. Canterbury has seen waves of migration since the 1950s, beginning with Greeks and Lebanese, and, more recently, people from China and the Pacific Islands. The Council's *Multicultural Social Plan* reflects its commitment to cultural diversity, embracing equity and access to quality services for all residents, and the promotion of harmonious and tolerant community relations (Thompson, 2003). The Plan defines the settlement needs of all of its diverse residents, after consultation with them, and then identifies actions that link multicultural considerations to all departments within the Council: engineering, corporate and community services, and environmental services. There are 'priority languages' of information and signage, cultural awareness training for staff, and a community worker for multicultural services. There is also a Multicultural Advisory Committee, whose membership is external to the Council, but whose activities are interwoven through all Council departments via their action statements. In these ways, the Council has begun to institutionalize its rhetorical commitments to serve its diverse community.

Under 'Environmental Services' the Council has embarked on several significant initiatives. The Town Centres Development Programme focuses on urban design guidelines and reviews the Council's public domain policies for open space, outdoor dining, festivals, temporary outdoor stalls, signage, and street furniture. The intention is that public spaces should be well used by all sections of the community, and the understanding is that this can only happen if they are well designed, with the community's input. There is also a recreation study that draws attention to the need for culturally sensitive recreation policies (from art works to cultural events to sports facilities to community gardens and landscaping), and a proposed Multicultural Oral History Project that would document the social history of migration into the area, acknowledging the contributions of migrant families to the economic and social life of the municipality.

Thompson (2003) concludes that this and other case studies from the national survey show that it is possible to develop innovative and well-funded projects 'that address cultural diversity as part of mainstream planning activity'. Of course, the fact that Canterbury is one of the most diverse districts in Australia has helped to prioritize this work. And the Council is mandated by state legislation to produce a multicultural social plan. Still, the Council has institutionalized staff positions and sought partnerships with state government to secure funding for projects, and they have used culturally appropriate consultative techniques. What this demonstrates, then, is the desirability of a multi-tiered governmental framework supporting cultural diversity, and of an internal, whole of Council, interdisciplinary approach. At this point, the multicultural project no longer relies on local leadership only, or on the vagaries of election cycles, which brought down the Frankfurt experiment.

VANCOUVER

Multiculturalism in Canada has served as a guideline for government policy since 1971, and also as a framework for national discourse on the construction of Canadian society (Mahtani, 2002: 68). Initially conceived as a way of accommodating the separatist impulse of Quebec's French-speaking population and Francophone culture, the policy has had to evolve to take on board, literally, the arrival of increasing numbers of immigrants from 'ethnically diverse' (non-Anglo, non-Caucasian) backgrounds. Canadian multiculturalism has encouraged individuals voluntarily to affiliate with the culture and tradition of their choice, and there has been significant spending, through multicultural grants, to support the maintenance of various cultures and languages and to encourage diverse cultural festivals in public places as well as the symbolic gesture of public art works that recognize and celebrate the multiple peoples who make up the nation. The intention has been to forge a workable national framework of 'unity within diversity', surely a remarkable change from conventional strategies of nation-building (Mahtani, 2002: 70).[8]

Still, there is a significant leap from multicultural rhetoric at the level of national politics and legal frameworks to what happens in the streets and neighbourhoods of

Canada's cities. As has been the case in Australia, provincial and local levels of government have been slower to respond to cultural diversity in terms of examining and changing their policies. Recent research in Vancouver (Edgington and Hutton, 2002) and Toronto (Wallace and Milroy, 1999; Milroy and Wallace, 2001) has shown that local policies in relation to the built environment have lagged behind the rapidly changing demographic realities. There are, however, exceptions, beacons of innovation, and it is to one of these that I now turn. The City of Vancouver (politically, a municipal government within the Greater Vancouver metropolitan region), with a population near 700,000, has developed a series of policy responses to its culturally diverse population, including staff hired within the City Planning Department as multicultural planners, and a multicultural outreach programme. One remarkable initiative supported by the City of Vancouver is the Collingwood Neighborhood House.[9]

Collingwood is a predominantly residential neighbourhood of significant ethnocultural diversity within the City of Vancouver, just east of downtown. It is home to 42,000 people, only 32 per cent of whom have English as their first language (compared to 51 per cent citywide). Over the past 20 years there has been rapid demographic change. In 1986, people of Chinese background comprised 21 per cent of the population and people of English background 51 per cent. By 1996 the area was 44 per cent Chinese, 10 per cent English, with Filipino and South Asian groups growing to 5 per cent and 8 per cent respectively. There are also Italians, Portugese, Vietnamese, First Nations, Scottish, Irish, and German residents, and the South Asian and Chinese communities can be broken down into distinct linguistic and other subcultural groups.

In the early 1980s, the provincial and municipal governments held consultations with local residents over the potential impacts of an elevated rapid transit line (and five stations) that was planned to cut through the neighbourhood. The process generated a new activism in the area and also highlighted intercultural tensions, as well as lack of local services. In 1985 a group of local volunteers established the Collingwood Neighborhood House (CNH) as a non-profit, non-government organization, initially to provide much needed family and childcare services. The funding agencies, the City of Vancouver and United Way, mandated a culturally diverse organization, and the founding members accordingly set out to diversify in terms of language and ethnicity.[10] As the organization developed, issues of access for other groups – in terms of age, ability, and socio-economic situation – were also addressed. The CNH was one of the first institutions in Vancouver to develop a multicultural policy, which is part of what makes its story significant. More important, though, are the details of how this was done, and the (local and national) circumstances that made it possible.

The CNH is now widely recognized for its innovative practice in diversification,[11] its ability to create and maintain 'a place for everyone' (Dang, 2002: 73). In 2002, the agency's programmes and services reached an estimated 25,000–35,000 residents (60–86 per cent of the neighbourhood's population). Among its successes, several different religious groups (Christian, Muslim, and various Chinese traditions) share the facility as a place of study and worship. Another is the establishment of its own community-leadership training institute that targets recruitment in under-represented and at-risk communities. A third is the success of outreach through the arts in its 'Building

Community though Cultural Expression' programme. Intercultural exchanges through children, food, and the arts seem to provide a less intimidating initiation into deeper, more long-term involvement in the community and in the organization (Dang, 2002: 84). An even more profound achievement, through the variety of outreach initiatives, has been an attitudinal shift. 'People are seeing each other as *assets*, not just clients or people in need' (Dang, 2002: 85). They are becoming contributors as well as recipients of services.[12]

On the surface, what CNH does is to develop and provide services according to perceived local needs. But there is more to it than that. First, the organization's real purpose (as reflected in its mission statement) is to *build community*, and its belief is that that cannot be achieved by providing culturally specific services. The very idea of a 'neighborhood house' implies a place with no subcultural affiliation, no shared interest other than *creating a community based on common residency*.[13] Thus the approach to programming is *intercultural*. Second, the services are not seen as merely services meeting a need. They are also seen as providing meeting places where people come together, and *connect through engaging in activities together*. Third, residents are engaged as researchers in the investigation of their own community, which further helps in establishing contacts and building relationships, as well as empowering locals to become involved in the decision-making and programming at the Neighborhood House.[14] The CNH also conducts regular anti-racism education programmes, and teaches through its consistent policies and actions that community is built through inclusion rather than through drawing boundaries. This is the daily negotiation of difference in the micro-publics of the city, in everyday activities, that was discussed in Chapter 4 as the most appropriate way to foster intercultural contact and exchange.

Dang (2002) conceptualizes the CNH achievement as a four-part organizational framework: achieving differentiated benefits; achieving inclusive participation; achieving varied discourse; and achieving inclusive definitions. Achieving differentiated benefits means building community through ensuring personalized flexibility within broad-based programmes; constantly monitoring the diverse needs of communities; and regularly evaluating programmes against these assessments. Achieving inclusive participation means conducting concerted outreach and building personal relationships in all communities to ensure diverse participation not only in programmes but also in decision-making processes. Achieving varied discourse means initiating and facilitating opportunities for dialogue that bring people together, enable them to talk through conflicts, and build community leadership capacity. Achieving inclusive definitions means creating a sense of ownership and belonging in the organization among all the neighbourhood's constituent communities, by making the organization accessible to and reflective of local diversity. Above all, these achievements have required patience, deliberate outreach (which involves personal cross-cultural communication skills), and a stable organization that residents get to know and come to trust over time (Dang, 2002: 95). Small decisions made each day by the Board, staff, volunteers, and user groups can matter a great deal to who is made to feel at home, who has access to community and identity. The art work on the walls, the language of a pamphlet,[15] the faces behind a desk, the height of a water fountain, can all signify inclusion – or exclusion. In all of these ways, and at all of these levels of detail, the CNH has succeeded in becoming an exemplary *intercultural organization.*

What circumstances brought this organization into being? The CNH was born in the mid-1980s amidst the emerging philosophies of diversity and multiculturalism at the national level. The City of Vancouver, under new left-of-centre leadership (the New Democratic Party) was engaged in redefining itself as both a global and a multicultural city in the lead-up to staging Expo in 1986. This City Council was eager to implement culturally sensitive policies. For example, the City of Vancouver created the Hastings Institute to provide leadership in diversity and improve race relations through anti-racist and diversity training programmes. As a new organization, the CNH was not burdened with inherited ways of thinking and doing. It defined itself, from the beginning, as a *learning* organization that would have to constantly reflect on its own programmes and ways of operating. It had strong internal advocates for diversity in its early development as an organization and strong leadership of its governing board. The founding President and the Executive Director had each received training in the practice of diversity through the Hastings Institute, and required that that be an ongoing practice of the organization. Care has always been taken in recruiting new staff, board members, and volunteers, who are expected to have cross-cultural experience and a demonstrated appreciation of the principles of diversification. Care has also been taken to ensure *ongoing* commitment by requiring that attention to diversity is integrated throughout the entire institution, from its strategic directives to its daily operations. Finally, the funding model is unusual. After initial dependence on the City Council and the United Way, the CNH successfully pursued a wide range of funding sources, so that if any one source is withdrawn, the operation does not collapse.

This intricate web of reasons for the success of the CNH cautions us against generalizing from it as a model to be imitated in other cities in other countries. Often, small local initiatives, especially ones that are sparked by strong and inspiring individual leadership, appear replicable if only comparably energetic and committed individuals can be found in different places, and some funding thrown at them. Clearly the situation here is far more complicated, involving philosophical, political, and/or financial support from two tiers of government, the engagement of a mobilized civil society, and the development of a complex funding model. Nevertheless, the story is instructive in what it takes to work towards living with diversity, beyond the model of 'indifference to difference', towards actually building an intercultural community. It is a living example of the principles discussed in Chapter 4, above all, emphasizing the daily and ongoing negotiation of difference through coming together on common projects and in everyday activities of survival and the reproduction of life.

*

I did not set out in this chapter to provide an exhaustive review of different approaches to integrating migrants and building intercultural communities. (That is beyond the scope of this book.) Rather, I have tried to concentrate on what is new and promising, what seems to be getting at the real issues. In this context it is worth mentioning, very briefly, the German federal government's efforts, under the Red-Green coalition elected in 1998, to tackle (rather than deny) migrant issues. This has operated on many fronts, including citizenship policy, and produced one impressive federal social policy initiative, which goes by the name of the 'Social City'. Money is available to cities to apply for neighbourhood regeneration projects. Many of the successful applications for the money are for projects in migrant neighbourhoods, where housing and other services are in need of additional support. When I visited one such project in the Kreuzberg district of Berlin in the Spring of 2002, what impressed me was the coordinated attempt to address migrant integration issues, from schooling to housing rehabilitation to the need for assistance in setting up small businesses. But what was disturbing, what the project has not been able to address, is the 'white flight' reaction of ethnic Germans, who are either leaving the neighbourhood, or removing their children from its schools. In this very tangible way, Berlin's problems are Germany's problems, and these are also Europe's present problems of integration. But before I go on to discuss these European issues from the perspective of citizenship debates, I want to ask what European cities might learn from the American city of Oak Park in terms of becoming 'diversity pioneers'.

OAK PARK, CHICAGO: CULTIVATING DIVERSITY

The goal of residential racial openness has rarely been pursued by cities or suburbs in the United States. But the residents of one municipality, Oak Park, in Chicago's western suburbs, initiated such a policy in the 1960s, despite surrounding local governments' policies of segregation. Racism, as a product of American history, reveals itself in many ways, from individual behaviour to institutional policies. One of its most insidious forms has been that of 'white flight', the departure of white residents from an area once Black families start to move in. What predisposes a city or suburb, or Village, as Oak Park refers to itself (as opposed to an individual household), to accommodation of difference rather than flight from it? While economists might argue that it is simply a rational choice related to property values, there is clearly something prior to this rational choice, and that is the *belief* that once Blacks (or Jews or foreigners . . .) move in, 'there goes the neighbor-hood' (Rotella, 1998). This takes us into the realms of prejudice, or pre-judgement, fears and anxieties, identity and security. It was, after all, the famous Chicago sociologist Robert Park who wrote, in the 1930s, that we hate because we fear (Park, 1967).

Oak Park has been solidly middle class for more than a century, but it borders blue collar communities to the south and east. By the late 1960s, it was clear to Oak Park residents that their Village was right in the trajectory on an outward-moving Black urban expansion. Oak Park residents collectively chose to fight exclusion by encouraging inclusion, rather than joining the forces of white flight. They chose to 'regard integration as a positive experience, defining the challenge as one of management rather than resistance' (Martin and Warner, 2000: 272). In 1972 the minority population was an almost invisible 1 per cent. By 2002, there was a 23 per cent black population. How did this positive transition occur?

According to the study by Martin and Warner, it was the creation of the Oak Park

Housing Center (OPHC) that was the critical instrument in the effort to manage change. Focusing primarily on the rental market (45 per cent of the housing stock), the OPHC set out to attract new residents who wanted to live in a diverse community; to counsel prospective residents; to maintain files on the availability of housing and on the lending institutions and realtors active in the residential market; to run community education programmes for residents; and to aid in legal referrals. The OPHC worked in a very detailed and people-oriented way, anticipating and managing fears as best it could, apartment complex by apartment complex, and block by block. This included escorting potential renters to apartment blocks, introducing them to residents, and speaking honestly about community responses to racial minorities.

The municipality's elected leadership supported the OPHC by adopting proactive integration policies.[16] Oak Park banks and mortgage lenders formed the Financial Institutions Special Committee for Area Leadership (FISCAL), which made mortgage information public, and the Oak Park Citizens Action Program initiated an anti-redlining campaign (Breems, 2002: 19). In 1978 the Village established an 'equity assurance' programme to assuage the fears of white home owners that their property values would decline in the face of rising diversity. (No claims have ever been made against this fund.) In 1984 a Diversity Assurance Program was started. It provides low-interest loans and matching grants to multi-family apartment building owners, and in return the owners agree to list their vacancies with OPHC. OPHC then 'places' people of varying races in apartments in a way that ensures that no building or block becomes racially segregated. If a 'suitable' renter is not found, the Program allows the OPHC to pay the apartment owner 80 per cent of their rent (between one and four months) until the apartment is rented (Breems, 2002: 19). A new Village hall was built in the neighbourhood that was quickest to diversify, as a symbolic statement of commitment to the entire population. In addition to financial programmes, the Village sponsors or supports programmes like 'Come to My House', in which people of all races and ethnicities meet in each other's homes to discuss racial issues of common concern.

This is very much a story of activism by and through the local state (city council). It was this city council that put in place a range of remarkable integration policies and that supported the OPHC, a non-profit civic institution, in its everyday commitment to making this suburb a 'diversity pioneer'. What is remarkable is that, over time, a 'culture of integration' evolved that pervaded local institutions and local life, from realtors to teachers to local lending institutions. Civil society was mobilized to support a collective goal of integration, which is all the more remarkable given the policies and attitudes of adjacent municipalities. In Oak Park, residents exercised a difficult democratic choice by being able to imagine an alternative to the usual story – the story of 'there goes the neighborhood'. They created community-based organizations and social institutions that contributed to the monitoring and maintenance of diversity. But they also recognized the need for a broader metropolitan attack on the challenge of integration, and began to promote a pro-integration programme (known as 'New Directions') in 50 surrounding suburbs, through a regional outreach office that does much the same work as that pioneered by the OPHC. The Chicago metropolitan area now has a Leadership Council for Metropolitan Open Communities, an advocacy group that searches out

discrimination and brings legal challenges when barriers to open housing are found. Still, Martin and Warner's study concludes that Oak Park needs more supportive state and federal policies to help the community succeed (Martin and Warner, 2000: 272–8).

The lessons of Oak Park in terms of striving for and establishing stable diverse communities include: strong local leadership; an active civic sector; institutions (such as schools and banks) whose primary goal is to promote stable diversity; the importance of a breadth of community-based organizations committed to this goal; enforcement of fair housing laws; strict control of the quality of housing stock; and a religious community actively promoting diversity (Nyden *et al.*, 1996, quoted in Breems, 2002: 22). Oak Park today tells us that, even in a racist society, strangers can become neighbours, but only through a block by block, street by street effort in which multiple institutions of civil society are mobilized, building on a collective faith that a new way of living is possible.

CITIZENSHIP: MULTICULTURAL AND URBAN

In a European Union of 350 million people, foreign (that is, non-EU) minorities are becoming an increasingly significant part of the urban landscape. The question of their acceptance, and citizenship rights, has suddenly become central to European politics and is crucial to the ongoing social stability of the region. What policy research has made clear in recent years (Sassen, 2000; Papademetriou, 2002) is the economic and demographic necessity of migrants, in part to do the dirty, dangerous and undesirable work that locals no longer want to do, or where there are not enough workers to fill such jobs; in part to provide high-end technological skills; and in part to ensure longer-term growth in the labour force, in order for taxes to support a rapidly aging population. As Papademetriou explains:

The demographic facts are clear. Because the baby-boom generation has failed to reproduce itself adequately throughout the advanced industrial world, its passage from the economic scene will create working age population voids. At the same time, a retirement age bulge will be created unlike anything we have witnessed in modern times – with the added 'wrinkle' of the aged now living much longer than ever before. This means that much higher old-age dependency ratios will follow, whereby the taxes of fewer and fewer workers will have to support ever-larger numbers of retirees. These facts suggest that over the next two decades, immigrants will likely be relied upon more and more heavily for many important social and economic purposes. Among them are tending to the needs of relatively affluent first-worlders through their labor, helping to keep retirement and public health systems afloat through their taxes, and, in many cases, keeping production and consumption systems humming.

(Papademetriou, 2002: 29–30)

Thus has postcolonial history come full circle, as the world's poor (many of them former 'colonial subjects') travel to the erstwhile metropolitan nations of empire to settle 'a new frontier' (Sassen, 2000: 156) in the midst of the West's prosperous societies, in the middle of 'White Nations' (Hage, 1998) that have yet to come to terms with their own colonial and neo-colonial pasts. For European nations to reconstitute themselves as multicultural societies is a profound reorientation which surely will take more than one generation. My optimism about the possibility of *cosmopolis* rests on the creative working through of new identities and the forming of new hybrid cultures by second generation immigrants. What I have emphasized thus far is the significance of *cities* in this process, and therefore of city governments, city planners, and city dwellers. I have also argued that it is as important to address the psychological challenges of integration (fear of, aversion towards, foreigners), as it is to address the material and communicative challenges. What remains is to discuss the importance and changing meanings of citizenship in multi-cultural societies.

The story of AMKA brings to the foreground the importance of debates about the meaning of citizenship as part of an *urban policy response* to the increasing presence of foreign migrants in global cities. In many parts of the world now, and not just in Germany, those loosely defined as 'guest workers' have become a permanent presence, yet survive as blatantly ambiguous groups, excluded by definition from the places where they live, and yet no longer at home in their 'homelands'. The problem of outsiders dwelling in a territory from which they are conceptually excluded as citizens, and often actively oppressed and subject to violent attacks from local citizens, has led to the 'return of the citizen' (Kymlicka and Norman, 1994) to the centre of political debate, both in the daily columns of newspapers and in the research papers of immigration scholars and political philosophers (Turner, 1993; Holston, 1998; Karst, 1986; Fried-mann, 2002).

Prominent immigration scholars Stephen Castles and Mark Miller (1998: 252) have argued that 'multicultural citizenship appears to be the most viable solution to the problem of defining membership of a nation-state in an increasingly mobile world'. Their multicultural model is a combination of a set of social policies to respond to the needs of new settlers – language policies and culturally sensitive social services provision – and a statement about the openness of the nation to cultural diversity. They contrast this multicultural model, which exists in Australia, Canada, Sweden and, to a lesser extent, the United States, with two other models predominant in Europe today, the 'differential exclusionary model' and the 'assimilationist model'. The former exists in countries in which the dominant definition of the nation is that of a community of birth and descent, and members of the dominant group are reluctant to accept immigrants and their children as members of the nation (examples are Germany, Austria, Switzerland). This unwillingness is expressed in the ideology of not being countries of immigration. Differential exclusion means that immigrants are accepted into certain areas of society, most notably the labour market, but not others, such as welfare systems, and political participation. The assimilationist model describes those countries that 'incorporate migrants through a one-sided pro-cess of adaptation: immigrants are expected to give up their distinctive linguistic, cultural, or social characteristics and become indistinguishable from the majority population' (Castles and Miller, 1998: 245). The price of citizenship is cultural assimi-lation. France is the best example of this model. Britain and the Netherlands have aspects of it, along with aspects of the multicultural model. While most liberal Euro-peans today would embrace this assimilationist model, seeing it as both a realistic acceptance of the necessity of immigration along with a reasonable (to them) tolerance of strangers (as permanent guests in 'their' nation), there is a long-term instability in such a position, since it is based on the absurdity of believing that immigrants who become, say, French citizens, lose their distinctive ethnic or cultural characteristics (including skin colour) by virtue of this fact. Since that clearly does not happen, the reality for immigrants in this situation is the lived experience of second-class citizenship.

Although I agree with Castles and Miller that the 'multicultural model' is the only model that is sustainable over the longer term, both from the perspective of social stability and from the perspective of the right to difference, I think there is more that needs to be said on the subject of citizenship. Their work, like most of the debates on citizenship, takes for granted that this is a right conferred by and related to the nation-state. What I am arguing, however, is that the lived complexities of migrant integration occur in the city, and usually in the largest or most economically dynamic cities of any nation (sometimes referred to as 'global cities'). Given this reality, some scholars as well as political activists have begun to talk of a new notion of urban or local citizenship (Siemiatycki and Isin, 1997; Isin, 1999), understood as the practices through which individuals and groups formulate and claim new rights or struggle to expand or maintain existing rights to the city, on the basis of their difference. This involves a more substantive notion of citizenship that goes beyond the formal, legal notion of *becoming a citizen* and extends to the lived, everyday, sociological experience of *being a citizen*. This in turn involves attempts by immigrant groups to establish collective cultural expressions of their identity in the form of places of worship, commercial environments, recreational facilities, community centres, as well as claims on and the use of public space in everyday life, the ability to transform the built environment in ways that reflect cultural diversity, and a subjective sense of belonging.

What is being spelt out here is a *normative ideal of urban citizenship*, but one that has political implications and urban policy consequences. The political implications include the encouragement of the political participation of migrants and the openness of the society to being redefined in the process, to new notions of an emerging common identity. This involves nothing less than expanding the spaces of democracy through participation at the local level, and a model of agonistic democracy (Chapter 4) in which there is no closure to the multicultural urban and political project; that is, no permanent state of integration and harmony towards which we are moving, *but an always contested engagement with and continually redefined notion of the common good and shared destiny of the citizens of the city.* Another crucial aspect of this normative ideal is the ethnographic reality of intercultural co-existence, the willingness of host society and immigrant groups and individuals to work together across cultural divides without the fear of losing their own identity. Thinking about Birmingham, for example, this means nothing less than a city-wide debate about what it means to be a Brummie today and in the future, and the working together across cultures to create the spaces for new 'mongrel' identities. One of the roles of urban policy and of urban planners is to create the physical and discursive spaces for such debates and renegotiations of collective identity.

CONCLUSIONS

In this chapter I have not attempted to be exhaustive about the range of existing or possible policy responses addressing the integration of migrants. I've asked how migrants might be integrated into cities that are not used to thinking of themselves as multicultural, and in answering that, I've looked to some recent experiments in Europe, as well as to several success stories from Australia and Canada which, as more traditional countries of immigration, have a longer experience with these issues. I also looked to the more intractable problem of integrating African Americans in the USA as another account of what it takes for a city to become a 'diversity pioneer'.

My discussion has provided at least seven policy directions. The *first* requirement is for commitment by political parties at the local level (city and neighbourhood) in developing integration initiatives as a central part of their mission. This can only be done cooperatively, involving a breadth of organizations in civil society. A *second* requirement is for multi-tiered political and policy support systems, from national through to provincial, city and local levels. The *third* requirement for addressing integration at the level of everyday life is to tackle the culture and practices of municipal workers such as the police, teachers, judges, planners, and service providers. Most bureaucracies need to undergo sensitivity training on gender issues in order to transform historic patterns of discrimination and domination. Now it is urgent that they address cultural difference and cultivate the qualities necessary to overcome discrimination and marginalization. A *fourth* requirement is reform and innovation in the realm of social policy, from the most obvious – language assistance – to the creation of new institutions such as Neighbourhood Houses, support for immigrant organizations, official recognition of immigrant rituals and naming rights, and provision of culturally sensitive social services, including culturally appropriate food and recognition rituals at official functions.

A *fifth* requirement is a better understanding of how urban policies can and should address cultural difference. This includes issues of design, location, and process. For example, if different cultures use public and recreational space differently, then new kinds of public spaces may have to be designed, or old ones re-designed, to accommodate this difference. Space also needs to be made available for the different worshipping practices of immigrant cultures: the building of mosques and temples, for example, has become a source of conflict in many cities. And when cultural conflicts arise over different uses of land and buildings, of private as well as public spaces, planners need to find more communicative, less adversarial ways of resolving these conflicts, through participatory mechanisms which give a voice to all those with a stake in the outcome. This in turn requires new skills for planners and architects in cross-cultural communication, a topic I address (amongst other things) in the next two chapters.

A *sixth* requirement is the elaboration of new notions of citizenship – multicultural and urban – that are more responsive to newcomers' claims of rights to the city and more encouraging of their political participation at the local level. This involves nothing less than openness on the part of host societies to being redefined in the process of migrant integration, and to new notions of a common identity emerging through an always contested notion of the common good and shared destiny of all residents. The *seventh* is an understanding of and preparedness to work with the emotions that drive these conflicts over integration: emotions of fear, and attachment to history and memory, as well as the status quo, on the part of host societies; and the (possibly ambivalent) desire for belonging, and fear of exclusion on the part of migrants. Not to acknowledge and deal with these emotions is a recipe for failure in the longer-term project of intercultural co-existence.

If mongrel cities are to be socially sustainable, their citizens, city governments, and city-building professions need to work collaboratively on all of these fronts.

PART III

TOWARDS A NEW PLANNING IMAGINATION

7

TRANSFORMATIVE PLANNING PRACTICES

How and why cities change

Cities change in unpredictable ways. Efforts to steer them in one direction or another, by property developers, business owners, residents, politicians, social movements, and the city-building professions themselves, inevitably meet with resistance and become a struggle. We might call this the struggle to define and shape the good city. That struggle takes place in city council chambers and newspapers; in banks and boardrooms; in bars and cafés; on the street and in schools. It is a struggle to shape and protect and improve places, to expand or contract accepted notions of belonging, to advance new or defend old notions of environmental care. All of these are issues that affect everyday life in manifold ways, and therefore evoke powerful emotions, like greed, fear, anxiety, anger, despair, hope, attachment, love. Consequently everyone has a stake in the city and how it is changing, and many people have theories about who has the power to do what, and just who are the real movers and shakers.

This book is concerned with the contribution of the city-building professions to the transformation of cities, but it recognizes that these professions do not act alone, and that they are most effective when they act in a transparently political way, in association with residents, politicians, and mobilized communities, negotiating an (always temporary) consensus about the best ways of living together. This chapter explores the possibilities and realities of transformative planning practices, asking what kinds of knowledges and know-how make transformation possible.

I have chosen three stories around which to build an analysis of transformative planning for the mongrel cities of the 21st century. The first concerns a recent land-use struggle between indigenous Australians and their white neighbours in an inner Sydney suburb. The second tells of a community mobilization in partnership with a university research effort in East St Louis, USA, that was successful in reversing structural and political processes of abandonment. The third, very much a work in progress, is the current attempt of the City of Birmingham to reinvent itself as *cosmopolis*, a city in which dynamic new sources of growth might be enjoyed across culturally diverse neighbourhoods in a more inclusionary approach to urban regeneration.

In telling these stories, my approach is not that of the comparative case study. There is very little that is comparable, structurally speaking, about these three situations. Rather I have searched for new approaches, for breakthroughs in dealing with long-standing problems of inequality and exclusion. And I have chosen examples that operate at different urban scales and with different time frames. Each story brings something different to my larger purpose: that of understanding why and how cities change, and who are the key change agents. Above all, I seek to eschew simple answers, or unified theory. Some believe that capital produces urban space and that (increasingly global) markets shape urban destinies. Others have faith that social movements are a counterforce. Some see expert knowledge and rational analysis as crucial. Still others see bureaucrats acting through state agencies as enforcers of societal norms and agents of control over who does what in cities, according to some larger forces that are able to impose class, patriarchal, cultural and other forms of power. The city-building professions jostle each other for pride of place as creators of cities, while inwardly agonizing that 'they' (whether landscape/architects, planners, engineers, urban designers) are really only cogs in some machine that others are in control of. The planning enterprise, to the extent that it has been normatively concerned with questions of social and environmental justice in relation to urban change, has been particularly self-critical of its role.

Planning theorists have argued that planning activity serves primarily to assist market forces or, alternatively, that planning is in the vanguard of social change, and every position in between. Urban researchers either start with a preferred theory and set out to prove it through a carefully selected case study, or they start with a case study from which they hope to build a general theory of planning and urban change. Both approaches are fatally flawed. The former approach is plainly biased from the outset. The latter, the attempt to see the whole world through one grain of sand – to build theory from one local government case study, or one policy sector involved in one project, or even a study of a national planning system – writes off what is arguably a crucial determinant of any change, namely contextual specificity. Compiling case studies and generalizing from them (to produce 'best practices', for example) does not overcome this problem, as the more we attempt generalizations, the further we remove ourselves from the specific historical, cultural, institutional, political and economic circumstances that shape place. Similarly, the question that has preoccupied a number of planning theorists, 'Is planning activity system-maintaining or system-transforming?' is a useless question when posed in that general way. It is quite conceivable that actions intended as catalysts of transformation, of urban regeneration, may have positive effects in some cities and negative effects in others, because of the different mixture of local ingredients.

In the process of understanding how planning activity might become, and when it actually is, transformative, then, I start from an openly normative position: I seek examples of planning working for greater social and environmental justice, and supporting culturally pluralist ways of living together. That is my definition of transformative (and I acknowledge that it will always be contested). But my goal is not a general theory of 'radical' planning or of urban change. It is a better understanding of the range of factors and players that are important: from leadership to discourse to ideas to institutions to governance practices to social mobilizations, to name just a few. As practitioners move from neighbourhood to metropolitan to regional arenas, and experience a range of cultural, political, institutional and economic circumstances (these things can change significantly in any one city, in even a single decade), they need not so much a general theory of transformative planning, as *a feel for the game*,[1] a repertoire of stories and experiences from which they have learnt and which enable them to become what Bourdieu (1977: 8) calls 'virtuoso social actors', in contexts rarely of their choosing and never entirely under their control.

The intention of the following three stories is to contribute in small part to that feel for the game. Hence my choice of examples. The first concerns a lone consultant, called in by a city council to 'put out a fire'. It was a site-specific conflict, and a relatively short-term gig for the consultant, but the effects of her intervention nevertheless may prove to be quite profound. The second concerns a ten-year involvement by university researchers with a marginalized community, during which relationships are developed, new processes become institutionalized, and habits of thought are changed. This is a bottom-up, community-based story of transformative planning. The third example is of a city, like an ocean-liner, trying to change its course. The captain is the City Council, but part of the change of direction is an effort to involve everyone on board, every section of the community.

Each story offers a different 'planning paradigm': the first I will call 'therapeutic planning', an extension of the communicative planning approach; the second, 'empowerment planning', inherits a more radical tradition of social mobilization. The third story is not so easily categorized, partly because we don't know the 'ending' yet, but it contains mixtures of institutional, social movement, and leadership components. Perhaps the labels are only important to theorists, staking out their turf. I am not seeking to engage in theoretical 'truth wars' here. I am more interested in what works, when, how and why, and I do not expect any one theoretical camp to have all the answers to these questions.

I am particularly interested in the capacity of the actors in each case to imagine themselves in a different story, to imagine alternatives to apparently insoluble conflicts or situations that appeared to be without hope. I ask what forms of planning, supported by what forms of urban governance, social movements, and modes of citizenship, are best able to accommodate difference and reverse exclusion and marginality. And I am mindful of the context of planning in the USA, UK, and Australia: as already racialized liberal democracies in which planning, as a state-directed activity, has always been implicated in a cultural (as well as class) politics, and almost always on the side of the dominant culture and class.

REDFERN, SYDNEY, AUSTRALIA: FROM FEAR TO HOPE[2]

You can't take people where you haven't been yourself ... we need, as individuals and as communities, to be about getting people to deal with the fears which immobilize us and bar us from our basic instincts towards growth, change, and harmony.

(King, 1981: 232)

What follows is an account of a recent cross-cultural conflict over land-use in inner Sydney, Australia, and its resolution through a *therapeutic process* in which a space is created for speaking the unspeakable, for talk of fear and loathing, as well as of hope and transformation. 'Therapeutic' needs a brief explanation, since its only previous use in the planning field was over 30 years ago, by Sherry Arnstein (1969) in her famous 'ladder of citizen participation'. Therapy featured in the bottom rungs of her ladder, which ascended from disempowering techniques of participation to more empowering ones. Arnstein was describing processes that made people feel good, by consulting them and appearing to listen to their concerns, and yet did not take their views seriously let alone give them any autonomy to act on their own behalf. For her, therapy was akin to manipulation. This is not the way in which I am using the term. For me, it denotes an essential quality of community organization and social planning. As Lee (1986: 21) has argued, 'people who are organized and who become effective in rendering their environment relatively more malleable will begin to perceive them-selves differently, as subjects not objects, as people who develop a vision of a better world and who can act coherently to achieve it'. The social planning endeavour can be seen as the process of bringing people together not only to share their experiences and work in solidarity, but also to work through their differences (some of which, in cities of increasing diversity, may be quite profound) in transformative ways. I am also using 'therapy' in its psychological sense, as part of an acknowledgement that many plan-ning disputes are about relationships, and therefore emotions, rather than conflicts over resources. That is certainly the case in the story that follows. I use the term 'transformative' to describe those actions which contribute to a more socially and environmentally just city, and one which is tolerant of difference, open and culturally pluralist.

The story concerns the future of a factory site immediately adjacent to the residen-tial area known as The Block in the inner Sydney neighbourhood of Redfern. The Block had been a 1970s federal government initiative that had granted urban Abo-riginal land rights. This area has received a lot of media and political attention in recent years as housing owned by the Aboriginal Housing Corporation deteriorated, and the area became a centre of drug dealing and drug taking. Local opinion has been dramatically divided regarding the Aboriginal presence. Some non-indigenous locals hoped that the state government would 'clean up' the area before the Olympic Games in 2000 (they didn't), while other non-indigenous residents remain firmly committed to a multi-racial neighbourhood, as a symbol of a wider reconciliation process in the nation.

In the 1980s the local (South Sydney) council had rezoned the factory site for com-munity use, which meant that when the factory closed down a decade later, the Council had to acquire the site. It then tried to rush through an approval to demolish the buildings on the site, in sympathy with the conservative white residents' faction who wanted the site to become a park with a prominent police station at its centre. This group expressed strong disapproval of any use of the site for Aboriginal purposes. A second group, the Redfern Aboriginal Corporation, wanted the buildings and site used for Aboriginal economic and community purposes, including a training facility. And a third group, white residents calling themselves Redfern Residents for Reconciliation (RRR), supported the Aboriginal group and the larger issue of ongoing Aboriginal presence in the area.

After being embarrassed by resident protests, the Council backtracked and hired a social planning consultant, Dr Wendy Sarkissian, to conduct a consultation process that would result in recommendations for a Master Plan for the 2200 square meter site.[3] The consultant's initial scoping of the situation suggested to her that there was such hostility between the three identifiable groups of residents that any attempt at a general meeting to start the process would either meet with boycott from one or more groups, or end up in violence. Her strategy therefore was to organize a series of meetings. For the first few months, separate meetings were held with each of the three 'camps'. These included small meetings in people's living rooms, larger meetings in more public settings, meetings with children, and meetings with members of the Aboriginal community using a Black architect as mediator. Eventually, after three months of dialogic preparation, a 'speak-out' was organized in which each group agreed to participate. This latter was the most risky part of the whole process in that it was the most likely to get out of hand. The point of participation in this event was for people to say what they felt, to speak their feelings, no matter how toxic, or painful, it might be for others to hear. The hope, implicit in such an event, is that as well as speaking the unspeakable – that is performing a sort of cathartic function for all those carrying anger or fear or betrayal inside themselves – the words will also be heard, in their full emotion, by those whose ears and hearts have previously been closed.

At the time that the speak-out was held, three months into the process, there had deliberately been no discussion (and certainly no drawings) of alternative uses of the site. The consultant's intention was to encourage the 'real issues' at stake to be aired, prior to any site-specific discussions. The 'real issues' ranged from sheer resentment on the part of conservative whites at the Aboriginal presence in 'their' neighbourhood, to concerns with personal safety and children's well-being related to the presence of drug-dealing and drug-taking. On the part of indigenous people, there was anger and sadness at 200 years of domination by 'white fellas' who even now had little understanding of their history and culture. At one point in the speak-out, the consultant herself was verbally attacked by a tearful Aboriginal woman storyteller, who demanded to know how the consultant thought she could shift 200 years of racist history in a few months, with a few meetings. There is no satisfactory answer to such a profound question, only the honest answer in this case, which was the attempt to create the space, in one place, at one point in time, where perceptions might shift, where public learning might occur, and some larger transformation take place.

And such a shift did in fact take place. Interestingly, before the speak-out, the consultant had been criticized by those white residents sympathetic to the indigenous desires for the site, for her overly 'therapeutic' approach, for too much talk about feelings. But clearly what had been happening during this initial period of meetings and listening was *the creation of a safe space in which parties could meet and speak without fear of being dismissed, attacked, or humiliated*. The speak-out would not have been possible without this preparatory work, which simultaneously involved the building of trust in the consultant and her team. The speak-out itself also had to be designed as a safe space, and this was achieved in part by formalizing and ceremonializing the activities.[4]

It was only after the speak-out (and the painstaking communicative preparation for it) that Sarkissian was able to move the process on, to enable joint group discussions and negotiations, to forge a set of principles for deciding the future use/s of the site, and finally to a set of meetings to draw up guidelines to present to the Council. One of the operating principles guiding the consultant was the determination not to force closure before there was the possibility of a genuine agreement rather than a mere 'deal', an unsatisfactory compromise. That agreement finally came, not without pain, after nine months of talk, and a budget of about $50,000. The outcome, ten guidelines for a Masterplan, was a breakthrough of sorts, in that the conservative white residents backed off from their opposition to *any* Aboriginal use of the site and agreed to some training facilities. This neighbourhood story of the micro-sociology of a land-use dispute may seem like small potatoes in the grand scheme of things, but its outcome actually signifies a remarkable shift in the willingness of one group of residents to co-exist with another. In that sense it was transformative, in unraveling previous notions of the unthinkable.

COMMENTARY: THERAPEUTIC PLANNING

There's a lot missing from this story as I've told it. I haven't filled in the institutional details of the local council planning process or explained the local political culture. I chose to focus on the transformative role of one practitioner because that seems to be the critical ingredient, *in this story*, in bringing about change. But before I go deeper into her work here (which I will argue is not unique), it is salutary to note that what made it possible for Sarkissian to be called in was the social mobilization by progressive sections of the local community. They had a different view of what their neighbourhood could be, and they chose to challenge the local council. That council, in turn, was more responsive than one might normally expect in Australian local government, perhaps because any conflict involving indigenous peoples was likely to draw national attention.

This kind of planning work, involving dialogue and negotiation across the gulf of cultural difference, requires its practitioners to be fluent in a range of ways of knowing and communicating: from storytelling to listening to interpreting visual and body language. It would seem to be a model that is very relevant to the new complexities of nation-building and community development in multicultural societies. It is an excellent model in situations where direct, fact-to-face meetings are unthinkable or unmanageable due to prior histories of conflict and/or marginalization. In such cases, the use of narrative, of people telling their own stories about how they perceive the situation, becomes a potential consensus-building tool for unearthing issues unapproachable in a solely rational manner.

For most complex and highly charged public policy issues, sound expert analysis plays an important role in shaping the possibilities for agreement. So, too, do well-planned, well-executed, face-to-face negotiations. But when the parties involved have been at odds for generations, or come from disparate cultural traditions, or where there is a history of marginalization, something more than the usual tool-kit of negotiation and mediation is needed, some 'method' which complements but also transcends the highly rational processes typical of the communicative action model developed in the 1990s.[5] In the case just discussed, that 'something more' was the speak-out, which provided an occasion for dealing with history in highly personal, narrative, and emotional ways. There are other possible methods, using drama, for example, or music, or other more symbolic or non-verbal means of story telling and communicating deeply felt emotions. Indigenous people are often, with good reason, preoccupied with the unacknowledged and therefore unfinished business of the past. It is particularly important for them to be able to tell their stories. But all parties involved in planning disputes have a story, and there is growing recognition of the importance of the telling and hearing of stories in the process of conflict resolution. Narratives about the past can be vital in navigating long-standing, cross-cultural disputes.

A more democratic and culturally inclusive planning not only draws on many different ways of knowing and acting, but also has to develop a sensibility able to discern which ways are most useful in which circumstances. What has been missing from most of the collaborative planning/communicative action literature is this recognition of *the need for a language and a process of emotional involvement*, of embodiment. This means not only allowing the 'whole person' to be present in negotiations and deliberations, but being prepared to acknowledge and deal with the powerful emotions that underpin many planning issues. By working patiently, attentively, and non-judgementally in the early stages of her handling of the Redfern conflict, Sarkissian was able to deal with the fears that were at the heart of the matter. Why has this crucial dimension of planning conflict so often been ignored in favour of 'rational discourse'?

It is tempting to answer this question by charging that the planning profession works, collectively, in a state of arrested emotional development, bracketing the realm of the emotions as being unmanageable, ungovernable, downright dangerous. To a profession that defines itself as concerned with rational decision-making over land-use and resource management conflicts, it is not surprising that the realm of the emotions has been perceived as troublesome territory. The origins of planning in the engineering sciences, and later in administrative and management sciences (see Friedmann, 1987), is another important factor in understanding this avoidance of the emotional domain. How can you make a rational decision if you allow the emotions to become part of the conversation?

There are two problems with this historic dividing line between reason and the emotions. One is that it poses reason and emotion as mutually exclusive, as binary opposites. There is now a significant and respected literature that makes a persuasive case for 'the intelligence of the emotions' (Nussbaum, 2001) and the foolishness of trying to bracket them out of 'serious' deliberations.[6] The other problem is that this historic dividing line precludes the possibility of understanding the nature of much conflict in the city, conflict that is generated by fears and hopes, anxieties and desires, memory and loss, anger about and fear of change. How can planners hope to resolve these conflicts unless they are prepared to get to the emotional heart of the matter?

Fortunately, there are signs of change: in the practice of people like Wendy Sarkissian, and in the writings of Howell Baum and John Forester. Baum has argued that when emotional language and behaviour is disallowed or discouraged by planners insisting that participants be rational, or that discussions follow a logical order, they will elicit only superficial participation. 'Told to be rational, people assume they have been told not to be themselves. They may feel relieved. Planning will not require them to reveal or risk what matters' (Baum, 1999: 12). Baum also suggests that it is important for planners working in emotionally charged situations not to try to suppress conflict, for to do so is to sabotage the work of grieving and healing which needs to be done as part of a process of change. Helping people to discuss their fears, he argues, is a way of seeing past them towards the future. Baum emphasizes that the planning process must create a transitional space, between past and future, 'where participants can share the illusion of being apart from time. They need to imagine stepping away from past memories without feeling they have lost their identity or betrayed the objects of memory. They must be able to imagine alternative futures without feeling obliged to enact any of them' (Baum, 1999: 11). This is what he calls the 'serious play' of a good deliberative planning process.

What particularly interests me about the philosophy underlying what I am calling a 'therapeutic' approach is the possibility of transformation: that is, of something beyond a merely workable trade-off or band-aid solution. Just as in successful therapy there is breakthrough and individual growth becomes possible, so too with a successful therapeutically oriented approach to managing our co-existence in the shared spaces of neighbourhoods, cities and regions, there is the capacity for collective growth. Or, to move from the language of therapy to that of politics, there is the possibility of social transformation, of a process of public learning that results in permanent shifts in values and institutions. In the case of Redfern, the values of local residents changed as they listened to the concerns and fears of others; and the local council, as an institution, changed its behaviour insofar as it was forced to recognize the importance of a genuine consultation process and the danger of listening to only one set of voices within its jurisdiction.

It hardly needs to be said that the success of this kind of planning work depends very much on the skills and wisdom of the practitioners involved. It would take a whole book to deal adequately with the kinds of preparation appropriate to this kind of work on deep-seated conflicts in cross-cultural contexts.[7] At the very least, it involves training in negotiation and mediation, facilitation and consensus-building, organizing and working with groups of different sizes and different kinds of internal conflict. It involves some understanding of individual, group, and community psychology, as well as group and community dynamics; and some experience doing research in and about communities, with community members. We could learn a lot from anthropologists' methods. They tell us that getting to know another (group, or culture) takes more than a few meetings and/or a needs assessment survey. Understanding, and building trust, depends on spending time in a community; and it calls for in-depth talk, and not just discussions with formal leaders. They also tell us that every group we encounter has a culture (as does every observer/planner), which may be thick or thin, thoroughly or only partially defining and directing actions. Learning about any culture is an empirical and time-consuming task that requires a special attitude (Baum, 2000: 133). Planners need to learn about culture: what it is and what shapes and maintains it, how and why it changes, and how one's own culture affects one's ability to understand that of others.

The task of fully listening in multicultural conversations may have consequences for our identities. This is so because fully participating requires an openness that exposes us to other beliefs and ways of being in the world that we must consider alongside our own, *not by transcending difference but by acknowledging and fully engaging with it.* In such a process, we may become more aware of ourselves as well as the unfamiliar 'Other', resulting in the possibility of mutual creation of new understandings and meanings. My customary mental horizon is the set of possibilities I can imagine from within the framework of my beliefs, habits and values. Any time I encounter a situation that tests my prejudices (in the sense of prejudgements, or a disposition to judge), my horizons are likely to be redefined, if I can bring openness to the situation. We broaden our horizons by observing and reflecting deeply on the landscapes of other people's lives. In any multicultural conversation there is likely to be tension between (at least) two sets of prejudices/prejudgements. The challenge for multicultural planning consists in not covering up this tension by attempting a naïve assimilation of the two, but in consciously bringing it out, exploring it, and working through it. That was Sarkissian's skill in Redfern.

What else might we conclude about the wider significance of this Sydney case study? One point often raised by critics of participatory processes is the cost and time involved. The Redfern process involved a significant commitment of resources, and this cannot be expected to be available for every dispute that arises. My argument is that this approach is the best model in cases where prior histories of conflict have made more traditional negotiation techniques irrelevant. A second point relates to scale and significance. The conflict in this case was ostensibly over the fate of a 2200 square meter site, within one local municipality. The symbolic stakes, however, were considerably greater, especially for indigenous people, whose ongoing presence in the inner city seemed to be the hidden agenda and longer-term threat. So this small, localized conflict was, in the minds of most of those involved, about core issues of (Australian) history, about historic injustices, and about how personal and national identity is deeply intertwined with these issues. At *whatever* scale such conflicts arise – neighbourhood, city, or region – there is a strong case for using this therapeutic approach.[8]

Another critical point that needs to be extracted from this story relates to my opening question: how does change come about? I do not want to leave the impression that planners, if only they become 'therapists' in their practice, will rid the world of racism, sexism and other plagues. Remember that the (politically conservative) South Sydney Council initially attempted to rush through its preferred solution, and would have succeeded had not those residents (Anglo and indigenous) who supported the indigenous community mobilized, confronted and politically embarrassed the Council into conceding a more consultative approach. *A political space had to be created for this approach through political action.* Occasionally, planners themselves can create such a space, but only with the support of progressive political regimes. But in highly charged, highly politicized conflicts, it is more likely that the planner's role will be to 'design' the space which has been created through political action. In the case of Redfern, once the space was created, the skills, courage, and commitment of the consultant were what made it possible to work through to a solution that dealt with the kinds of fears and anxieties previously discussed, rather than ignoring, marginalizing or overriding them. The courage, or risk factor, also needs to be emphasized. Sarkissian clearly took personal risks, including the risk of failure, in choosing this approach. *Daring to take risks* is one of the qualities I will emphasize in the final chapter (along with this therapeutic approach), as critical to a 21st-century planning imagination.

A final critical ingredient of the Redfern story was the *building of trust*, between the social planner and the various community factions, then among community factions, and finally between community and social planner and local council, developing new working and neighbouring relationships, and mending broken ones. One should not underestimate the inspirational value of such a story. And there are many more like it. There are Wendy Sarkissians in every city, but very few of their stories get told. That's a pity, because collectively they constitute a new breed of planner, sharing a transformative philosophy and always looking for opportunities to put it into practice.

Thinking critically, however, there is a clear limitation to this kind of practice. In this instance, it produced a better outcome, and seems to have transformed the values of some residents, creating the possibility for longer-term peaceful co-existence of indigenous and non-indigenous groups in the neighbourhood. But it's in the very nature of such a consultancy engagement that the practitioner is unlikely to have a more enduring effect on institutional practices. Has the South Sydney Council changed the way it makes decisions as a result of this one-off intervention? Probably not. Has the planning process itself become more inclusionary? No. For these broader changes to come about, there would have had to be more of a working relationship between consultant and council and planning staff and an openness to the possibility of a long-term, as opposed to a short-term fix. Political leadership is an important ingredient in, and institutional change an essential component of, lasting transformation. Our next two stories move in these directions.

EMERSON PARK, EAST ST LOUIS, USA: FROM ABANDONMENT TO HOPE

There's no such thing as a poor community. You can't talk about 'resources' in isolation. The greatest resources are human physical and psychological ones.

(King, 1981: 234)

The city of East St Louis was one of the hardest hit local economies in the USA during the deindustrialization decades of the 1970s and 1980s. The number of local businesses fell from 1527 to 383 and the number of locally employed residents from 12,423 to 2699 between 1970 and 1990 (Reardon, 1998: 324).[9] The municipal unemployment rate increased from 10.5 per cent to 24.6 per cent and the citywide poverty rate rose from 11 per cent to 39 per cent during this same period. As increasing numbers of working-class and middle income whites moved to the suburbs, the city's total population declined from 88,000 to 43,000 and the African American portion increased from 45 per cent to 98 per cent. As the property tax base declined drastically, the city was forced to cancel all but essential services, including a six-year halt in municipal trash collection. By 1991, when the city was unable to pay a court-mandated settlement to a person injured in the city jail, it was compelled to seek state bankruptcy protection. In the absence of city funds, a local judge ordered the transfer of the title to City Hall and 240 acres of city-owned waterfront property to the injured person to satisfy his claim (Reardon, 1998: 324).

The city may have reached rock bottom, but residents trapped in East St Louis by poverty as well as attached by historic ties were not about to give up on their neighbour-hoods, in spite of increasing levels of drug-dealing on their streets, illegal dumping of garbage, and municipal abandonment. In the late 1980s, three dozen local churches formed the Metro-East Coalition of Church-Based Organizations to lobby municipal and state officials to do something about the substance abuse and illegal dumping prob-lems. At the same time, in the state legislature, Wyvetter Younge, a representative from East St Louis, became chairperson of the Illinois House of Representatives Standing Committee on Education Appropriations. During a customarily routine presentation by the President of the University of Illinois at Urbana-Champaign (UIUC), requesting continuing state aid for the university, Representative Younge indicated that no money would be forthcoming until the university articulated its urban service commitment to distressed communities like East St Louis. Thus was put in motion what was to become, after a faltering start, a community-university partnership (the East St Louis Action Research Project, ESLARP) that would reverse the cycle of decline and bring hope to this abandoned community.

The remarkable story of this reversal begins with the hiring of Ken Reardon in 1990 by the UIUC Department of Urban Planning. Reardon had a decade of community organ-izing experience behind him in various US inner cities and was committed to an *empowerment* approach. This approach 'integrates the principles and methods of par-ticipatory action research, direct action organizing, and education for critical conscious-ness into a powerful new planning paradigm (Reardon, 1998: 326). Reardon's first step was to interview community leaders to get their views on the university's activities in the area over the past three years. What he learnt was a shock. Many community leaders had no idea there had even been a university project in existence. Those who were aware were extremely critical, describing university researchers as 'ambulance chasers' and 'carpet-baggers'. 'These interview findings prompted the faculty to abandon their top-down approach in favor of a more participatory, bottom-up, bottom-sideways approach to community planning in which residents identify the issues to be examined, participate in the collection of data, and collaborate in the analysis of this information' (Reardon, 1998: 325).

The first challenge was to overcome the suspicions, among residents, of the university and its researchers. Reardon's meetings with community leaders produced a five-point

protocol for the proposed partnership. The community insisted that the university agree to these points. First, the residents of Emerson Park and their organization, the Emerson Park Development Corporation (EPDC), would determine the issues that the university would work on. Second, local residents would be involved with the students through every step of the research and planning process. Third, UIUC's Department of Urban Planning must make a minimum five-year commitment to Emerson Park. Fourth, the University must help the EPDC gain access to regional funding agencies to secure the resources needed to implement local development projects. Fifth, the University must help the EPDC establish a non-profit organization to sustain the community revitalization process once the campus left the community. This resident-driven protocol, with its shrewd evaluation of previous failures of university 'assistance', drew on the principles of empowerment planning, insisting on participatory action research and community capacity-building.

When the first class of students arrived in East St Louis with Reardon in autumn 1990, this is what they saw: 'Two-thirds of the city's downtown office buildings and retail stores were vacant. All of the city's street lights and traffic signals were dark because of the municipality's inability to pay its electric bill. The air smelled of burning garbage due to a six-year hiatus in residential trash collection . . . Forty per cent of the city's building lots were vacant and thirty per cent of its existing buildings were abandoned' (Reardon, 2003). The students already knew that Emerson Park's median family income was $6738 and 75 per cent of its households were female-headed families with children. The poverty rate was 55 per cent. What they didn't know was that, alongside these grim statistics, was the reality of a feisty and grimly determined group of residents in Emerson Park, led by women like Ceola Davis and others at the Neighborhood House and through church-based organizations. At the first meeting with students, Miss Davis told how these local women had already launched their own community revitalization initiative by recruiting unemployed workers to convert three abandoned buildings across the road from the Day Care Centre into a playground. To do this, the women first had to determine who owned these derelict structures. Miss Davis led a neighbourhood delegation on a bus excursion to the County Administration Building to find out. When they discovered that the County had acquired the properties after tax default by their owners, Miss Davis organized a larger group of residents to attend a public hearing of the County Property Tax Disposition Committee, to request site control of the properties. Once that was granted, local volunteers began to demolish the derelict structures, brick by brick, and haul the materials to a salvage yard, where they garnered $3000. Then residents sought matching funds from the city and charitable organizations. Nobody gave them a cent. The playground project was seen as 'too risky'. So another $1000 was raised by selling fried chicken and catfish dinners on Friday nights. Then the residents, with the help of local contractors and settlement house volunteers, did the work themselves, constructing a 5000 square foot green space that, 15 years later, remains a source of great pride and inspiration.

On the one hand, the playground story tells us of the depths of hopelessness of the situation in this neighbourhood, and its total abandonment by the region's public and private institutions. On the other hand, the determination shown by the residents is a clue to the success story that followed from this first small step. In the winter of 1991, residents again mobilized their own labour, but this time with the help of hundreds of student volunteers from UIUC, to clean up the trash-filled lots. These first working bees were followed by others over the next two years that began repairs to residents' houses, using architectural expertise from UIUC and student and resident labour. Gradually state officials began to take note, and to offer small parcels of financial assistance for home improvement loans. Step by small step, one improvement was followed by another: neighbourhood beautification projects, public safety projects, and a concerted assault on drug-dealing activities with the help of the United States Attorney's office (Reardon, 2003).

There were several minor and major turning points in this story. One was a two-year Community Outreach Partnership Center Grant (COPC) for $500,000 in 1995, followed by a one-year institutionalization grant, both from the US Department of Housing and Urban Development, which enabled ESLARP to expand its neighbourhood planning, community development, and technical assistance and leadership training activities. With the additional resources provided by COPC grants, ESLARP was able to extend its work to other neighbourhoods, again working with local residents to create a community stabilization plan, and then to devise specific projects to resolve specific community development challenges: such as crime prevention, youth development, housing improvement, and job generation. Another turning point was the ongoing challenge from the community to the university researchers to fully engage with the empowerment model by establishing a free 'neighbourhood college' where residents could be trained in a range of community organizing and development skills: community-based crime prevention, environmental racism, non-profit management, grantsmanship, direct action organizing, and so on. In the spring of 1995, 43 community leaders completed the first course on community organization offered through this new adult education programme. Courses were designed to provide community activists with the knowledge and skills required to better understand the structural factors that were driving the uneven patterns of development within the Greater St Louis Metro Region (Reardon, 1998: 326).

A third turning point was the initiative, yet again from the amazing Miss Davis, to lobby for a light rail route through Emerson Park. Miss Davis had learnt that the region's transportation authority was preparing plans to extend St Louis's highly successful light rail line from downtown St Louis across the river to Scott Airforce Base in Southwestern Illinois. Miss Davis saw this as an opportunity to use an abandoned, state-owned, railroad right of way that ran through East St Louis's poorest neighbourhoods, as the route for the proposed light rail. If this was successful, and a station could be built in East St Louis, it would give local residents access to living-wage jobs in St Louis's central business and international airport districts. Miss Davis asked Reardon to recruit planning and design colleagues to prepare a cost-benefit study of using the existing right-of-way. She also requested assistance in securing funds to purchase land around potential rail station sites, so that community organizations could then bargain with would-be investors. All this came to pass. The route was approved. The land was acquired, and subsequently a developer was found who wanted to turn the land around the Emerson Park station into a mixed housing project (the Parsons Place project), with 40 per cent afford-able housing. By 1999, $30 million had been raised to go ahead with that project and the City of East St. Louis completed the sewer, street, sidewalk, lighting and other improve-ments required for the project to go ahead.

By 2000 the EPDC/UIUC Partnership had produced plans that led to more than $45 million in new public and private investment in this once devastated neighbourhood that only a decade earlier could not raise a thousand dollars of outside assistance for its playground. The EPDC had been transformed from a voluntary organization into a well-respected community development corporation. Thanks to federal funding, the Univer-sity's Neighborhood Technical Assistance Center, established in 1995, has helped more than 60 non-profit agencies in the region. The EPDC secured funding for a YouthBuild Program to train unemployed residents in the building trades. A foundation has opened a state-of-the-art youth recreation and development centre within walking distance of the Parsons Place housing project. A local chemical plant that had been a major problem to the neighbourhood was bought by a Scandinavian company with an excellent environmental and labour record and an intention of training local residents for jobs in the plant. Last, but not least, over this decade some 3500 UIUC students have had powerful and, for some, life-transforming learning experiences that have challenged their values and beliefs as well as their intellects and planning skills (Reardon, 2003).

COMMENTARY: EMPOWERMENT PLANNING

These incredible achievements in the space of a decade can be attributed to a number of factors. Reardon's various accounts attribute success primarily to the extraordinary lead-ership of Miss Davis and others from within the East St Louis community. That was clearly a major factor. The capacity of that community to imagine alternatives, to come up with daring schemes, and to follow through on details and with hard work, is a lesson to anyone who doubts the capacity of communities to shape their own destinies. In Emerson Park, whose households were predominantly female-headed, the role of the church and of faith-based organizations has to be noted as providing one source of strength. Another was the experience of these older women in the civil rights movement over the previous three decades. Still, this has been the story of a partnership, a collabor-ation with the university, in which Reardon's own skills and commitment were crucial to the positive outcomes. Reardon himself would say that the key to success was the *empowerment model*, the commitment to participatory action research, direct action organizing, and education for critical consciousness. I would add two things to this analysis. One is the importance of the participatory action researcher's interpersonal skills: Reardon had the capacity to establish trust, working in this cross-cultural context in which there was initially great suspicion and scepticism on the part of the community. Part of that capacity was his radical openness, including openness to criticism from the community, and a real capacity to listen. Listening to Reardon tell this story to a work-shop in the summer of 2000, I was struck by his capacity to inspire and motivate, to tell an inspiring story, and that capacity no doubt played a part in motivating students to become involved in this challenging project.

Another key factor in this success story of empowerment planning is that the mobilized community cannot do it all by themselves. Building a playground from scratch through local sweat is one thing, but new housing and light rail projects do not get built that way. At some point, mobilized communities have to engage with various arms of the state, and with private investors, to realize these larger projects. The residents of East St Louis knew (at least) two things. One was the power of demonstration, through their own early efforts, in attracting attention and interest from state agencies. The other is the importance of entering negotiations from a position of strength, as when they acquired land likely to increase in value once a light rail station was built. Their community stabilization and revitalization depended, along the way, on financial resources from the State Treasurer, on the added capacity created by the federal HUD grant, on the federal drug enforcement agency's undercover action in tackling the city's crack-cocaine dealing areas, and finally on attracting 'quality' companies and developers into the area, who would share the residents' commitment to endogenous development, that is, to developing local resources. The older residents also knew that it was important to train a new generation of leaders from within the community, so they pressed successfully for the 'neighbourhood college'.

Finally this story represents two things. There is a core story that is about *the organization of hope*. The work of the community leaders, and of the leading activist planner through this decade-long struggle, can be described as the work of organizing hope. That is a very human story in which individuals support and inspire each other against massive odds. And then there is the story about those massive odds, the story of structural change that decimates communities, the story of an already historically marginalized community which is further excluded by technological changes over which it has no control. But the residents of East St Louis refused to accept the plot that had been scripted for them by these forces. They were able to imagine another story, and envisage themselves as actors in that alternative story. In such ways do apparently impervious structures become porous and somewhat malleable.

BIRMINGHAM, UK: CREATING COSMOPOLIS IN THE 'POSTCOLONIAL WORKSHOP OF THE WORLD'

I now resume the Birmingham story where I left it off in Chapter 1, at the turn of the 21st century. Since the mid-1980s the City Council had been engaged in an ambitious and expensive physical regeneration of downtown that had achieved some of its aims (like making the downtown more attractive as a tourist and convention destination) but had also depleted the budget available for schools and housing and thus had increased social deprivation and jeopardized the next generation of Brummies, the human capital of the city. Further, this assumed link between the urban economy and the urban fabric (fix up the physical city and the investors will come) had ignored the ethno-cultural complexity of the 'metropolis of the midlands'. On the one hand, the new physical environment that was in place by the mid-1990s was the platform from which to tell a new story about the city, a city now opening itself to the outside, a lively and attractive metropolis, open to the 'new economy'. On the other hand, this new vision reproduced not only the socio-economic exclusions of the previous era, but also the socio-cultural marginalizing. Birmingham's multi-ethnic, multi-racial society was not part of the new image.

All this began to shift in the late 1990s. A new generation of political leadership in the Council encouraged the hiring of key new council staff, who in turn started to shake up a rather traditional city bureaucracy that had been too cosily Labour and clientelist in the past. Nationally, a Labour government in power since 1997 had produced money for innovative social policies, and these funds had brought community programmes and thus activists to the foreground. These activists challenged the vision of the Council as being a very partial one, neglectful of the needs of the poorest neighbourhoods and of the cultural diversity of the city. The Council responded with Highbury 3, a three-day workshop in February 2001 to revisit the city's strategic vision. This extraordinary participatory event (designed with the help of the consultants Charles Landry and Phil Wood of Comedia) engaged over 100 local activists from all sections of the city. It symbolized the Council's acknowledgement that the economic development vision of the 1980s had failed to create economic prosperity beyond a narrow range of middle-class beneficiaries, and had not provided a culturally inclusive representation of the city. The challenge was to work together to create a new vision and a new set of strategies that would shift attention from downtown regeneration to the neighbourhoods, and would involve all residents of this postcolonial city. A consensus emerged that the new emphasis should be on 'place making' (nurturing the neighbourhoods), not rather than, but as well as, 'place marketing' (the necessary promotion of the city to investors). One aspect of this consensus was recognition of the need for multiracial and multiethnic coalitions to struggle against established patterns of exclusion, to end the competition between ethnic groups, and to link immigrant and poor neighbourhoods with downtown politics and urban economy.

I was a speaker at that event, and followed up a year later spending some time in the city, getting to know people (politicians, planners, community activists, youth, musicians . . .), visiting some pilot projects that had emerged out of Highbury 3, and running some workshops for the city council, on cultural diversity and on economic development. What was immediately significant was that in the intervening year since Highbury 3, at a time when three northern British cities had experienced what were being called 'race riots', Birmingham was calm, and was even referred to in the national press as a positive example of a city trying to come to terms with its diversity and social exclusion issues. Had something changed in Birmingham? Arguably what had made some symbolic difference was the fact that Birmingham had held its own Stephen Lawrence inquiry (see Chapter 1) and that inquiry had publicly named a long-standing problem, the history of institutionalized racism. What I saw at neighbourhood level were some interesting and brave efforts to tackle this.

In Handsworth – a multiethnic neighbourhood where three generations of immigrant

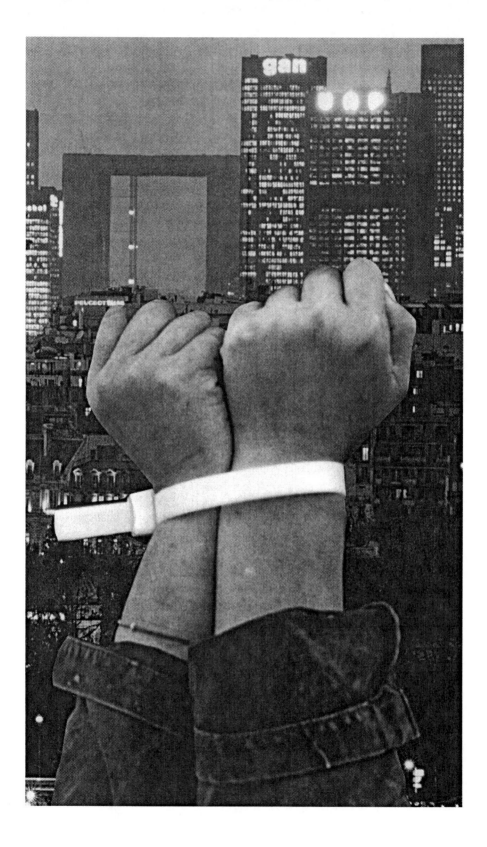

exclusion is visible on the streets and in the run-down housing – a series of innovative programmes were growing out of the Community Fire Station. This local institution is also a community centre, and from it run a variety of promising programmes: anti-racist and anti-gang programmes staffed by young (and not so young) Black men, some of whom have done time and don't want the next generation to repeat their mistakes, others of whom have made it in the music business and provide classes for local youth on how to follow in their footsteps, how to 'learn the biz'; cooperative street-beat policing by the Metropolitan Police working alongside the Rasta-inspired Haile Selassie Peace Force, working in pairs, responding to racial tension on the streets and breaking down stereo-typed views on both sides (police and community); significant efforts to diversify the racial and ethnic composition of the police and fire brigade; the training of locals as community safety wardens; and an effort by the professional football clubs to reach out to Black and Asian youths. The talk, at this grass roots level, was of 'breaking down barriers and stereotypes' and 'connecting communities'. People of different ethnicities, ages, gender, religious and class backgrounds were working on a common project: the desire to build a more cohesive and prosperous local community, and one that would be more integrated socially and economically into the larger city around it.

What I also heard and observed were levels of internalized anger among young people of colour in Birmingham that would be familiar to anyone who has worked in an American inner city: anger over exclusion and lack of recognition; anger over their decaying neighbourhood; anger that new wealth being generated in the city is not com-ing to their neighbourhood. Alongside this anger is fear: fear of travelling beyond their neighbourhood; fear of entering 'white space' downtown; fear of gangs and violence; fear of succumbing to gang culture. And alongside this fear is desire: desire to make it, through self-employment; and desire for the city to make it, through a successful transi-tion from a city of exclusion to a truly multicultural city. As long as this desire exists (rather than alienation or despair), there is hope for Birmingham, but . . .

There is not enough support yet, from the city or the central government, to give these local innovations time to grow and stabilize and make a difference; there are not enough connections between these marginalized communities and the city's planning mechan-isms and horizons; and there are still too many voices in the city referring to themselves as 'indigenous' and expressing the belief that 'newcomers' or 'outsiders' (even if they've been around for three generations) should not have the same rights as 'real Brummies'. Within city hall there is a familiar institutional split between those who do economic development and those who do community and social development, exemplified in the prioritizing of a Master Plan for the redevelopment of Eastside (an old industrial neigh-bourhood adjacent to downtown), an all-too-familiar 'megaproject' approach that appears to have no connections with social development goals or with the multicultural, endogenous economic base of the city. There is unresolved conflict around who should 'own' any new programmes focusing on 'community cohesion', the new central govern-ment buzz phrase. There is an also familiar tension in the desire to empower local communities (including letting them make their own mistakes) and the reality that resources are centrally controlled and thus centrally accountable. I also had a sense that while community cohesion is the new slogan, there are not enough people (beyond the

Handsworth Community Fire Station) who know how to do it. Not enough Wendy Sarkissians. Not enough Ken Reardons. And certainly not the necessary links between the universities and communities, for capacity-building purposes. The admirable goals and efforts embodied in the Community Fire Station's programmes – programmes that understand the importance of working street by street, in cross-cultural coalitions, in order to rebuild neighbourhoods – are not yet receiving sufficient support from either city or central governments.

What is novel and exciting about Birmingham is the willingness on the part of city government to open up debate about the collective future of the city, and to rethink notions of a civic identity based on more inclusive ideas about who is and who isn't considered a Brummie. The Leader (Sir Albert Bore) and the then Deputy Leader (Andy Howell) of City Council have shown real leadership on this and other matters. Part of the art of leadership is the ability to recognize the need for change, and to welcome outsiders as well as encouraging insiders to help think a way through it. Ideas are crucial. So is a new discourse and symbolism about civic identity. So too is institutional reform, whether that be tackling racism or addressing the historic underprivileging of social versus economic development in the council's bureaucratic power structure. Birmingham's leadership is aware of and working on all of these issues.

In all of this 'work in progress' that is Birmingham trying to reinvent itself as a multicultural city (a story for which I have no ending), there is one conspicuous absence. That is the absence of any official city discourse around Birmingham as a postcolonial economy.[10] But as economic geographers Henry, McEwan and Pollard (2000) have pointed out (based on census data), something like 33 per cent of Birmingham's business activity is within minority ethnic-owned enterprises. These are not 'third world comes to first' through ethnic entrepreneurial sweatshops. Rather they are examples of what geographers call 'new industrial spaces' and 'networks', and the production of new hybrid products (*ibid.*: 13). For example, there is a historic Chinese Quarter in Birmingham that signifies the traditional route of early Hong Kong migrants into the catering industry in the 1950s. But there is also a transnational Chinese community in the city, which has expanded its activity into property development, banking and supermarkets. A key element of the investment strategies of some transnational capital is through global, ethnic, community-based networks: the diaspora. Birmingham, as a multicultural city, is one such meeting place of the global diaspora (*ibid.*: 8).

The areas of Sparkbrook and Sparkhill include Pakistani banks operating within the usury laws of Islam and aimed at the UK's 1.5 million practising Muslims. Sparkhill is also the centre of the South Asian jewelry quarter, the retailing of clothes, saris, and other textiles. The city has a Greek-Cypriot fish-frying network which constitutes 25 per cent of the city's 300 fish and chip shops. There are more than 50 halal butchers, and Birmingham's National Halal Centre exports goods such as halal baby food all over Europe. One company makes a range of halal Chinese meals for British Muslims who otherwise cannot eat in Chinese restaurants. Birmingham is now famous for its Kashmiri balti, which is a hybrid product of British-Asian cultures. Other ethnic food producers supply Asian and Caribbean basics and delicacies for national markets. And then there is music. Birmingham is recognized as the centre for Banghra music in Britain, a sound based on the fusion of Asian (specifically Punjabi), western and broader styles (such as reggae, soul, jazzfunk, hip-hop and rock). There are a large number of bands in the city, several recording and distribution companies, and a vibrant club scene. Birmingham-based Apache Indian was the first South Asian British musician to break into the mainstream British charts in the early 1990s. His music 'epitomizes the hybrid nature of the fusion musical scene in Birmingham' (*ibid.*: 10).

What all this suggests to Henry, McEwan and Pollard is that Birmingham is home to a diversity of 'cultural capitalisms' that makes its economy both local and global. They see a unique occurrence of and opportunity for a kind of 'globalization from below' that could combat the social and economic polarization that has accompanied the 'globalization from above' scenarios of the flagship projects (*ibid.*: 15). They describe Birmingham as a 'locus of ethnic community-based economic networks' that may be producing a distinctive competitive advantage for the city. Exploring these networks offers a more relational way of thinking about Birmingham as a city and its insertion in the national/ global economy. It also suggests that City Council's economic development planners need to embrace the notion of multicultural economic development. 'This is about recognizing the cultural diversity of economic activity in policy terms and encouraging it in the expectation that such diversity brings with it a broadening of the economic base' (*ibid.*: 16). Further attention to this hitherto invisible sector might reveal how to 'mobilize diversity as a source of both social cohesion and urban economic competitiveness' (Amin, 1997: 134).

CONCLUSIONS

From these three very different stories of change, both achieved and in progress, in contexts where change for the better often seemed highly unlikely, we can tease out some conclusions about the 'who and how' of transformative planning practices: about the intersecting roles of residents, planners, mobilized communities, powerful stakeholders, and city governments; about power and power imbalances; about the role of emotions in dealing with difference and exclusion; and about the importance of institutionalizing apparently transformative initiatives.

In the story from Sydney, I focused on the conflict resolution and mediation skills of the planner, arguing that without her insight into and attempt to get at what was *really* going on in this dispute over land use, no land use solution could have been arrived at that would have been acceptable to the conflicting parties. I described her approach as 'therapeutic'. But I also noted that without the prior resident mobilization that put pressure on the local council, the political space would not have been created for her intervention. So resident mobilization – in response to lack of community consultation from council – was the catalyst for a new approach. The skill of the social planner was in designing a safe space in which antagonistic residents could speak the unspeakable, but could also listen to others doing the same, and hear what mattered to those others. She created the space for a multicultural conversation, out of which new meanings emerged.

In Redfern, there was space and scope for mediation, for community learning, and these produced changes. But it would be foolish to suggest that mediation should *always* be the strategy of choice. Forester talks about this, remarking on the question of power, and power imbalances, which has long been a sore point with critics of communicative action approaches (see Huxley and Yiftachel, 2000; Flyvbjerg, 2002). 'Collaborative problem-solving can only be truly collaborative when the power of parties is balanced enough to make them interdependent, to make their problem-solving a joint enterprise, not the decision of one party visited upon the others' (Forester, 2000: 167). He does not deny that courts and legislatures are sometimes the more appropriate avenue to redress or protect the rights of those with less power. Susskind *et al.* (1999) have made a similar argument, that mediation processes can complement, but not substitute for, legal and political processes in which weaker parties might gain real protections of their resources or entitlements.

In the Redfern story, I intentionally foregrounded the work of an individual planner because I wanted to demonstrate that individuals do have agency and can make a difference. The difference in that case was that a more culturally inclusive solution was found to a local land-use dispute because the planner was able to create the space in which values were questioned, and attitudes shifted. That is vitally important work. But, I also noted that there was no apparent legacy of this intervention in terms of institutional change. The city council that brought in the consultants did so in order to put out a fire, rather than to rethink their own *modus operandi*. The South Sydney council, unlike that of Birmingham, had not questioned its own practices or understandings. Absent that kind of shift, enduring change is unlikely.

If the planning enterprise is to be a transformative one (irrespective of whose definition of transformative is at work), then there must be 'some institutional position from which to articulate and prosecute a transformative agenda' (Healey, 2003: 1).[11] What is missing in the Redfern story is such an institutional base. In the East St Louis story, that base begins as a coalition between a university and a community organization, but ripples out over time to embrace state and local politicians, government agencies, and the business community. In East St Louis we saw that to bring about significant change involves a mix of ingredients, from individual qualities and leadership skills, to long-term commitment to strengthening the organizational capacities of community-based organizations, to the politics of involving and interacting with state agencies and representatives of the private sector, such as housing and commercial project developers. When historically marginalized groups mobilize to fight their exclusion they need all the help they can get: from capacity-building to coalitions, from planners with multicultural skills to planners with plain old technical skills, from sweat equity to federal funding.[12]

In the ongoing saga of Birmingham's reinvention of itself, the lead role has been taken by an action-oriented yet self-critical city council. At the scale of a city-region like Birmingham, many forces need to be in alignment for successful transformation. These include new ideas about economic development, new discourses about identity and belonging, new sources of funding for community-based programmes, new institutional arrangements within city council, and between council and the variety of ethno-cultural capital networks. All of this might be thought of as planning work, but not all of it is done by planners. Some of it is done by politicians, some by residents and community organizations, some by combinations of these acting together. The effort of social transformation, in other words, of building *cosmopolis*, is a necessarily combined effort, by residents, planners, and politicians at local, state, and national levels. What remains to be underlined is that this effort is not only about mobilizing resources and power, and changing institutions, but also about *organizing hope, negotiating fears, mediating collective memories of identity and belonging, and daring to take risks*. In the next chapter, I take these cases further in my exploration of the importance of story and storytelling in transformative planning.

8
THE POWER OF STORY
IN PLANNING

INTRODUCTION: THE ROAD TO WOLLONGONG

A rhyme's
a barrel of dynamite.
A line is a fuse
that's lit.
The line smoulders,
the rhyme explodes –
And by a stanza
a city
is blown to bits.

(Mayakovsky, 1975)

I had an epiphany on the road to Wollongong almost 20 years ago. I was doing research on the social impacts of economic restructuring in the coastal steel town of Wollongong, 100 miles south of Sydney, when I realized, with a power of epistemological detonation akin to Mayakovsky's poem, that the research as formulated wasn't going anywhere. My political economy framework appeared to me as a ghostly ballet of bloodless categories (class, labour, capital) that could only be animated by the power of story, or stories – the stories of the men who had lost their jobs. I changed the research plan, hired a research assistant to do in-depth interviews, read a book of poems by a Wollongong lad that told obliquely of the ordeals of some of the retrenched miners and steelworkers. But after two years of a research grant I was unable to write the expected academic book. I had a macro-political economic framework (that carried one narrative), and a micro-sociological and psychological set of field data, and I didn't know how to put the two together. I didn't know how to make a good academic story out of these two discrepant sources. I gave up on the project, and before long resigned from my Chair in Urban Studies in Sydney and moved to Los Angeles, where I enrolled in a Masters in Screenwriting at UCLA. My epistemological crisis was such that I didn't believe it could be resolved from within academia. I wasn't aware of any models at that time that suggested otherwise.

For the next half dozen years, once I'd graduated from Film School, I led a somewhat schizophrenic life as a part-time screenwriter and part-time academic in Los Angeles, before choosing to return full-time to the academic fold. Ever since then, I have tried to apply what I learnt in film school to my academic teaching and writing. I believed in the power of stories, but in a completely fuzzy and stubbornly un-analytical way. I was afraid I might spoil the magic if I thought too much about why story is important, how it works, in what circumstances, and what kind of work stories do. This artificial binary that I'd created for myself came partly from previous academic conditioning. For the longest time, 'story' was thought of in the social sciences as 'soft', inferior, lacking in rigour, or, worst insult of all, as a 'woman/native/other' way of knowing.[1] There was even a time, in the academic discipline of history (my starting point), in which story was demoted and more 'analytical' approaches were sought. In response to this kind of marginalizing of story, feminists, historians, and workers in the cultural studies field, not to mention anthropologists, have reasserted its importance, both as epistemology and as methodology. We shouldn't be forced to choose between stories and so-called more rigorous (positivist, quantitative, etc.) research, between stories and census data, stories and modelling, because all three 'alternatives' to story are each imbued with story.

In order to imagine the ultimately unrepresentable space, life and languages of the city, to make them legible, we translate them into narratives. The way we narrate the city becomes constitutive of urban reality, affecting the choices we make, the ways we then might act. As Alasdair MacIntyre put it: 'I can only answer the question "What am I to do" if I can answer the prior question, "of what story or stories do I find myself a part?" ' (quoted in Flyvbjerg, 2001: 137). My argument will be deceptively simple. Stories are central to planning practice: to the knowledge it draws on from the social sciences and humanities; to the knowledge it produces about the city; and to ways of acting in the city. Planning is *performed* through story, in a myriad of ways. I want to unpack the many ways in which we use stories: in process, as a catalyst for change, as a foundation, in policy, in pedagogy, in critique, as justification of the status quo, as identity and as experience. By 'story', I mean 'verbal expressions that narrate the unfolding of events in some passage of time and some particular location' (Eckstein, 2003).

My approach is not uncritical. Despite increasing attention to and use of story in some of the newer academic fields (feminist and cultural studies, for example), I don't see it as the new religion, and I take to heart Eckstein's caution that stories' ability 'to act as transformative agents depends on a disciplined scrutiny of their forms and uses' (Eckstein, 2003). We still need to question the truth of our own and others' stories. We need to be attentive to how power shapes which stories get told, get heard, carry weight. We need to understand the work that stories do, or rather that we ask them to do, in deploying them, and to recognize the moral ordering involved in the conscious and unconscious use of certain plots and character types. A better understanding of the role of stories can make us more effective as planning practitioners, irrespective of the substantive field of planning. Story and story telling are at work in conflict resolution, in community development, in participatory action research, in resource management, in policy and data analysis, in transportation planning, and so on. A better understanding of the role of stories can also be an aid to critical thinking, to deconstructing the arguments of others. Stories can also sometimes provide a far richer understanding of the human condition, and thus of the urban condition, than traditional social science, and for that reason alone, deserve more attention.

In short, I want to make two bold arguments in this chapter. One is about the importance of story in planning practice, research, and teaching. The other is about the crucial importance of story in multicultural planning. Much of what planners do, I will argue, can be understood as performed story. Yet the importance of story has rarely been understood, let alone validated in planning. Story is an all-pervasive, yet largely unrecognized force in planning practice. We don't talk about it, and we don't teach it. Let's get this out of the closet. Let's liberate and celebrate and think about the power of story. And let's appreciate its importance to the 21st-century multicultural planning project, as a way of bringing people together to learn about each other through the telling and sharing of stories.

HOW STORIES WORK

Very few scholars within the planning field have investigated the work of story in planning, and, even then, only aspects of it (Forester, 1989; 1999; Mandelbaum, 1991; Throgmorton, 1996; Marris, 1997; Eckstein and Throgmorton, 2003).[2] In coming out of the closet about the importance of story, I want to be systematic about the ways, implicit and explicit, in which we use story, and to demonstrate what I mean when I say that planning is performed through story.

But first I need to say something about story itself, because 'story' conveys a range of meanings, from anecdote, to exemplar, to something that is invented rather than 'true', in the sense of strictly adhering to widely agreed-on facts. All three of these meanings are present and demonstrable in the way story is used in planning.[3] In their most developed form, stories have certain key properties, and here I draw on my film school training, and also on Ruth Finnegan (1998), to sketch some of them. *First*, there is a temporal or sequential framework, which often involves a ticking clock to provide dramatic tension. *Second*, there is an element of explanation or coherence, rather than a catalogue of one damn thing after another. *Third*, there is some potential for generalizability, for seeing the universal in the particular, the world in a grain of sand.[4] And *fourth*, there is the presence of recognized, generic conventions that relate to an expected framework, a plot structure and protagonists. Aristotle's *Poetics* was our bible on this subject in film school. We learnt from him that stories have plot as well as characters, both equally important: and that stories have a beginning, middle, and end, a shape or structure. Perhaps a *fifth* observation should be that moral tension is essential to a good story.[5] Finnegan (1998: 9–13) notes that the moral ordering of the more familiar fictional genres is equally present in stories in and about planning.

I want to elaborate briefly on the second and fourth of these properties of story, the elements of *coherence or explanation*, and plot structure. Historian Hayden White wrote that narrative is a 'form of human comprehension that is productive of meaning by its imposition of a certain formal coherence on a virtual chaos of events' (quoted in Eckstein, 2003). Literary, folklore and myth analysts have argued that there are a number of widely recognized plots: most obviously, the hero's tale, the rags-to-riches tale, the fall from grace, the effects of villainy, the growth to maturity, the Golden Age lost, the pioneer's tale, the stranger comes to town, and the young man leaves home in order to find himself/make his place in the world/escape from the provincial straightjacket. To take a few examples from planning:

1. The conflict between settlers and indigenous peoples in New World countries over land uses and land rights. For indigenous peoples there is a core story that is about paradise lost, or an expulsion from paradise. For the settlers, the core story is the pioneer's tale of bravery and persistence in the face of adversity.

2. The story of the young man leaving home to escape the provincial straightjacket. This may evolve into the urban story of the young gay man who seeks out the big city to find a community of those like him. Or it may become the story of a squatter settlement in the hills outside town or on the banks of a river, or a homeless encampment in skid row on the edge of downtown. Each is a potential domain of planning action.

3. The Golden Age lost. This is a story that recurs in writings about communities and their destruction. Sometimes the villains in this plot are developers. Other times, they are planners.

And so on. Stories in and about planning, even the most seemingly abstract, embody quite familiar and recognizable plots.

If we think about the East St Louis story as told by Ken Reardon (Reardon, 1998; 2003) and which I re-told with a slightly different emphasis in Chapter 7, it's possible to see all five story conventions at work. There is a *temporal sequence* that begins when the University of Illinois is challenged in the State House regarding its community service work, and proceeds through early tentative efforts to do something, followed by setbacks, turning points, crises, obstacles, and finally reaches dramatic resolution when we learn that a decade later, $45 million in funds has been committed to the revitalization of the hitherto abandoned neighbourhood. There is certainly an *element of explanation*. In Reardon's version, this achievement was primarily the product of the faith of certain community leaders, and secondarily the result of hard work on the part of community members. (In my version, Reardon and his students play a significant role also.) There is *potential for generalizability* in the way that Reardon draws lessons from this story that may have applicability for other poor communities as well as for university/community partnerships. There is the presence of the *generic conventions of plot and character*. At one level, the 'plot' is about deindustrialization and globalization, abstract and impersonal forces, but it is also about community resistance and mobilization, coalition building, and the triumph of the human spirit. There are individuals who embody some, but not all, of these abstract forces. The 'noble community activists' have names and brief biographies, as do the 'few good men' who come forward to invest in the community with public or private funds, whereas those who had abandoned the community remain unnamed villains. Finally, the moral ordering of the story is clear. Faith produces a will to act. The capacity to act is enhanced by the university/community partnership. There is also blindness/self-deception in the university's involvement, and that has to be over-

come, through the courage, honesty and compassion of the community leaders, as well as the humility and self-criticism of the researchers. An ethic of service to others drives the story . . .

I want to turn now to the ways in which I see *planning as performed story*: in process, in foundational stories, in stories as catalysts for change, in policy, and, finally, in academic stories, as method, as explanation, and as critique.

PLANNING AS PERFORMED STORY

STORY AND PROCESS

For many planning practitioners, the role of story is central, although not always consciously so. Those who do consciously make use of story do so in diverse, often imaginative and inspiring ways. The best way to demonstrate this is by using some examples – of story as process, and of story being used to facilitate process. These examples are so varied that I'll use sub-headings as guides.

Community participation processes

In community or public participation processes, planners orchestrate an event in such a way as to allow everybody, or as many people as possible, to tell their story about their community, neighbourhood, school, or street. We tend to refer to this as drawing on local knowledge, and there are various techniques for eliciting people's stories, such as small group work with a facilitator for each group, or doing community mapping exercises.[6] What is not always clear is how these collected stories will be used in the subsequent process, but the belief operating here is that it is important for everybody to have a chance to speak, and to have their stories heard. This is linked with an argument about the political and practical benefits of democratizing planning.

If a participatory event is a way of *starting* a planning process, its purpose is most often about getting views and opinions, so the story-gathering is likely to be followed by an attempt to find common threads that will help to draw up priorities. If, on the other hand, the participatory event is a response to a pre-existing conflict that needs to be addressed before planning can move ahead, then the gathering of rival stories takes on more import. In such a situation – like the Redfern story discussed in Chapter 7 – practitioners will usually meet separately with each involved person or group and listen to their stories of what the problem is before making a judgement about when and how to bring the conflicting parties together to hear each other's stories. In extreme cases, where the conflict is long-standing, relating to generations or even centuries of oppression or marginalization, this is very difficult work, but when done well can be therapeutic, cathartic, even healing.

Mediation, negotiation, and conflict resolution

In one growing branch of planning practice – mediation, negotiation, and conflict resolution – there is a raft of techniques and procedures for facilitating story telling, and the hearing of stories, in conflict situations.[7] In this kind of work, the ability of a practitioner to make the space for stories to be heard is more important than the ability to tell stories. And it is here that the importance of listening to others' stories, and the skills of listening in cross-cultural contexts, is at a premium.[8]

In Sarkissian's mediation and social planning work in the cross-cultural conflict in Redfern, there were two stages in the process when story telling was critical. The first was in the preparatory phase, when Sarkissian was scoping out for herself what was going on in this neighbourhood. She went from house to house, and from one small group of residents to another, listening non-judgementally to each of their stories, hearing people speak bitterness, speak anger, speak fear and resentment. The purpose of this first phase was not only for the consultant to learn about the issues and the emotions surrounding them, but also somehow to convey to all of the conflicting parties that the consultant had really listened to and heard their story. After reflecting on the intensity of feelings involved in this conflict, Sarkissian judged that conflicting parties needed to hear each other's stories, but initially in a situation where they could not interrupt or argue with those stories. Thus she designed an event, the Speakout, with carefully established rules of procedure that everyone understood and agreed to before the event. At the Speakout, everyone in the neighbourhood had the opportunity to tell their story, and also had to respect others' rights to speak theirs. From that event, more trust was generated, and there was a subtle shift in perspective among the conflicting parties. They were now prepared to engage in some form of dialogue with their neighbours. 'In telling stories, parties tell who they are, what they care about, and what deeper concerns they may have that underlie the issues at hand' (Forester, 2000: 166). Without using these two forms of storytelling, Sarkissian would not have been able to bring the conflicting parties into the same room to discuss the issue that the Council wanted discussed – some agreed-on principles for a Master Plan for the factory site.

Forester describes a similar case in Washington State, where the mediator, Shirley Solomon, brought together Native Americans and non-Native county officials to settle land disputes. A critical stage in that mediation was the creating of a safe space in which people could come together and 'just talk about things without it being product-driven' (Solomon, quoted in Forester, 2000: 152). Solomon ceremonialized this safe space by creating a talking circle and asking people to talk about what this place meant to them. Everyone was encouraged to tell their story, of the meaning of the land, the place, to them and their families, past, present, and future – the land whose multiple and conflict-ing uses they were ultimately to resolve. It was this story-ing that got people past 'my needs versus your needs' and on to some 'higher ground', moving towards some com-mon purpose. Solomon describes this stepping aside to discuss personal histories as both simple and powerful, as a way of opening surprising connections between conflicting parties. Or, as Forester has it, story telling is essential in situations where deep histories of identity and domination are the context through which a present dispute is viewed. Stories have to be told for reconciliation to happen (Forester, 2000: 157). In terms of process, too, the design of spaces for telling stories makes participants from different cultures and class backgrounds more comfortable about speaking, and more confident about the relevance of the whole procedure. A tribal elder who was present at Solomon's mediation said to her: 'In those meetings where it's Roberts Rules of Order, I know that I either have nothing to say, or what I have to say counts for nothing' (quoted in Forester, 2000: 154).

Intercultural collaboration in participatory action research

In the case of the university/community partnership in East St. Louis which involved an intercultural collaboration, Ken Reardon is not explicit about his use of story in the participatory action research process, but I can imagine it by extrapolating from his account. In order to recruit students into this project, Reardon would have had to tell a particular kind of persuasive story about why this work was important and what might be achieved. In order to persuade the sceptical community leaders that they should allow university researchers to work with them, Reardon had to tell other stories, about his track record, and tell them as convincingly as possible. Further into the project he describes a speech he gave on a public occasion at the University in St Louis, in which he appealed for 'a few good men' to come forward and invest in the East St Louis community: another occasion on which persuasive story telling, this time about progress already made, was crucial. Throughout the decade of his involvement in this project, Reardon was using story telling skills in a wide variety of circumstances, to a wide variety of audiences, and part of this involved a skill in translating from one cultural context to another, knowing what 'language' to use in which circumstances. Finally, when Reardon speaks his account of these events,[9] he weaves them together in the manner of a true story teller, using all five conventions of story, as I described earlier.

Core story

Another interesting development of the use of story in practice is what Dunstan and Sarkissian (1994) call 'core story'. The idea of core story as methodology draws on work in psychology which suggests that each of us has a core story: that we do not merely tell stories but are active in creating them with our lives. We become our stories. When we tell stories about ourselves we draw on past behaviour and on others' comments about us in characterizing ourselves as, say, adventurous, or victims, or afraid of change, or selfish, or heroic. But in telling and re-telling the story, we are also reproducing ourselves and our behaviours. Social psychologists argue that communities, and possibly nations, have such core stories that give meaning to collective life (see Houston, 1982; 1987). Culture is the creation and expression and sharing of stories that bond us with common language, imagery, metaphors, all of which create shared meaning. Such stories might be victim stories, warrior stories, fatal flaw stories, stories of peace-making, of generosity, of abandonment, of expectations betrayed.

In their work in evaluating the success of community development on a new outer suburban estate developed by a public agency in an Australian city, Dunstan and Sarkissian used an array of research tools: attitude and satisfaction surveys, interviews, focus groups, as well as census and other 'hard' data. When they came to analyse this material, they found contradictions that were not likely to be resolved by collecting more details. In order to go beyond the details and the quantitative scores on 'satisfaction', they explored the notion of core story, drawing on heroic, mythic and meta-poetic language.

They scripted such a story of heroic settlers, of expectation and betrayal, of abandon-ment, and took the story back to the community, saying 'this is what we've heard'. The response was overwhelming, and cathartic. 'Yes, you've understood. That's our story.' The task then, as the social planners defined it, was to help the community to turn this doomed and pessimistic story around. They asked them how they thought their story might/could/should be changed. Underlying this was a belief that core stories can be guides to how communities will respond to crisis, or to public intervention. As with individuals, some tragic core stories need to be transformed by an explicit healing pro-cess or else the core story will be enacted again and again. Renewal and redemption are possible, Dunstan and Sarkissian believe. New 'chapters' can be written if there is the collective will to do so. They suggest four steps towards renewal. The first is a public telling of the story in a way that accepts its truth and acknowledges its power and pain. The second is some kind of atonement, in which there is an exchange that settles the differences. The third is a ceremony or ritual emerging out of local involvement and commitment by government (in this case municipal and provincial) that publicly acknowledges the new beginning. The fourth is an ongoing commitment and trust that a new approach is possible and will be acted on (Dunstan and Sarkissian, 1994: 75–91).

This fascinating case study offers some illumination to a more general puzzle in participatory planning: how to turn a raft of community stories into a trustworthy plan, one that is faithful to community desires. To turn the light on inside the black box of that conversion surely requires planners to take their plan back to the community and say, 'this is how we converted your stories into a plan. Did we understand you correctly?': In a community or constituency where there is only one core story, this is a more straight-forward process than in a situation where what the planners have heard is two or more conflicting stories. In the latter situation there is far more working through to do, in order to prioritize and to reach some consensus about priorities.

Non-verbal stories

Less 'verbal' story telling approaches have been developed using people with community arts experience to be part of a community development project that creates the opportunity for residents to express their feelings and tell their story vividly and power-fully. The Seattle Arts Commission matches artists with communities to engage in just such projects. At their best, they can create a new sense of cohesion and identity among residents, a healing of past wrongs, and a collective optimism about the future. A com-munity quilt, and quilting process, has proved to be a successful way to bring people together and for a group to tell their story. Depending on the community involved in an issue, video or music, or other art forms, may be more powerful forms of story telling. In his violence-prevention work with youth in the Rock Solid Foundation in Victoria, British Columbia, Constable Tom Woods initiated a project to create an outdoor youth art gallery and park site along a 500-meter stretch of railway right-of-way between two rows of warehouses. This area, which had a long history as a crime corridor, is now home to the Trackside Art Gallery, where local youths practise their graffiti on the warehouse walls. Woods realized that these teenagers needed a safe site for their graffiti. More profoundly, he realized that they needed a space to express themselves through non-

violent means, and that graffiti is a communicative art form, a form of story telling (Macnaughton, 2001: 5). The potential of planners working with artists in processes like these that encourage story telling has only just begun to be tapped.

Future stories

Peter Ellyard is another consultant who uses story in an imaginative way in his 'preferred futures process'. Working with an array of clients, from institutions and corporations to place and interest-based communities, he helps them to develop their own 'future myth', a preferred future scenario; he then takes them through a process of 'backcasting' or reverse history, as they unfold the steps from the future back to the present, which got them to where they want to be. On the way, there are missions, heritages, disasters, triumphs and pitfalls. He consciously employs these narrative devices as an aid to imagination. Once the future myth task is complete, they proceed to SWOT (strengths, weaknesses, opportunities, threats) analyses and to the development of capacity building strategies and action plans (Ellyard, 2001).

What emerges then is the use of story in both obvious and imaginative ways in planning processes: an ability to tell, listen to, and invent stories is being nurtured as well as the equally important ability to make the space for stories to be heard.

STORY AS FOUNDATION, ORIGIN, IDENTITY

I've already discussed the notion of core story and how it might be used by planners. There's a related but not identical notion of foundational story, a mytho-poetic story of origins, a story that cities and nations tell about themselves. This is particularly relevant to planning in multiethnic, multicultural contexts in which conflicting notions of identity are at play. Take Australia. The foundational story that Anglo-Australians have been telling for the past 200 and some years concerns the arrival of the brave Captain James Cook, who landed with the First Fleet at Botany Bay in 1788 to establish a colony, and of subsequent heroic pioneers who explored and tamed the land – a familiar story in New World settler societies. On one level this story is mytho-poetic, but on another it is also politico-legal. The founding institutions, and specifically the system of land ownership, were based on the legal concept of *terra nullius*, that is, empty land. This concept rendered invisible the previous 60,000 years of indigenous occupation, as well as their continued presence on the continent.

Towards the end of the twentieth century, growing numbers of non-indigenous as well as indigenous Australians grew increasingly uncomfortable with this founding fiction. Momentum grew for the rewriting of the story of origins. Many of those concerned with celebrating nation-building at the turn of the 21st century wanted to tell a more complex origins story, and the foundational myth became contested terrain. Part of the battle was legal and was fought through the High Court. Another part was symbolic and emotional, concerning apology and atonement. That was handled in part by the placing of 'Sorry Books' in all public libraries across Australia. Anyone who wished to could sign one of these books, and thereby publicly apologize to the Aboriginal people for their dispossession. There were also a series of 'Sorry Day' marches throughout 2001, one in each capital city. Half a million people participated in Sydney and 300,000 in Melbourne. The refusal of the Prime Minister (since 1996), John Howard, to make an official apology on behalf of the government continues to anger many Australians, and to be seen as unfinished business in the reconciliation process.

Having participated in the Melbourne march, this was in the back of my mind in the winter of 2002 when I was working in Birmingham, at the invitation of the City Council. Partly in response to race riots in other northern British cities in the preceding summer, Birmingham's politicians were concerned about 'getting it right' in relation to 'managing' ethnic diversity (see Chapter 7). As I met with various groups in the city, from the city planning staff to workers in a variety of community development programmes, to young black men and Muslim women, I began to hear very different versions of Birmingham's identity. There was a fairly widely accepted founding story on the part of some Anglo residents (who referred to themselves as the 'indigenous' population) that Birmingham was an *English* city (not a multicultural city) and that those who were there first had greater rights to the city than the relative newcomers from the Indian subcontinent, the Caribbean, and so on. This profoundly political question of the city's changing identity clearly needed the widest possible public debate. I suggested that at some point the city was going to have to re-write its foundational story, to make it more inclusive, and open to change. The planning staff were very much implicated in this debate. At the community coalface, and especially in non-Anglo neighbourhoods, these predominantly Anglo-Celtic planners were either reproducing the founding story of 'British Birmingham', or helping to change that story by making their policies and programmes reflect and respect the diversity of the 'new city'.

This is not an isolated example any more, but a situation increasingly common across Europe in this age of migrations. The need to collectively change (and represent in the built environment itself) these old foundational stories is one of the contemporary challenges facing planners.

STORY AS CATALYST FOR CHANGE

Stories and story telling can be powerful agents or aids in the service of change, as shapers of a new imagination of alternatives. Stories of success, or of exemplary actions, serve as inspirations when they are re-told. I've lost count of the number of times I have told 'the Rosa Parks story',[10] either in class, or in a community or activist meeting, when the mood suddenly (or over time) gets pessimistic, and people feel that the odds are too great, the structures of power too oppressive and all-encompassing. When Ken Reardon tells or writes his East St Louis story, he is amongst other things conveying a message of hope in the face of incredible odds. This 'organizing of hope' is one of our fundamental tasks as planners, and one of our weapons in that battle is the use of success stories, and the ability to tell those stories well, meaningfully, in a way that does indeed inspire others to act.

In multicultural contexts, there is usually a dominant culture whose version of events, of behaviour, and practices, are the implicit norm. It is also usually the case that those engaged in planning – as a state-directed activity – are members of the dominant culture, and therefore less likely to recognize, let alone question, current cultural norms and practices. For a society to be functionally as well as formally multicultural, those norms occasionally have to be held up to the light and examined and challenged. One effective way to do that is through story. Describing his first experience with participatory action research, Rajesh Tandon (in Forester, Pitt and Welsh, 1993) recalls his PhD fieldwork in rural Rajasthan, working for a local development organization that wanted someone to do some training for village-based groups of tribal youths. Tandon stayed in the village and interacted with local people while he developed his data collection instruments. The locals began to ask questions. Why was he trying to get a PhD? Why was he developing a data instrument that was alien to the context? Why was he pretending to be more objective than he really was? Why did he think that only outsiders could be objective, while insiders could only be subjective? One night after dinner he was sitting with some local people in the darkness, chit-chatting as was the local custom. One of the elders told him a story: about a trader who came several generations back from Afghanistan to their area, how he lived there quite a while but took away a lot of their jewelry and things like that, never to return. They trusted him and he stayed in the village. He said he'd bring spices back with him, but he never did. After a while, the elders turned to Tandon and said: 'What lessons did that story teach you?'. Tandon wasn't prepared for the question. He thought they were telling stories to each other to pass the time. But the elders were actually confronting him, he a city boy with a different class and cultural background, and forcing him to examine the ethical dimension as well as the methodology of his research. In this case, the use of story in confrontation was life-transforming for Tandon, forcing him to question his own training, and to critique what role knowledge plays in society. It propelled him to invent a participatory action research approach (Tandon, interviewed in Forester, Pitt and Welsh, 1993: 101–102).

Canadian planner Norman Dale has written of the critical importance of hearing the stories of the Haida Gwaii (an indigenous community on the Northwest coast of Canada) in what was meant to be a cross-cultural community economic development project in the Queen Charlotte Islands, sponsored by the provincial government (Dale, 1999). After a series of formal meetings with local residents, Dale was struggling to create a space in which the lone Haida representative (whose name was Gitsga) would feel empowered to say anything. Gitsga seemed to have taken a vow of silence, and was on the verge of pulling out of the consultation process when Dale sought him out and encouraged him to return. At the next consultation meeting, there was some informal chat among the white folks, before the real meeting began, about the artistic and environmental merits of a sculpture that had been erected on a rock offshore. It hadn't occurred to anybody to ask the Haida people what they thought. When Gitsga broke his silence to volunteer the information that the rock was sacred to the Haida, there was genuine shock and consternation, leading to an opening up of the whole community economic development planning process to the involvement of the Haida. Planners have a tremendously important role in acknowledging the voices of minority groups, designing meetings in which such groups are comfortable speaking, and encouraging them to speak

Depending on the context, success stories may not be enough to disrupt existing habits of thought and bring about profound change, as we've seen in the last two examples. We may need different kinds of stories: stories that frighten, stories that shock, embarrass, de-familiarize (Eckstein, 2003). Deciding what stories to tell in what circumstances is part of the planner's art. The puzzle of how to change the stories that people tell themselves everyday, often repeating familiar stories from the media, absorbing and internalizing the messages of the dominant culture or class, is an old one. For Marx, this was a problem of 'false consciousness' (that is, a group, or class, not understanding what was in its own best interests in the long run), and called for a revolutionary vanguard to enlighten the proletariat. This answer is no longer acceptable, partly because it prejudges and demeans the actual life experience and knowledge of oppressed groups, and their capacity to analyse their own circumstances and organize themselves. Faced with a situation where people appear to be telling themselves 'the wrong stories', there are two things that planners can do. One is, in good conscience and with humility, to suggest alternative stories. The second is to build 'education for a critical consciousness' into their participatory approaches.[11] Planners are, after all, just one of the actors in the force field of public conversation.

I have one more example of the use of story in planning practices – in the process of policy analysis, formulation, and implementation – before I turn to academic story telling about planning.

STORY AND POLICY

Here I am aided by James Throgmorton and Peter Marris, each of whom has done a lot of thinking about the connections between story and policy. In *Witnesses, Engineers and Storytellers: Using Research for Social Policy and Community Action* (1997), Peter Marris argues that the relationship between knowledge and action is not straightforward, and that knowledge itself cannot, has not ever, determined policy. In analysing various types of and approaches to social policy research, Marris asks why so little of the research produced on poverty, for example, has affected policy. His answers are several. One is that academics are powerful critics but weak story tellers. That is, they fail to communicate their findings in a form that is not only plausible but persuasive. (By contrast, he notes that community actors have great stories to tell, but no means of telling them, except to each other. So the wrong stories win the debates.) Story telling, he says, is the natural language of persuasion, because any story has to involve both a sequence of events and the interpretation of their meaning. A story integrates knowledge of what happened with an understanding of why it happened and a sense of what it means to us. (If it fails to do all this, we say things like 'but I still don't understand why he did that' or 'why are you telling me this?' or 'so what's going to happen?'.) Stories organize knowledge around our need to act and our moral concerns. The stories don't have to be original, but they must be authoritative (that is, provide reliable evidence marshalled into a convincing argument). The best are both original and authoritative.[12]

To be persuasive, the stories we tell must fit the need as well as the situation. Policy researchers compete with everyone else who has a story to tell, and their special claim on public attention lies in the quality of their observation as well as the sophistication of the accumulated understanding through which they interpret their data. But this truthfulness is not, in itself, necessarily persuasive. Good stories have qualities such as dramatic timing, humour, irony, evocativeness and suspense, in which social researchers are untrained. 'Worse', says Marris, 'they have taught themselves that to be entertaining compromises the integrity of scientific work' (Marris, 1997: 58). Writing up policy research is hard work: it's hard to tell a good story while simultaneously displaying conscientiously the evidence on which it is based. But, Marris insists, the more social researchers attend to the story teller's craft, and honour it in the work of colleagues and students, the more influential they can be. We have to be able to tell our stories skilfully enough to capture the imagination of a broader and more political audience than our colleagues alone.

There are two notions of story at work here. One is functional/instrumental: bringing the findings of social research to life through weaving them into a good story. The other is more profound: story telling, in the fullest sense, is not merely recounting events, but endowing them with meaning by commentary, interpretation, and dramatic structure.

While Marris seems to confine his advocacy of story telling to the publishing of research results, James Throgmorton's work addresses the next step, the arts of rhetoric in the public domain of speech and debate. The lesson he wants to impart is that if we want to be effective policy advocates, then we need to become good story makers and good story tellers, in the more performative sense. In *Planning as Persuasive Storytelling* (1996), Throgmorton suggests that we can think of planning as an enacted and future-oriented narrative in which participants are both characters and joint authors. And we can think of story telling as being an appropriate style for conveying the truth of planning action. However, what should be done, he asks, when planning stories overlap and conflict? How can planners (and other interested parties) decide which planning story is more worthy of the telling?

Throgmorton (1996: 48) draws on the concept of 'narrative rationality' in claiming that humans are story tellers who have a natural capacity to recognize the fidelity of stories they tell and experience. We test stories in terms of the extent to which they hang together (coherence) and in terms of their truthfulness and reliability (fidelity). But Throgmorton is unhappy with this, reminding us of situations in which two planning stories, both of which are coherent and truthful on their own terms, compete for attention. What then makes one more worthy than another? Throgmorton suggests that the answer to this question lies in part at least in the persuasiveness with which we tell our stories. Planning is a form of persuasive story telling, and planners are both authors who write texts (plans, analyses, articles) and also characters whose forecasts, surveys, models, maps, and so on, act as tropes (figures of speech and argument) in their own and others' persuasive stories. A crucial part of Throgmorton's argument is that this future-oriented storytelling is never simply persuasive. It is also constitutive. The ways in which planners write and talk help to shape community, character and culture. So a critical question for planners is what ethical principles should guide and constrain their efforts to persuade their audiences.

I am unsatisfied by Throgmorton's argument here on two grounds. First, there is the question of values. I cannot accept that it is 'persuasiveness' that makes one story more 'worthy' than another in a public policy conflict. I want to bring in the notion of 'value rationality' and suggest that ultimately, in public policy, we are arguing over values rather than facts.[13] We can rarely marshall all of the relevant facts in complex public policy decisions, in part because of complexity itself, in part because there will never be agreement on what are the relevant facts. Judgements about 'relevant facts' are just that, judgements based on a values-informed notion of what is important, what matters, what is in the public interest. We should stop pretending that there is any such thing as an objective answer to any public policy issue, and acknowledge that all available answers are informed by values. The public debate can then be around those values (what kind of city do we want, what kind of transport system, how much are we prepared to pay, and so on) rather than around contested data. This would help to clarify policy choices as political choices, but it doesn't resolve the problem of knowing when policy stories are based on lies and deception, or on what Flyvbjerg (1998) calls the 'the rationality of power'. This brings me to my second problem with Throgmorton, the question of power. We are all too aware of the capacity of spin doctoring, or manipulating facts and arguments in order to make them more persuasive. Powerful people and organizations also tell stories (about why we need budget cuts, or why we need more roads and less public transport, or why any one project is better than another) and use all of their material as well as persuasive powers to get their stories heard and to silence, trivialize or marginalize others. Are planners' counter-stories going to make a difference when power is not on their side? Here stories suffer the same limits as 'rational argument' does in the direct face of power. But counter-stories can serve to mobilize opposition, to bring people on to the streets or to organize any number of attention-grabbing and potentially embarrassing (to politicians answerable to a constituency) forms of protest. And such oppositional stories are likely to be more powerful than rational argument in defeating naked power, because they appeal through their ability to mobilize emotions, to reach out to what matters most to people.

Marris's and Throgmorton's work has very important implications for policy research and recommendations. If planners want to be more effective in translating knowledge to action, they argue, then we had better pay more attention to the craft of story telling in both its written and oral forms. That means literally expanding the language of planning, to become more expressive, evocative, engaging, and to include the language of the emotions. 'Academic story telling', writes Finnegan, 'is ugly in its stark, clichéd monotone manner. We tell the dullest stories in the most dreary ways, and usually deliberately, for this is the mantle of scientific storytelling: it is supposed to be dull' (Finnegan, 1998: 21). What Finnegan alleges of academic story telling is equally true of bureaucratic story telling. Policy reports produced by government planning agencies, and also by consultants for those agencies, are cut from the same clichéd cloth. They are dry as dust. Life's juices have been squeezed from them. Emotion has been rigorously purged, as if there were no such things as joy, tranquillity, anger, resentment, fear, hope, memory and forgetting at stake in these analyses. What purposes, whose purposes, do these bloodless stories serve? For one thing, they serve to perpetuate a myth of the objectivity and technical expertise of planners. And in doing so, these documents are nothing short of misleading at best (dishonest at worst) about the kinds of problems and choices we face in cities.

To influence policy, then, as well as to be effective in planning processes, planners need to learn story, or rather, an array of story telling modes. But where to learn this? What to learn? How to learn to critically scrutinize stories? What is the academy teaching?

STORY AS CRITIQUE AND/OR EXPLANATION

There is a false binary in our heads that separates planning documents, social scientific research and theorizing from story telling, rather than allowing us to appreciate the ways in which each of these employs story. Planning documents, from maps, to models, to GIS, to plans themselves, do in fact all tell a story. Sometimes the story is descriptive, or poses as descriptive – 'this is how things are', 'these are the facts'. But there is no such thing as mere description, or pure facts. There is always an author who is choosing which facts are relevant, what to describe, what to count, and in the assembling of these facts a story is shaped, an interpretation, either consciously or unconsciously, emerges. Facts are usually marshalled to explain something and to draw some conclusions for action.

Scholars also use story in their critical writings about cities and planning, sometimes consciously, but usually not. Even unconsciously, however, academic urban stories – even the most seemingly abstract – often exhibit some of the five familiar properties of story that I described in the introduction, drawing on familiar plot lines. There are heroes and antiheroes, victims, and other familiar character types: the witch figure/demon of international capitalism; the two-faced fairy of progress; the insubstantial and ambiguous trickster called postmodernity; and the darling love, long-lost, but in some stories found again, of community (Finnegan, 1998: 21). There is a temporal ordering, often on a grand scale, taking us from pre-industrial to industrial to postindustrial cities, or from deindustrialization to the knowledge economy and the space of flows. The most familiar plot is change itself, and the desire to explain it.

Along with the explaining usually comes a valuing. Things were better before, or after, such and such, which then suggests we should go backwards or forwards. Evocative plots, of rural superseded by urban, community by alienation, tradition by modernity, or community triumphing over capital, residents over bureaucracies, squatters over the forces of law and order, are moving stories with which individual readers can identify, positioning themselves in a larger historical narrative. There are stories of times of transition, of new eras, of an old order passing, of lost Golden Ages. And there are some stories, but not many, which foretell a happy ending, if only . . . If only 'we' would do such and such, then we could live happily ever after. One of the reasons for the appeal of the New Urbanism is that it tells just such a story with a happy ending, rather than the more familiar bleak urban stories in which the bad fairy of political, economic, or environmental exploitation triumphs yet again.

In other words, academic urban stories and theories evoke basic narrative plots that are familiar to us from other contexts (from fairy tales to movies) and which resonate with us morally as well as intellectually, satisfying or disturbing or challenging us. My point here is not to say that these stories are therefore worthless. On the contrary, they are illuminating and instructive precisely because of these underlying plots, which are all exercises in valuing human activities, in a moral ordering of life and social organization. As with planning documents, the more alert we can be to the underlying story or stories,

the better we are able to evaluate them. We need to understand the mechanisms of story, both in order to tell good stories ourselves, to be more critical of the stories we have to listen to, and to be able to resist persuasive stories as well as create them. How to do this?

Rein and Schön (1977: 5) argued that the validity of stories is measurable, and offered five criteria: stories should be consistent, testable by empirical means, actionable, beautiful, and lead to a moral position. This is a curious list of criteria, part normative, part aesthetic, and part quantitative. It fails to get at a number of important issues. First, when planners are listening to stories, and depending on the context, the most important thing to listen for may be the story truth rather than the data truth, that is, to get at the emotional core of an issue, rather than to worry about whether all the facts alluded to are accurate. Second, Rein and Schön don't advise us to ask who is telling the story. But, as Eckstein (2003) argues, identifying the author/s is the first step in determining who or what 'authorizes the authors'. What power is being invoked by the story teller? For whom, and with what justification, are they claiming to speak? What is their place in the prevailing systems of power? We have to interrogate story tellers and the powers behind them. When public decisions are afoot, 'every story teller is narrating to control others' actions' (Ecktein, 2003). Third, if we need to interrogate the story teller, we also need to interrogate the story. Rein and Schön's criteria don't help us to get inside the construction of a story, the real engine of its persuasive power, to which I now turn.

Stories do their work, make themselves compelling, by manipulating time, voice, and space (Eckstein, 2003). So we need to attend to all three when hearing or constructing stories. *Time* is 'manipulated' through the device of duration. How much story 'space' is given to specific time intervals or periods of time? Which parts of a chronological story are collapsed into relatively few sentences, pages, or minutes, compared with other parts of the story that are given extended treatment? Paying attention to this issue of duration can allow the listener/reader to hear what matters most to the teller, as can listening for repetition, which produces patterns of significance. *Space* ranks with time as a component of and in story, and is critically important for urban scholars and practitioners. We must be able to ' "see" time in space' (Balzac, quoted in Eckstein, 2003). Geographic scale is an important factor in the production of meaning. Stories operate at different geographic scales, sometimes metaphorical, and interpretation requires careful attention to those scales. The most obvious example would be whether one is viewing the city from the windows of an aeroplane or skyscraper (the bird's-eye view) or from the street. Stories also sometimes ask us to adopt a different spatial perspective than the one we're most comfortable with. For example, residents and local activists may be most familiar with looking at issues from the local or neighbourhood perspective. Some stories ask us to take a global perspective. If this is beyond our familiarity, the story teller will have to be very skilful in helping us to do this.

Voice is also central to story telling. Is the story being told in the first person, third person, or first person plural (I, s/he, we), and what does that signify about who is speaking on behalf of whom? Whose voices are given prominence, whose are repressed? As with the myths of other cultures, our planning and academic stories function as sanction and justification for the current order, but also as launching pads for counterversions. Academic stories about planning usually take sides, although not always overtly.

Sometimes this is revealed by asking, of any narrative, what voices are missing here? In *Making the Invisible Visible* (1998), I critiqued what I call the 'Official Story' of planning's history, by pointing out what that story leaves out. The 'Official Story' portrays planning as a heroic pursuit, often without any fatal flaws, always on the side of the angels, and those who oppose it as irrational, reactionary, or just plain greedy. What this leaves out, as I explained in Chapter 2, are the gender, class, race, and cultural biases of planning practices; the ways in which planning has served as an agent of social control, regulating (certain marked) bodies in space; and the many stories of oppositional practices, grass roots planning by excluded groups, in opposition to a state-directed mode of planning that has always disadvantaged them.

To imagine the future differently, we need to start with history, with a reconsideration of the stories we tell ourselves about the role of planning in the modern and postmodern city. In telling new stories about our past, our intention is to reshape our future. If we can uncouple planning history from its obsession with the celebratory story of the rise of the planning profession, then we may be able to link it to a new set of public issues – those connected with a dawning appreciation of a multicultural heritage and the challenge of planning for a future of multicultural cities and regions.

Stories matter. They can make a difference. Whether that difference is for the better depends, to a not inconsiderable extent, on the capacities of listeners to hear and critically interpret the elements of time, space, and voice in the narrative.

STORY AND PEDAGOGY

There are a variety of ways of using story in pedagogy: that is, specifically in the training of planners. I will mention a number of them, and then concentrate on the contribution of one outstanding educator. It is not new for planning educators to use story in the form of role-play in the classroom (or in problem-solving workshops). The intent is to nudge people beyond their own horizons, into the worlds of others with whom they are in conflict. I have a number of reservations about role-play. One is that the effect of asking participants to take on roles with which they are unfamiliar, or opposed to, may simply be to mobilize the worst kind of stereotyping of others' views and positions and behaviours. Another is that some people feel extremely uncomfortable having to be anybody but themselves. This may be more than shyness. For example, the mediator Shirley Solomon, in the case discussed earlier in this chapter, tells how in one case the attempt at a role-play turned into a near-disaster. 'The people couldn't get into it because they just wanted to be themselves . . . all these people are very much engaged in these issues, and it's passionate for them. They learned not at all from having to take the other's role . . . One of the tribal leaders never got it, couldn't get into it, and just couldn't believe that he wasn't able to represent himself . . . The (county) general manager was asked to be a developer. He just didn't want to be a developer. So he tried to do it for a while and then just got aggravated with it' (Solomon, in Forester, 2000: 158–9).

I have been inspired by new teaching ideas emerging from feminist studies in the 1980s. During my decade teaching graduate students in the Urban Planning Program at UCLA, I used the device of 'life stories' as a way to explore difficult issues of identity and difference. My students, in their diversity, mirrored the social and cultural diversity of that city, and this occasionally led to tensions in classes. I began each semester asking students to write short stories about the ways that race, or gender, or ethnicity, or disability, had shaped their lives. We then shared those stories in class, and drew on them during the semester, as a way of connecting the personal with the political. I have also used the idea of (what I called) a 'housing autobiography' when teaching undergraduates about housing issues, asking students to craft a story about the houses they've lived in and how that might have shaped their ideas of the ideal house and neighbourhood. When I did this at the University of Melbourne, with students from Hong Kong, Singapore, and Malaysia in class as well as Anglo-Australians, it worked very well in bringing out cultural and class stereotypes of the 'normal' house and neighbourhood. In general, I have found that the more creative I can be in the classroom (by using music, images, and so on) the more creative is the response of my students in their own papers and in their thinking. It was partly feminism, partly my film school experience, and partly the need to find as many ways as possible to connect with my multicultural student group that led me to experiment with story. The results, in terms of wonderful papers and presentations from my classes, have taught me a lot about the creativity that so often lies dormant, or is undernourished or even discouraged, through our academic straightjackets of 'appropriate', 'objective', 'scientific' papers.

For two decades, John Forester has been a story-gatherer, collecting the details of the working days and lives of a wide range of practitioners in North America and a handful from Israel and Europe, using interviews to get them to describe what it is that they do, always in terms of action rather than theorizing. With minimal editing, these 'work stories' have been published both as transcripts for pedagogical purposes and also, with detailed commentary and interpretation, incorporated into Forester's books as the foundation of his understanding of and theorizing about planning (Forester, 1989; 1999).[14]

Over the past decade, Forester has been dedicated in his pursuit of an understanding of difference in planning. I see his larger project as an attempt to reshape planning as a practice of deliberative democracy. But, as part of that quest, he recognizes 'the challenges of a multicultural planning practice – the ability to anticipate and respond sensitively and creatively to complex differences of standpoint, background, race and gender, cultural and political history' (Forester, 2000: 147). He puzzles over what it means to 'respect difference'. He sees the danger of respect conceived as the mere acceptance or appreciation of difference: in that form, respect can stymie dialogue and mutual learning. He is acutely aware that planning conflicts are often about more than resources (such as land, money, facilities). They are also about relationships, and this involves not only personality and politics, but also race, ethnicity, and culture. To learn about how to work successfully in such cross-cultural or multicultural situations, he has sought out practitioners with good stories to tell. One such story, that can do double duty for me in writing here about pedagogy and story, is the work of Marie Kennedy, who teaches community development planning at the University of Massachusetts in Boston.[15]

Kennedy's undergraduate students are primarily of working-class background, urban, and older (average age 39). The class works with grass roots community organizations in the Boston area, around issues defined by those organizations, and in the process

students learn planning skills. The project that Kennedy describes in her interview
(Forester, Pitt and Welsh, 1993: 110–22) was in the city of Sommerville, adjacent to
Cambridge and Boston, population around 100,000. Sommerville was in transition from
a predominantly white ethnic working-class district to a city with a significant new
immigrant population, as well as a new liberal/radical, more educated white group who
were moving in from Cambridge. (This latter group had become politically active and
pushed the agenda of Sommerville as a Sanctuary City.[16]) In the previous ten years the
population had changed from 95 per cent white ethnic working-class to 25 per cent
foreign born (Haitian, Vietnamese, Central American) and this was accompanied by
increasing racial tension and incidence of racial violence. Kennedy was approached by
the Mystic Welcome Project, an organization of newcomers in the Mystic housing project, the largest public housing project in Sommerville. The question was how to build, or
rebuild, a sense of community cooperation and support in this neighbourhood. There
was also the challenge of how to bring together several neighbourhood-based organizations in the same area who had nothing to do with each other. For Kennedy the agenda
was clear. 'We are explicitly going in with an agenda to build a healthy multi-racial,
multi-ethnic community. So the goal is out front. We will have many discussions, and
some of them will be heated' (*ibid.*: 118).

What I want to draw from this story is how Kennedy prepared her students to work in
this situation. The students themselves were diverse in terms of age, gender, race, and
ethnicity, and mostly working-class. For the first month (of a one-year course) she met
with the students and concentrated on their own attitudes towards immigrant communities and newcomers, and their own attitudes towards Sommerville as a place. 'We
spend the initial time getting their biases and preconceptions on the table . . . I feel
strongly that no matter who we are, we bring our previous experience, our baggage, our
preconceptions with us into any planning situation. The first step is to get real clear
about what you are bringing . . . You can either set your baggage aside in order to clearly
hear and listen to other people's experience, or you can check it out against other
people's opinions and against facts to see whether your preconception is born out or not'
(*ibid.*: 113).

The students all individually took walking tours through the neighbourhood and had
to figure out how the neighbourhood affected them, whom they saw there, what racial
and ethnic and socio-economic groups, what they saw in the physical environment, what
their assumptions about it were, whether they thought it would or would not be a 'nice'
place to live. Kennedy got all the students to write about Sommerville, and to write about
their attitude to newcomer groups and individuals. The writing was done anonymously,
and discussed collectively. There was a lot of disagreement among students about their
impressions. What came out in the discussions was how different students' backgrounds
(growing up, or not, in a public housing project; living, or not, in a neighbourhood of
newcomers, and so on) had shaped their reflections on Sommerville. Students were
asked to think about the experience of becoming a minority newcomer, maybe the only
family that is different from the now-majority community. Some could draw on their
backgrounds as minority members to talk about this, and educate their fellow (white)
students. Gradually this led into discussions on housing policy, immigration policy, a

needs analysis of the area, and so on. But a whole semester was spent in this kind of preparation, before the students started to work with the community group, in the community.

This is a deeply informative account of what it takes to work as an agent of social change in a changing neighbourhood, and how important it is to examine one's own preconceptions. It gives us some idea of the detailed personal work that needs to be done in preparation for working in multicultural environments. In this learning stage, the stories that students tell about themselves, and hear from each other, are crucial in peeling back layers of preconceptions and assumptions about 'others', and about physical, residential environments different from whatever one is accustomed to. In turn, when I read this account of Kennedy's work, I learn new ways of approaching the training of community development planners. Her 'work story' helps my work. Forester's gathering of such stories helps us all. Stories teach. But what do they teach?

Forester's work is both empirically based and ethically and normatively saturated. Despite his disclaimer that 'we sought no particular philosophy or style' when seeking out potential interviewees, he is not merely describing what planners do, in their own words. He wants planners to do good and make a difference, and he searches for stories from practitioners which demonstrate these possibilities (and correspond with his understanding of doing good). His purposes shape his collection of stories. His pedagogical aims in passing these stories on to his students are not simply to convey the skills of these practitioners but also to inspire his students with how those skills are used, that is, for what moral purposes. In Kennedy's case, the purpose is building healthy multiracial, multiethnic communities. And herein is perhaps the oldest and most traditional use of stories, as moral exemplars.

CONCLUSIONS

There are of course limits to the power and reach of stories and story telling in planning. Two need to be mentioned in closing this chapter. One concerns scale: the other, power itself. I am not claiming that story telling works in situations of extreme conflict that divide nations, such as contemporary conflicts between Zionists and Palestinians in Israel, or Hindus and Muslims in India. My examples are drawn from local and regional contexts and from scenarios where planners have a role and some leverage. Nor am I claiming that story telling is so powerful that it can or should replace other planning tools. Persuasive story telling is one form of power at the disposal of planners, but it takes its place in a force field in which there are other powers at work, including the powers of misinformation, deception, and lying, which are deployed within planning as well as by outside forces opposing planning interventions.[17] Encountering and countering such stories is another layer of the process of judging and judgement that is part of all planning work.

Nevertheless, this chapter has argued that stories and story telling are central to planning practice, that in fact we can think about planning as performed story. We have seen stories working as, and in, *planning processes*, where the ability to tell, to listen, and to invent stories is being nurtured as well as the equally important ability to create/design the spaces for stories to be heard. When stories work as *catalysts for change*, it is partly by inspirational example, and partly by shaping a new imagination of alternatives. We've explored the notion of *foundational stories* that need to be rewritten, whether at the level of the nation, the city, or the neighbourhood. We've heard how story could be critical in *policy research and analysis*, as well as how the mantle of scientific story telling may be handicapping our policy causes. We've seen how academics use story, *as explanation and as critique* of planning practices, and how these stories too can make a difference, can uphold as well as question the status quo. We've explored various ways that stories are used in the *training of planners*, personal stories, practical stories, moving and inspiring stories. Specifically, I have argued the crucial importance of story in multicultural planning, and demonstrated in each section of this chapter how particular applications of story contribute to the multicultural planning project.

But there are still too few practitioners or academics who are conscious of or creative about the use of story. My purpose in drawing attention to the centrality of story is, among other things, to suggest that the role of the story telling imagination could be given far more prominence in the education of planners. A better understanding of the work that story does, or can do, and how it does it, could produce more persuasive plans and policy documents. It could help us to analyse such documents. And the creative use of or responsiveness to stories in planning processes can serve many purposes, including widening the circle of democratic discourse, and shifting participants in such discourses out of their entrenched positions and into more receptive or open frames of mind.

As cities become more multiethnic and multicultural, the need to engage in dialogue with strangers must become an urban art and not just a planner's art, if we are concerned about how we can co-exist with each other, in all our difference. This most ancient of arts begins with the sharing of stories, and moves towards the shaping of new collective stories. 'The storyteller, besides being a great mother, a teacher, a poetess, a warrior, a musician, a historian, a fairy, and a witch, is a healer and a protectress. Her chanting or telling of stories . . . has the power of bringing us together' (Minh-ha, 1989: 140).

I am advocating both a creative and a critical approach to stories and story telling. Using stories in planning practice must be done with an alertness to the ways in which power shapes which stories get told, get heard, and carry weight. Critical judgement will always be necessary in deciding what weight to give to different stories, as well as what stories are appropriate in what circumstances. *The telling of stories is nothing less than a profoundly political act.*

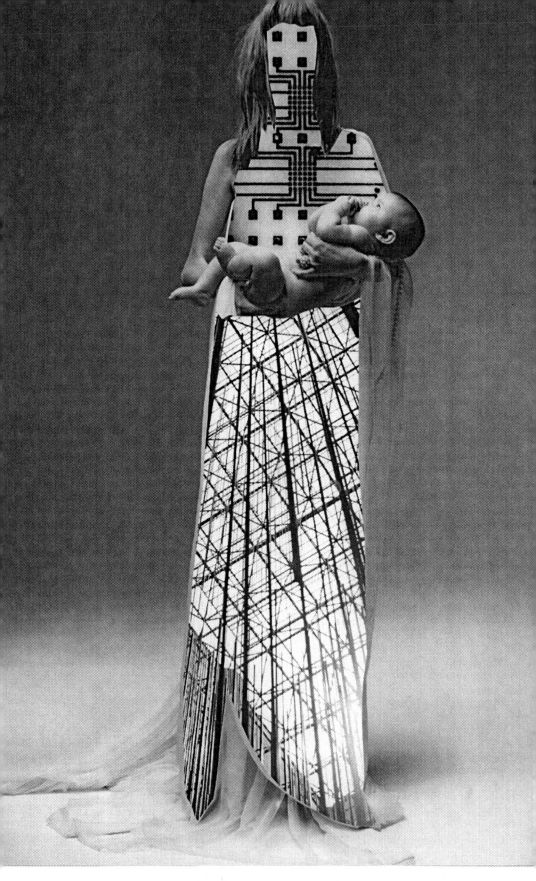

9

CITY SONGLINES

A planning imagination for the 21st century

The ancients sang their way all over the world. They sang the rivers and ranges, salt pans and sand dunes. They hunted, ate, made love, danced, killed: wherever their tracks led, they left a trail of music. They wrapped the whole world in a web of song.

(Chatwin, 1987)

INTRODUCTION

I look into my crystal globe, and I dream of the carnival of the multicultural city. I don't want a city where everything stays the same and everyone is afraid of change; I don't want a city where young African Americans have to sell drugs to make a living, or Thai women are imprisoned in sweat shops in the garment district where they work 16 hours a day, six days a week; where boys carry guns to make them feel like men, and suspicion oozes from plaster walls, and white neighbourhoods call the police if they see a black/stranger on their street. I don't want a city where the official in charge refuses to deal with the man standing at his desk because everything about him is different; where immigrants are called 'blackheads' and forced to find shelter in the industrial zone; where whites pay more and more of their private incomes to protect themselves from 'strangers', and vote for officials who will spend more of everyone's taxes on more law and order rather than more schools and health clinics; where political candidates run on promises of cutting off services to 'illegal immigrants'; where the media teach us to fear and hate one another and to value violence in the name of 'patriotism' and 'community'. I don't want a city where I am afraid to go out alone at night, or to visit certain neighbourhoods even in broad daylight; where pedestrians are immediately suspect, and the homeless always harassed. I don't want a city where the elderly are irrelevant and 'youth' is a problem to be solved by more control. I don't want a city where my profession – urban planning – contributes to all of the above, acting as spatial police, regulating bodies in space . . .

I dream of a city of bread *and* festivals, where those who don't have the bread aren't excluded from the carnival. I dream of a city in which action grows out of knowledge and understanding; where *you* haven't got it made until you can help others to get where you are or beyond; where social justice is more prized than a balanced budget; where I have a right to my surroundings, and so do all my fellow citizens; where we don't exist for the city but are seduced by it; where only after consultation with local folks could decisions be made about our neighbourhoods; where scarcity does not build a barb-wire fence around carefully guarded inequalities; where no one flaunts their authority and no one is without authority; where I don't have to translate my 'expertise' into jargon to impress officials and confuse citizens. I want a city where the community values and rewards those who are different; where a community becomes more developed as it becomes more diverse; where 'community' is caring and sharing responsibility for the physical and spiritual condition of the common living space.

I want a city where people can cartwheel across pedestrian crossings without being arrested for playfulness; where everyone can paint the sidewalks, and address passers-by without fear of being shot; where there are places of stimulus and places of meditation; where there is music in public squares, and street performers don't have to have a portfolio and a permit, and street vendors co-exist with shopkeepers. I want a city where people take pleasure in shaping and caring for their environment and are encouraged to do so; where neighbours plant bokchoy and taro and broad beans in community gardens. I want a city where my profession contributes to all of the above, where city planning is a war of liberation fought against dumb, featureless public space; against STARchitecture, speculators, and benchmarkers; against the multiple sources of oppression, domination and violence; where citizens wrest from space new possibilities, and immerse themselves in their cultures while respecting those of their neighbours, collectively forging new hybrid cultures and spaces. I want a city that is run differently from an accounting firm; where planners 'plan' by negotiating desires and fears, mediating memories and hopes, facilitating change and transformation.

That is my love song to our mongrel cities of the 21st century. But how do we get to there from here? How can citizens, city governments, and the city building professions help to construct this *cosmopolis*? To paraphrase the Chinese sage, a journey of a thousand miles begins with the first step. Many steps have already been taken, some of which have been discussed in previous chapters. Using them as a springboard, it is not hard to imagine a metamorphosis of planning as we have known it, a liberation from its twentieth-century Kafkaesque castle/prison of regulation and normalization – in a word, bureaucratic planning. I see planning as an always unfinished social project whose task is managing our co-existence in the shared spaces of cities and neighbourhoods in such a way as to enrich human life, to work for social, cultural, and environmental justice.[1] This social project has an imperfect past and an uncertain future, but as an enduring social project it needs to come to terms with the new social realities of the 21st century, the demands of an insurgent citizenship on the one hand, and fear of and reaction to those demands, on the other. Is there a planning imagination that can be harnessed to this task?

In this concluding chapter I suggest that there is such an emerging imagination and that, among other things, it involves an expanded language for planning, the language of memory, desire, and spirit: and *five qualities* that are quite distinct from the skills, or even literacies[2], that have obsessed twentieth-century planning education. I propose a different sensibility from the bureaucratic or regulatory planning that dominated that century – a sensibility that is as alert to the emotional economies of cities as it is to the political economies; as alert to the city senses (of sound, smell, touch, taste, and sight) as to city censuses; as alert to the soft-wired desires of citizens as it is to the hard-wired infrastructures; as concerned with the ludic as with the productive spaces, indeed seeing these as inseparable and complementary; a sensibility as curious about the spirit of place as it is critical of capitalist excesses; a sensibility that can help citizens wrest new possibilities from space, and collectively forge new hybrid cultures and spaces.

There are, and will continue to be, multiple roles for planners, but the normative position which this book argues is for a more radical approach, one which is prepared to address the issues of social, cultural, and environmental justice in cities that are being shaped by global economic and demographic forces. This amounts to no less than a paradigm shift for planning. In the next section, I outline that shift, suggesting five qualities of a new planning imagination for the 21st century: *political, therapeutic, audacious, creative,* and *critical.* In the following section I sketch a new language for planning, the language of memory, desire, and spirit. Finally, I explain 'city songlines'.

A PARADIGM SHIFT: FROM METROPOLIS TO *COSMOPOLIS*

Chapter 1 outlined six pillars of modernist planning wisdom that have dominated the planning of modernist cities. The analyses in Chapters 2 through 8 undermined the stability of these pillars and suggested the need for their replacement with a more normative, open, democratic, flexible, and responsive style that is sensitive to cultural difference.

In the old model, planning was concerned with making public decisions more rational. The focus was predominantly on advanced decision-making; on developing blueprints for the future; and on an instrumental rationality that closely considered and evaluated options and alternatives. While means-ends rationality may still be a useful concept for tasks like building bridges and dams, we also need a different, substantial rationality that focuses on debating values and goals. Rather than being technically based, this is a more *communicative and value-driven rationality* with a greater and more explicit reliance on practical wisdom.

In the old model, planning was regarded as most effective when it was comprehensive. Comprehensiveness was written into planning legislation, and referred to multi-functional and multisectoral spatial plans as well as to the intersections of economic, social, environmental, and physical planning. Planning's task was understood as coordinating and integrating, and was regarded as necessarily hierarchical. Today, planning is no longer seen as being exclusively concerned with integrative, comprehensive, and coordinating action and is increasingly identified with *negotiated, political, and focused planning* (Christensen, 1993), a planning less oriented to the production of documents and more interactive, centred on people.

In the old model, planning emerged out of the engineering mindset of the late nineteenth century, and drew its authority from a mastery of theory and methods in the social and natural sciences. Planning knowledge and expertise were grounded in positivist

science, with its propensity for quantitative modelling and analysis. Today there is growing acknowledgement that there are many kinds of appropriate knowledge in planning.
New epistemologies – among them hermeneutics, action research, social learning, feminist, and other ways of knowing (Chapter 3) – are displacing the sole reliance on the
powers of positivist social science as a basis for action. Local communities have
grounded, experiential, intuitive, and contextual knowledges that are more often manifested in stories, songs, and visual images than in the typical planning sources. Planners
need to learn and practise these *other ways of knowing.*

In the old model, planning was a project of state-directed futures, part of a 200-year
modernization project that began with the industrial revolution. As we saw in Chapters
6, 7 and 8, there is now a thriving, community-based planning practice, in which planners link their skills to the campaigns of mobilized communities, working as enablers
and facilitators. Rather than speaking for communities, as in the older advocacy model,
this new style of planning is geared to community empowerment. Planners bring to the
table skills in research and critical thinking, knowledge of legislation and the workings of
state agencies, specific skills in fields like housing and local economic development,
organizing and financial skills, and a commitment to social and environmental justice.

This is not an argument for the rejection of state-directed planning. There are transformative *and* oppressive possibilities in state planning, just as there are in community-
based planning.

Victories at community level almost always need to be consolidated in some way
through the state, through legislation and/or through the allocation of resources. State-
directed, but participatory, planning is important for providing strategic directions. But
in the new model, there will be more in the way of *partnerships between the state and
community-based organizations and NGOs.* Flexible and creative solutions and adapta-
tions are far more likely to emerge from the bottom-up, and processes of learning to live
together have to be worked out from street to street and neighbourhood to
neighbourhood.

In the old model, at least until the late 1960s, planning was held to operate in 'the
public interest', and it was assumed that planners' educations entitled them to identify
that public interest. In the wake of Marxist, feminist, and poststructuralist dismantlings
of this concept, it seems more useful to talk about planning for *multiple publics,* or for *a
heterogeneous public.* Planning has never been value-neutral. It ought now to be explicitly
value-sensitive, working on behalf of the most vulnerable groups in multicultural cities
and regions, accommodating rather than eradicating difference. In this new arena of
planning for multiple publics in multicultural societies, new kinds of multi- or cross-
cultural literacies are essential.

In the old model, planning stood apart from politics, distancing itself from that which
was believed to pollute its pure rationality and objectivity. Since decades of research have
now shown planning to have been neither purely rational nor purely objective, it is now
time for it to become transparently political, open about the values and visions it stands
for and defends.

These, then, are the bare bones of a shifting paradigm, a brief overview. The world of
planning education and practice at the beginning of the 21st century uneasily straddles

the two, the old and the emerging, in a way that is evocative of Matthew Arnold's great mid-nineteenth-century image of 'wandering between two worlds, one lost, the other yet to be found'. The old planning served modernist cities in a project that was, in part, dedicated to the eradication of difference. Metaphorically, this planning can be linked with the machine images of the great Fritz Lang film *Metropolis*. The emerging planning, defined in Chapters 6, 7 and 8, is dedicated to a social project in which difference can flourish.[3] The metaphorical image of *Cosmopolis* is meant to suggest that diversity. To ensure planning's continued relevance as a significant social project, contributing to the creation of cosmopolis, it is important to give more flesh to these bones. This will be done by elaborating the five qualities already mentioned: political, therapeutic, audacious, creative, and critical sensibilities.

EXPANDING THE POLITICAL HORIZONS OF PLANNING

In shifting beyond the modernist paradigm there must be an end to the pretence – still held in some quarters – that planning is, or could ever be, a-political and value-neutral. In this age of global economic integration and multiple migrations there are continuous and conspicuous redistributions of wealth and power which have manifest spatial expressions, and which planners help to bring into being, or to resist. At the moment, these global forces and top-down processes are increasing economic, social, and cultural polarization in an overall climate of increasing uncertainty and decreasing legitimacy of governments everywhere (Marris, 1996; 1998). In response, mobilized communities within civil society launch struggles for livelihood, in defence of life space, and in affirmation of the right to cultural difference. In this context, planners must make choices. For whom to work, on behalf of which set of forces or struggles? The choice is not a simple one, in the sense that it is often posed, as a choice between top-down and bottom-up, between working for the state or working for 'the community'. Not all communities practise a progressive, inclusionary politics (Abu-Lughod, 1998), and the state is not always repressive and reactionary. Further, while community mobilization is the necessary first step of an insurgent/radical planning, it is rarely sufficient for lasting change. The most promising experiments in insurgent planning have involved mobilized communities forging coalitions to work for broad objectives of economic, environmental, social and cultural justice, and in the process resisting, engaging with, and participating in 'the state'. As I argued in Chapter 6, the real work of managing our co-existence in cities of difference takes place at the local level. This means drawing on the creativity and local knowledge of community-based organizations and planners working for the local state, but the national or regional state agencies are still critical as strategic thinkers and enablers of the local work. The German 'Social City' programme, federally funded but locally proposed, designed, and implemented, is a good example of more creative roles between different levels of the state and local communities.

If planning's constituency is to continue to be, at least in part, those groups who are most vulnerable, whether from economic or political disadvantage or from cultural discrimination and oppression, then these new forms of planning will be increasingly important. Current political processes (in the racialized liberal democracies of the West) represent people's needs only in the crudest and most partisan way, even in an open democracy. If we want to achieve greater social justice, less polluted environments, and broader cross-cultural tolerance, and if planning is to contribute to those social goals, then we need a broader and more politicized definition of planning's domain and practices. These practices will have to include mobilizing constituencies, protests, strikes, acts of civil disobedience, community organization, professional advocacy and research, publicity, as well as the proposing and drafting of laws and new programmes of social intervention (Marris, 1996; 1998).

Serious thought has to be given to the institutional location of planning. If we want planning to be more responsive to the pressures that a mobilized civil society is able to exert on the state (in its various guises), then the planning function needs to be located more directly within city councils, rather than protected as yet another line agency. Making planning more overtly political has risks associated, but is surely better than the behind-the-scenes machinations that have typically characterized planning decisions. Planning, to the extent that it is a function of the state, is very dependent on the quality of institutions responsible for implementing it (Chapters 6 and 7). Imagining utopian possibilities, we must be able to imagine the institutions that we desire, as well as imagining the citizens and planners who will maintain and transform them. The following sections on risk-taking and creativity partially address this problem. So too does the section on critical thinking, which tackles how we think about the state itself.

Operating in an always political climate has at least three implications for planners. One is the impossibility of ignoring politics, and thus the need to develop political skills. Another is the need for choices: choice in terms of arenas of practice, as opportunities arise or are foreclosed. But the major choice concerns the vision of the good society to which planners might dedicate themselves. I have argued for planning as a social project in which difference can flourish – difference in all of its multiplicity – as we continue to struggle for economic and environmental justice, for human community, and for the survival of the spirit in the face of the onslaught of a global consumer culture, and growing concern for security at all levels. I have outlined a set of principles to guide the construction of and create the space for this emergent 'utopia', a utopia which has more to do with process and becoming than with achievement and being – principles of social justice, of multicultural and urban citizenship, of coalitions building bridges of cooperation across difference. The creation of *cosmopolis* must be a partnership between citizens, city governments, and the city-building professions. Planners could be midwives at the birth of *cosmopolis*. But they won't be, unless their practice is politically informed and consciously based on values.

DEVELOPING A MORE THERAPEUTIC APPROACH TO URBAN CONFLICTS

When John Forester (2000: 147) wrote that 'planning conflicts often involve not only resources like land and money, but relationships that involve personality and politics, race, ethnicity and culture, too', he was saying something with profound implications for how we think about and practise planning. If it is *relationships* between people that are driving a land use or resource management conflict, then something more than rational discourse among concerned stakeholders, or the usual toolkit of negotiation and mediation, is necessary to address what's really going on. Conflictual relationships involve feelings and emotions like fear, anger, hope, betrayal, abandonment, loss, unrecognized memories, lack of recognition, and histories of disempowerment and exclusion. I have argued throughout this book that when planning disputes are entangled in such emotional and symbolic as well as material battles, there is a need for a language and process of emotional involvement and resolution. In her fieldwork with indigenous people in southern Australia, planning research by Elizabeth Porter shows that while the ostensible issue is co-management (by indigenous and non-indigenous Australians) of national and state parks, what most concerns this group of indigenous people is the matter of lack of recognition – of their historic presence, and their ongoing special knowledge of and relationship to the land (Porter, 2002). Cooperation is unlikely until that issue has been dealt with, but this is not something that planners have been trained to expect or attend to. There are a variety of ways of dealing with this lack of recognition, some of which are necessarily formal and ceremonial and involve various levels of local, regional and national politics, including (in this instance) the need for an official apology from the Australian government. Obstinacy or blindness about such emotional matters can stall reconciliation or conflict resolution indefinitely.

There are many interesting examples of recognition of the need to deal with memory in order for reconciliation, healing, or social transformation to occur. Best known perhaps are Maya Lin's Vietnam War Memorial in Washington, DC, and Daniel Liebeskind's Jewish Museum in Berlin. South Africa's Truth and Reconciliation Commission was a process rather than a memorial. Lesser known is the case of Liverpool, England, a city which, by the 1980s, after two decades of economic decline, was on the brink of 'city death', with disastrous levels of unemployment, out-migration of young people, appalling race relations, and a deteriorated and neglected built environment. How can a city regenerate from such despair and demoralization?

There were, according to Newman and Kenworthy's account (1999), three catalysts. The first was community mobilization around housing rehabilitation. The second was a major effort to combat racism – starting an arts anti-racism programme, and tackling racism in the police force. But it was the opening of the Museum of Slavery in the new Albert Dock tourism complex that had the greatest symbolic and spiritual impact. This award-winning museum shows how Liverpool was central to the slave trade. It graphically depicts the whole process of slavery, and names the many established Liverpool families who made their fortunes from slavery. Here is a case where the telling of a buried story provides some grounds for healing a divided city, and, in so doing, acts as a catalyst for regeneration and growth.

My detailed analysis of a social planner's response to a cross-cultural planning dispute (in Chapter 7) argued that her therapeutic approach was able to create new understandings and meanings through multicultural conversations. But I also argued that the political space had to be created for such an intervention, and this refocuses our attention on the critical role of mobilized communities, putting pressure on politicians and political institutions, which in turn redirects the works of planning staff. Citizens and their political representatives are always key players in the planning environment, partners in the struggle to build *cosmopolis*.

TOWARDS AN AUDACIOUS PLANNING PRACTICE: DARING TO BREAK THE RULES

If there's any organization that's notorious for being risk-averse, it's 'the bureaucracy'. But so too are politicians and thus, of necessity, the planners who serve them. The essence of twentieth-century planning was regulatory, rule-bound, procedure-driven, obsessed with order and certainty: in a word, inflexible (Jacobs, 1962; Sennett, 1970). But when the world's changing around you, it's often not appropriate to stick to the rules, to the tried and true, nor for that matter to cling to whatever is the main oppositional ideology – to simply assert the opposite of what's currently conventional wisdom/dominant ideology. Neither anti-globalization nor anti-state intervention postures contain the mix of imaginations required for the complexities of 21st century urban life.

For politicians involved in urban governance, the greatest risk of all is to think beyond the short term, yet that is precisely what's necessary when the sustainability of cities is at stake. The second greatest risk is to involve the public in decision-making (as opposed to mere consultation), because that involves surrendering some control, and people who hold power are not usually predisposed to share or devolve it. Building better cities depends on both these things happening, and the most likely way to bring it about is through an active citizenry applying pressure at all levels of government, along with a critical media. The now much-celebrated, decade-long, successful experiment in municipal participatory budgeting in the Brazilian city of Porto Alegre (Abers, 2000) was originally a huge risk, not least because the city had minimal financial resources. But the Workers Party was elected to office on such a promise, and carried it out, and the results have demonstrated the capacities of ordinary, not highly educated citizens to debate among themselves, neighbourhood by neighbourhood, and to establish regional and metropolitan spending priorities for urban infrastructure, all of which has pleasantly surprised the most sceptical advocates of participatory democracy.

Another extraordinary example of risk-taking on the part of politicians in partnership with planners and citizens began in the city of Oak Park, on the western political boundary of the city of Chicago. Middle-class Oak Park initiated a policy of residential racial openness in the late 1960s, in the face of surrounding municipalities' policies of racial segregation. Collectively, residents chose to fight exclusion rather than join the forces of white flight (Chapter 6). They chose to become 'diversity pioneers', to regard integration as a positive experience, defining the challenge as one of management rather than resistance (Martin and Warner, 2000: 272). In 1972, the minority population was an almost invisible 1 per cent. By 2002, it was 23 per cent, and the key institution behind this success, the Oak Park Housing Center (OPHC), had initiated a regional outreach programme to clone Oak Park's efforts in the wider western metropolitan region. The OPHC worked in a very people-oriented, micro-political way, apartment block by

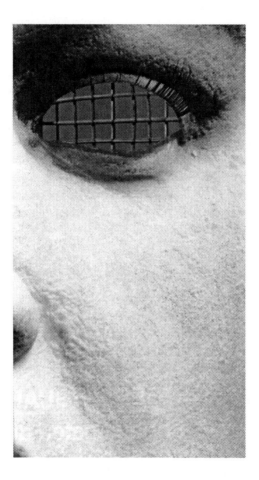

apartment block, street by street, anticipating and managing fears in whatever creative ways it could.

The shifts in institutional cultures that are required in order to create *cosmopolis* call for strong, visionary leadership that encourages and rewards exposure to new ideas and risk-taking. That in turn calls for listening to a wider range of voices, for fostering a vibrant public realm, and for the democratizing of decision-making. People don't usually participate for the sheer exhilaration of exercising their democratic rights. They participate when there is a likelihood that their time commitment will have consequences, set new things in motion.

When Wendy Sarkissian was hired by the South Sydney Council to sort out the conflicts between residents in the Redfern neighbourhood, she took huge personal and professional risks in choosing the path of therapeutic planning. But in so doing, she showed that it is possible to find other ways to resolve conflicts. When Ken Reardon took his white students from Urbana-Champaign into the Black neighbourhoods of East St Louis he was similarly taking personal and professional risks in forging new solutions (a community-university partnership) to exclusion and poverty. For planners, the essence of risk-taking is learning to surrender the obsession with control and certainty and developing the ability to listen to the voices of multiple publics. It would be safe to say that nothing new enters the world without a certain amount of risk-taking on someone's part, and that encouraging a culture of risk-takers is essential for managing our co-existence in the mongrel cities of the 21st century.

EXPANDING THE CREATIVE CAPACITIES OF PLANNERS

But risk-taking by itself is useless without creativity, without new ideas about how to do things. Creativity itself comes in many forms, and this brief discussion cannot do justice to the subject. Where do new ideas come from? How can creative thinking be encouraged? How can our cities and planning institutions be more creative places?

Visionary leadership can be important in creating a climate conducive to new ideas. A good leader or manager is a person who recognizes creativity and gives it space to flourish, who creates an environment in which exposure to new ideas and experimentation is rewarded, and who demonstrates by example, taking risks herself. Constable Tom Woods of the Victoria, BC, Police Force, stepped way outside his job description in coming up with the idea of the Rock Solid Foundation as a way of addressing violent behaviour among local youths. Woods became a *de facto* community development planner, in providing a venue and activities for teenagers (Chapter 8), but he also became a therapeutic planner in his willingness to listen to the teenagers talk about their lives, and by recognizing their artistic creativity. One or more of his superior officers had to recognize the value of Woods' idea, and provide the time for him to implement it. That was good leadership, thinking beyond customary job descriptions and addressing a problem in new ways.

In participatory action research, planners place their trust to some extent in the creativity of residents. Ken Reardon and his planning crew in East St Louis were inspired by the creative solutions, including the political creativity, of local residents in a situation of minimal material resources. The ability to make space for the creativity of ordinary folks to emerge might be considered another important planning skill. A number of community-based planners in North America have discussed their successful experiences with this way of working.[4]

Consultant Charles Landry has written specifically about the creative city (Hall and Landry, 1997; Landry, 2000). Having worked with Landry, I've noticed that one of his talents is the ability to see apparent weaknesses as potential strengths. For example, working in Helsinki he learnt that there is an illness, referred to as SAD, which descends on many residents as winter sets in. SAD stands for seasonal affective disorder, and is a depression caused by light deprivation. Landry and his colleagues undertook an 'image survey' among residents that was based on associative thinking, in order to find a means of discussing the city in new terms. He asked residents what Helsinki would be in terms of 40 associations, including: if Helsinki were a colour, a car, a fruit, a musical instrument, or a song, what would it be? (It came out as dark blue, a Volvo, a raspberry, a flute, and the song 'Silence is Golden'.) Looking at the meanings in the subsequent analysis helped Landry to define a cultural strategy for the city based on the importance of light, inclusiveness, and female strengths. None of this would have come about using traditional thinking paths.

Landry began to explore light in all its guises, quickly picking up on such local traditions as candles burning in windows, the placing of candles on graves, the Lucia candle parade, and the lights that mark Independence Day. He also noticed that Finnish lighting design was cutting edge, but not as well known as that of the Italians. He conceived a winter Festival of Light, a two-week event that could turn the weakness of the dark into a strength. The first festival was staged in November–December of 1995 with a budget of £30,000. It is now an annual event that has grown ten-fold, and in unexpected ways. The original concept involved lights fanning out from the central station square, and lantern projects and parades spreading inwards from the suburbs, thus linking, through the symbolism of light, the different parts of the city. Today the festival not only generates a whole series of local projects (including trade events that feature lighting), but also attracts international collaboration as well as becoming a brand name for Helsinki (Landry, 2000: 87–9).

Landry has spent more time than most planning practitioners, I suspect, in thinking about creativity. Creating new ideas, he writes, may involve originating completely new ideas or developing new ideas from old ones. Association, analogy, and metaphor are ways of bringing together by force seemingly incompatible concepts: by making the familiar strange, and the strange familiar (Landry, 2000: 179). Other techniques range from brainstorming to mindmapping, daydreaming to visualization: and a whole slew of techniques developed by Edward de Bono to encourage thinking laterally (De Bono, 1971; 1996). Landry has used a 'survey of the senses' to analyse the city through its sounds, smells, panoramas, at different times of the day and night. This changes conventional ways of discovering possibilities by getting decision-makers to connect with their visceral experiences of city life (Landry, 2000: 180). The senses can be a creative resource.

There is another form of creativity that I have drawn out of some of the stories discussed in Chapters 6, 7 and 8. This is the capacity to *imagine* a different story, a different outcome, a different way of being or relating. The community leaders in East St Louis had that capacity, and the faith to act on it. Wendy Sarkissian had that capacity, as did the people of Oak Park in Chicago, along with their politicians, and housing policy folks. Can this kind of imagination be taught? Possibly. It can certainly be discussed, encouraged, and nurtured through story (Chapter 8).

Another way of tapping, releasing, and nurturing imagination in planning is by working collaboratively with artists. The Welfare State International (WSI) is a company of artists formed in the UK in 1968, now internationally acclaimed for its work with and in communities in processes of change and transformation (Coult and Kershaw, 1990). Initially oriented to popular and political theatre, WSI subsequently became interested in myth, ritual, carnival, festival, street parades, puppetry, feasts, and more. Emblazoned on the side of the company's touring truck is the logo, 'Engineers of the Imagination', reflecting their belief that recovery of imagination is a vital partner and precondition of change through more analytical and rational methods. In a world where local and diverse cultures are increasingly threatened by a largely imposed electronic culture, WSI's mission is to rediscover and invent new hybrid myths and archetypes, new celebrations, and new forms of protest. Working for political and social change in and with communities, these 'civic magicians' (Kershaw, 1990) understand empowerment, teaching people the skills necessary to make their own celebrations and protests as part of the company's 'process'. In their 35-year life, these artists have worked in an extraordinary variety of scales, types of 'performance space', operational modes, and cultural contexts, from one-man back-pack story telling to giant processional imagery; from cathedrals to London docksides; from touring shows in the company's bus, the 'Lantern Coach' (the second smallest theatre in the world), to long-term community residencies; from international festivals to intimate local events. They have survived on grants from arts agencies, local and national governments, and increasingly find themselves in international demand from local planning departments not only to organize public celebrations and transform public space, but also to train local communities in these diverse skills (Coult and Kershaw, 1990).

Vancouver has its own version of WSI, in the Public Dreams Society (PDS), founded by Dolly Hopkins who, like the artists in WSI, has a background in theatre performance. The PDS brings together artists and the public (at the instigation either of local communities or the City of Vancouver, or both), incorporating art, music, theatre, dance, puppetry, pyrotechnics, street and circus performance in the creation of interactive community events like the Lantern Parade around Trout Lake on the evening of the Day of All Souls, or the First Night celebrations on Granville Island. The mandate of the PDS is to 'revive and redefine community arts and the role of the artist in the community' (Hii, 2002). The appearance of PDS productions in the eastern neighbourhoods of the city is not accidental. These are lower-income areas that have previously not shared in city celebrations (Brock 2002). PDS events encourage people of diverse backgrounds to celebrate difference in public arenas; ignored public spaces are re-born; creative impulses are released; fears are confronted and embraced. Communities reclaim the streets and

public spaces through these events, and the skills and experiences of individuals are broadened.

Often there are groups of people who have been excluded from 'the urban conversation' (Landry, 2000) for silly reasons – like age (being too old, or too young), or gender (being a woman, in some cultures), or being newcomers. Working with artists is a way of bringing such groups into the urban conversation, as well as introducing new forms of expression and new ways of thinking into planning processes. Organizations like WSI and PDS, working in and with residents and planners, have the capacity to build community, to cross cultures, to confront fears and nurture hopes, and to transform public spaces through their magic and mystery, their intuitive and visceral methods, their 'celebratory excesses' and 'radical criticism' (Kershaw, 1990).

Yes Ebenezer, the recovery of imagination is possible, and it is coming to a city near you.

MAINTAINING A CRITICAL SENSIBILITY

One of my arguments in preceding chapters has been that we need to reconceptualize planning as a process that involves organizing hope, negotiating fears, mediating memories, daring to break the rules, and so on. But what changes simply by reconceptualizing planning's tasks? A critical planning theorist might ask what power relationships have changed or are changing? Where is the understanding of political interests: of class, gender, race and ethnic power? My reply is twofold. First, social representation matters. If we only talk or write books documenting the hegemonic power of capital, or patriarchy, or governmentality, we are not simply reflecting reality but helping to constitute or reproduce it.[5] My discursive struggle in this book has been to emphasize, rather than to sweep under the carpet, alternative forms of planning, alternative imaginations and practices.

My second response is that, ultimately, a critical sensibility is always asking who is getting what, where, and how (is power operating) in the distribution of goods, services, and opportunities in a specific place at a specific historical moment. Maintaining a critical sensibility in planning does not mean adopting one or more of the many varieties of critical theory at large in the world, and boxing the operations of planning into its iron cage. It means maintaining a critical awareness of and openness to those theories for what they can illuminate in specific contexts about the operations of power. It also means maintaining a scepticism about the 'will to plan' and the 'improving impulse' out of which it grew,[6] best expressed in twentieth-century confidence about scientific and technological progress – a mentality that was unscientifically optimistic about the possibilities for the comprehensive planning of human settlements.

It was not only capital, or patriarchy, which got in the way of those dreams. The administrative ordering of society and nature proved an equally formidable enemy. The seemingly unremarkable tools of modern statecraft, tools of measurement, accounting, mapping, record-keeping, are tools vital to our well-being and freedom. They undergird the concept of citizenship and the provision of social welfare. But they are also constitutive of a new social order: privileging the centre and the synoptic view, and marginalizing local knowledges. As James C. Scott puts it in his marvelous book, *Seeing Like a State*, 'the builders of the modern nation-state do not merely describe, observe, and map: they strive to shape a people and landscape to fit their techniques of observation' (Scott, 1998: 82). Thus, categories that begin as artificial conventions of cartographers, census takers, police officers, and urban planners can end by becoming categories that organize people's daily existence, precisely because they are embedded in state institutions that structure that experience. The state is thus the vexed institution that is the ground of both our freedoms and unfreedoms (Scott, 1998). A critical vigilance about the operations of the state must be second nature to planners. But so too must there be a symmetrical vigilance about the operations of mobilized communities, always asking who is excluded from the 'we' of any self-defined community, and the causes for which they are mobilized.

EXPANDING THE LANGUAGE OF PLANNING

I've talked so far about five qualities that would help reshape 21st-century cities and planning. In Chapter 8, I made a case for the importance of story and story telling. In this final section, I want to connect the idea of story with the notion of an expanded language for planning, a language that can encompass the lived experience of mongrel cities: the joys, hopes, fears, the senses of loss, expectation, adventure. In planning's postwar rush to join the social sciences, some of its capacity to address important urban issues was lost because it turned its back on questions of values, of meaning, and of the arts (rather than science) of city-building. The language, and the mental and emotional universe of planning, was thus constricted. We can and must expand this universe by being more attuned to the city of memory, the city of desire, and the city of spirit: these are what animate life in cities, and they are also what animate urban conflicts (whose memories are respected? whose desires are fulfilled? what spirit of place seduces us?). Planners with those five qualities that I've described above are more likely to be attentive to these vital dimensions of urban life than those who are obsessed with technical skills or wearing the protective armour of the policy sciences.

CITY OF MEMORY

Why do we visit graves? Why do we erect sculptures to dead leaders or war heroes or revolutionaries? Why do we save love letters for 30 or 40 years or more? Why do we make photo albums, home movies, write diaries and journals? Why do we visit the sites of cave paintings at Lascaux, at Kakadu? Because memory, both individual and collective, is deeply important to us. It locates us as part of something bigger than our individual existences, perhaps makes us seem less insignificant, sometimes gives us at least partial answers to questions like 'Who am I?' and 'Why am I like I am?'. Memory locates us, as part of a family history, as part of a tribe or community, as a part of city-building and nation-making. Loss of memory is, basically, loss of identity. People suffering from amnesia or Alzheimer's are adrift in a sea of confusion. To take away a person's memories is to steal a large part of their identity. Whether or not we are one of those people who likes to 'dwell on the past', the past dwells in us and gives us our sense of continuity, anchoring us even as we move on. Cities are the repositories of memories, and they are one of memory's texts. We revisit the house(s) we grew up in, we show our new lover the park where, as a kid, we had our first kiss, or where students were killed by police in an anti-war demonstration . . . Our lives and struggles, and those of our ancestors, are written into places – houses, neighbourhoods, cities – investing them with meaning and significance.

Modernist planners became thieves of memory. Faustian in their eagerness to erase all traces of the past in the interest of forward momentum, of growth in the name of progress, their 'drive-by' windscreen surveys of neighbourhoods that they had already decided (on the basis of objective census and survey data) to condemn to the bulldozer, have been, in their own way, as deadly as the more recent drive-by gang shootings in Los Angeles. Modernist planners, embracing the ideology of development as progress, have killed whole communities, by evicting them, demolishing their houses, and dispersing them to edge suburbs or leaving them homeless. They have killed communities and destroyed individual lives by not understanding the loss and grieving that go along with losing one's home and neighbourhood and friends and memories (Marris, 1974). Since nobody knows how to put a monetary value on memory, or on a sense of connection and belonging, it always gets left out of the model.

This is not an argument against change. (Change can be for better or worse, depending in part on how it happens. Decaying and growing, cities can't choose to stay the same. They have to choose all the time between alternative changes – blight or renewal, replacements or additions, extensions outwards or upwards, new congestions or new expenditures.) It is rather an argument for the importance of memory, for the need to pay attention to it, to understand that communities can and do go through grieving processes, to acknowledge these in some sort of ritual way. We need to remind ourselves of the importance of memory, and of ritual in dealing with loss. If we need to destroy, as part of our city-building, we also need to heal.

Recent work by planner-historians Gail Dubrow (1998; Dubrow and Goodman, 2002; Dubrow and Graves, 2002), Dolores Hayden (1995), and John Kuo Wei Tchen (1990), among others, indicates that there is a new multicultural sensibility at work in planning. Hayden's work in public history and public space dwells on the ways in which public space can help to nurture a sense of cultural belonging and at the same time acknowledge and respect diversity. She writes of the power of ordinary urban landscapes to nurture citizens' public memory, and notes that this power remains untapped for most working people's neighbourhoods in most American cities, and for most ethnic history and women's history. Urban landscapes are storehouses for individual and collective social memories. Moving beyond the familiar architectural approach to cultural heritage which favours individual buildings, Hayden argues for a deeper understanding of the entire urban cultural landscape as an important part of American history, emphasizing the social and political meanings of vernacular buildings (factories, union halls, tene-ments); ending the invisibility of the history of all but the white Anglo occupiers; and connecting the history of struggle over urban space with 'the poetics of occupying particular places' (Hayden, 1995: 12).

Both individuals and communities need to find ways to connect to the larger urban narrative. Some urban planners are now working with artists, anthropologists, land-scape architects, archaeologists, and communities to do just that in public history and public art, community mapping, and urban landscape projects that seek a more socially and culturally inclusive approach to our urban memories. One beautiful example of this is research by Dubrow and Graves (2002) on the previously undocumented built environment and cultural landscape associated with Japanese communities on the West coast of the United States – community halls, temples, hospitals, language schools, midwiferies, and the Japanese-style public bath houses known as *sento*. Drawing on vintage photographs, personal memories culled from oral histories, and research on historic places, the authors of this study have made visible the once-thriving urban communities that were destroyed after Executive Order 9066 in 1942 forced the internment of all Japanese residents on the West coast for the duration of World War II. By contributing to a deeper knowledge of this history, the authors hope to assist in new claims of historic preservation of what remains of Japanese American heritage.

CITY OF DESIRE

Why do we enjoy sitting alone in a coffee shop, or outdoor café, or on a park bench, apparently day-dreaming? If city dwelling is in part about the importance of memory and belonging, it is also about the pleasures of anonymity and of not having to belong. These are closely related to desire, to sexual desires and fantasies. We sit on a bus, empty seat beside us, watching new passengers come on board, wondering whether anyone will sit next to us, and, if so, who? This is the thrill and the fear of the chance encounter (Epstein, 1998). We sit on the beach or stroll through a park, watching others and being watched, and in that watching are hidden fantasies and desires, sometimes unacknow-ledged, other times a conscious searching.

This is the eroticism of city life, in the broad sense of our attraction to others, the pleasure and excitement of being drawn out of one's secure routine to encounter the novel, the strange, the surprising. We may not want to partake. But we enjoy the parade. If city life is a coming together, a 'being together of strangers' (Young, 1990: 237), we need to create public spaces that encourage this parade, that acknowledge our need for spectacle – not the authorized spectacle of the annual parade or the weekly football game, but the spontaneous spectacle of strangers and chance encounters. Yet the oppos-ite is happening. Planners are systematically demolishing such spaces in the name of the flip side of desire – fear (Chapter 5).

The city of desire – and its place in city planning – is one of the aspects of city life that has only just begun to (re)surface in writings about the city.[7] There are many themes to be unraveled and stories yet to be told relating to desire and the city, to sexuality and space. Elizabeth Wilson's *The Sphinx in the City* (1992) argues that the anonymity of big cities has been liberating for women (at the same time as it increases our jeopardy from sexual assault); and George Chauncey (1994: 135) makes the same point with respect to gay men, in his history of gay New York, noting how many gays have moved from the oppressive, homophobic atmosphere of small towns to the anonymity of New York, with its many identifiable places for cruising, looking for dates, for simply being freer to be one's true self. In Barbara Hooper's account of the origins of modern planning in nineteenth-century Paris, 'The Poem of Male Desires', the role of desire on the one hand, and fear of it on the other, produces the desire to control desire, which Hooper argues has been a central organizing theme of planning practice.

In making the hitherto invisible visible – that is, the significance of desire, of eros, in urban life – we also make it discussable. In breaking the taboo, the silence, we move slowly towards a richer understanding of urban life and of what has been left out of planners' models and histories. But there is much more to the City of Desire than eros, as philosopher Iris Young has suggested:

> The city's eroticism also derives from the aesthetics of its material being: the bright and colored lights, the grandeur of its buildings, the juxtaposition of architecture of different times, styles and purposes. City space offers delights and surprises. Walk around the corner, or over a few blocks, and you encounter a different spatial mood, a new play of sight and sound, and new interactive movement. The erotic meaning of the city arises from its social and spatial inexhaustibility. A place of many places, the city folds over on itself in so many layers and relationships that it is incomprehensible. One cannot 'take it in', one never feels as though there is nothing new and interesting to explore, no new and interesting people to meet.
>
> (Young, 1990: 240)

The city of desire is also an imagined city of excitement, opportunity, fortune. It is what brings millions of people from the countryside to the big city – Nordestinos to São Paolo, Turks to Frankfurt, Anatolians to Istanbul, Michoacans to San Diego, the Hmong to Chicago, the people of the Maghreb to Paris. It fuels dreams. By not understanding the power of such dreams, or by dismissing them as irrational, planners' own dreams of rational control of migration processes, of orderly human settlements, will remain just that – dreams. The daily stories of border-crossings (for example, from Mexico into the United States), crossings in which people all too often risk, and sometimes lose, their lives, illustrates the point. Such is the power of the city of desire, a power strikingly rendered in Gregory Nava's movie *El Norte*, and John Sayles' *Lone Star*, both of which also show how easily the city of desire may become the inferno.

One symptom of the narrowness of modernist planners' horizons is the fact that they find it very hard to focus on desires rather than needs. A need is supposedly an objectifiable entity, identified in 'needs surveys': 'I need a more frequent bus service'; 'I need more police patrols in my neighbourhood'. A desire, by contrast, involves the subconscious, a personal engagement, dreams and feelings, an ability to intuit the atmosphere and feeling of a place. How does the city of desire translate into planning? Perhaps by giving more attention to places of encounter, specifically those which are not commercialized – the street, the square – and which are not placed under the gaze of surveillance technologies. Perhaps also by recognizing that some places of encounter must necessarily be appropriated, and not trying to regulate the uses of all public spaces.[8]

CITY OF SPIRIT

What draws many of us to visit places like Machu Picchu, Stonehenge, the Dome of the Rock or the Wailing Wall in Jerusalem, the Kaaba stone at Mecca, Chartres, or Uluru, in the apparently empty centre of Australia? Why do certain mountains, springs, trees, rocks, and other features of landscape assume symbolic and sacred values to certain peoples and cultures? Historically we have invested our surroundings, urban as well as non-urban, with sacred or spiritual values, and we have built shrines of one sort or another as an acknowledgement of the importance of the sacred, the spiritual, in human life. The completely profane world, the wholly desacralized cosmos, is a recent deviation in the history of the human spirit. Beginning perhaps in the nineteenth century we have created landscapes, cityscapes, devoid of the sacred, devoid of spirit. The tall chimneys that arose in the nineteenth-century factory landscape (Mumford's 'Coketown') and the skyscrapers of the late twentieth-century city, perhaps symbolize the excessive dominance of the masculine *yang* force and its values. From East Germany and Russia to California or the Mississippi Delta, parts of the devastated countryside are left sterile and dead, a monument to the consequences of human rapacity unchecked by considerations of spirit. We are so deadened by our western industrial landscapes that we now go in search of comfort to Aboriginal songlines or Native American sacred places.

Perhaps it's time to re-introduce into our thinking about cities and their regions the importance of the sacred, of spirit. In his superb book about black and white Australians' relationship to the Australian landscape, *Edge of the Sacred* (1995), David Tacey calls for such a 'resacralization' as a social and political necessity. 'White Man Got No Dreaming' was the partial title of a book by anthropologist W. E. H. Stanner (1979). The Aboriginal Dreaming and western rationality stand to each other as thesis to antithesis. What the one affirms, the other denies. In Aboriginal cosmology, landscape is a living field of spirits and metaphysical forces (Tacey, 1995: 148). Our English word 'landscape', as the Australian poet Judith Wright has pointed out, is wholly inadequate to describe the earth-sky-water-tree-spirit-human continuum that is the existential ground of the Aboriginal Dreaming. Obviously white Australians cannot appropriate Aboriginal cosmology, tacking it on to their own overly-rational consciousness, and nor can alienated North Americans adopt the cosmology of Native Americans (although much of so-called new-age spirituality, the world over, seems to be attempting something very much like that). But there are western traditions of re-enchantment to which we might connect, and one way of connecting is through the collaboration between artists and communities outlined in the previous section. Perhaps our modernist/progressive longing for freedom from the non-rational is inherently flawed, out of date and out of touch with enduring human needs.

How can cities/human settlements nurture our unrequited thirst for the spirit? In the European Middle Ages, it was in the building of cities around cathedrals. But that was long ago. In the more secular cities of today, at least in the West, life does not revolve around the cathedral, although in many communities the church, synagogue or mosque continues to play a vital role in social organization. But if we look at cities as centres of spontaneous creativity and festival, then we come closer to an appreciation of the presence of spirit around us. Our deepest feelings about city and community are expressed on special occasions such as carnivals and festivals. Creativity is not only found in art galleries or heard in symphony halls. The nourishing of the spirit, or soul, needs daily space and has everyday expressions: a group of students in a coffee shop discussing plans for a protest; an elderly Chinese man practising his tai chi on the beach or in a park; amateur musicians performing in front of cafés and museums; an old woman tending her flowers in a community garden; kids skateboarding among the asphalt landscaping of sterile bank plazas; lantern parades through city streets on the winter solstice . . . Rational planners have been obsessed with controlling how and when and which people use public as well as private space. Meanwhile, ordinary people continue to find creative ways of appropriating spaces and creating places, in spite of planning, to fulfil their desires as well as their needs, to tend the spirit as well as take care of the rent.

There is another dimension to the city of spirit that has begun to actively engage some planners, in collaboration with artists and communities. That is the process of identifying what we might call 'sacred places' in the urban landscape. The works of Hayden (1995), Dubrow (1998), and Kenney (1995; 2001) are suggestive. Kenney's work in mapping gay and lesbian activism in Los Angeles reveals the connections between place and collective identity which are at the heart of gay and lesbian experience of the city (Kenney, 2001). In her essay 'Remember, Stonewall was a riot', she evokes Stonewall – the scene of three days of rioting in Greenwich Village in 1969 in protest at police entrapment and harassment in a bar frequented by African American and Puerto Rican drag queens – as essentially a sacred site for the gay and lesbian movement (Kenney 1995). The labour movement, the women's movement, African Americans, Japanese Americans, and Native Americans could each name such 'sacred urban places', and have begun to do so, and to commemorate such sites.

In a creative twist on this theme of sacred sites, '*The New Charleston*' project is an exhaustive look at one city and the spatial history of African Americans within it over three centuries (Hayden, 1995: 69). This is a project in which an artist, in collaboration with a poet and an architect, developed a detailed map of historic places of importance to African Americans – slave markets, the hanging tree, community centres – and painted this map onto the wooden floor of a public room. The map serves as a stage for performances by African American musicians. The map is actually a complex layering of physical and social history. There are 14 places, 'Spiritual Signposts', each marked with a crossroads sign of Congolese origin. The art work functions not only as a performance space but also as a cosmogram, a 'description of the universe of the African American story', and as an image of a water journey, delineating the waterways that slaves travelled, from Sierra Leone all the way to Charleston Harbor (Hayden, 1995: 72). We might describe this as a *created* sacred space, as opposed to the struggle for the recovery of actual, erased sacred spaces.

What the above discussion suggests is the need for a diversity of spaces and places in the city: places loaded with visual stimulation, but also places of quiet contemplation, uncontaminated by commerce, where the deafening noise of the city can be kept out so that we can listen to the 'noise of stars' or the wind or water, and the voice(s) within ourselves. An essential ingredient of planning beyond the modernist paradigm is a reinstatement of inquiry about and recognition of the importance of memory, desire, and spirit, as vital dimensions of healthy human settlements, and a sensitivity to cultural differences in the expressions of each.

THE WORK OF THE SONGLINES

I've argued that in working towards more creative and sustaining multicultural cities, we need some new models of planning practice which expand the language of planning beyond the realm of instrumental rationality and the system world, and speak about (and develop the skills for) organizing hope, negotiating fear, mediating memory, and daring to break rules, as well as developing the habits of a critical/analytical mind. This transformed language would reflect the emotional breadth and depth of the lived experience of cities: cities of desire, cities of memory, cities of play and celebration, cities of fear and paranoia, cities of struggle. The new planning imagination embodied in this work is political and critical, creative and therapeutic, and audacious.

The sensibility underpinning this transformation includes the ability to tell, to listen to, and, above all, make space for stories to be heard. We use stories in various ways: to keep memory alive, to celebrate our history/identity; to derive lessons about how to act effectively; to inspire action; and as a tool of persuasion in policy debates. We uncover buried stories. We create new stories. We invent metaphors around which policy stories pivot. Stories, carefully told and carefully heard, have the potential to act as a bridge between ingrained habits and new futures. Stories can (usefully) disrupt habits of thought and action that control everyday life. The will to change has to come from an ability – a planner's ability and also a city user's ability – to imagine oneself in a different skin, a different story, a different place, and then desire this new self and place that one sees. An effective story telling practice is perhaps that which is able to conscript readers or residents to *suspend their habits of being and come out in the open and engage in dialogue with strangers.*

I've provided examples of this kind of planning work, from all over the world, which I think of as the work of the Songlines. So let me finally explain this allusion. Pre-colonial Australia was the last landmass on earth peopled neither by farmers nor by city dwellers but by hunter gatherers. Along a labyrinth of invisible pathways, known to us as Songlines, the Aboriginals travelled in order to perform all those activities that are distinctly human – song, dance, marriage, exchange of ideas, and arrangements of territorial boundaries by agreement rather than by force. The Songlines, in Aboriginal culture, are what sustain life. The task of a new planning imagination is to search for the *city's songlines*, for all that is life sustaining, in the face of the inferno.

NOTES

INTRODUCTION

1. For example, according to the 2001 census, in the City of Vancouver, the population is divided almost equally between residents with English as their mother tongue and those whose language is other than English, with Chinese being the next largest group, at 26 per cent, followed by Punjabi (2.6 per cent), Tagalog (2.3 per cent), Vietnamese (2.1 per cent), and French (1.9 per cent). Of metropolitan Vancouver's 1.9 million population, there were 754,800 residents for whom neither English nor French was their mother tongue. In the municipalities of Richmond and Burnaby, fewer than half the residents report English as their mother tongue. Looking at Collingwood, a neighbourhood of 42,000 people within the City of Vancouver that will be the subject of attention in Chapter 6, the Chinese population has grown from 21 per cent in 1986 to 44 per cent in 1996, while the English-speaking population in that period went from 52 per cent to 10 per cent (Dang, 2002). Such significant demographic changes are requiring municipalities to address cultural diversity in every dimension of local policy and service delivery.

2. But see Castells (1997) for a counter-argument about the power of social movements, which he refers to as 'the power of identity'.

3. The present and future multiculturalism, diversity, and emerging pluralism in Asia has been noted in the following: Denoon, et al., 1996; Nirwan, 1997; Wu, McQueen and Yamamoto, 1997; Lim, 2001; Douglass, 1999; Douglass and Roberts, 2000; Zhang, 2001. Douglass (2002) discusses the implications of lowered fertility on notions of national identity and citizenship in Asia.

CHAPTER 1: MODERNIST CITIES AND PLANNING

1. For a useful distinction between modernism, modernity, and modernization see Berman (1982). For a clear exposition of postmodernism as an architecture, a state of mind, an epoch, and a philosophy, see Dear (1986). For a brilliant provocation on whether we have ever been modern, see Latour (1993).

2. A recent reminder was the movie *Rabbit Proof Fence*, directed by the Australian Phil Noyce. It tells the true story of an Australian government policy of forced removal of so-called 'half-caste' Aboriginal children from their parents, a policy that was in place for more than half of the twentieth century. Those children are now referred to in Australia as 'the stolen generations'. The policy was the product of an Enlightenment mindset that imagined European civilization and the White Race as the saviour of the 'lesser races', in this case through the 'benign' approach of allowing full-blood Aborigines to die out, while selected half-castes could breed with white folks, whose children would then, over several generations, ultimately become white. With no irony intended, the government official overseeing this policy was called the Protector of Aborigines.

3. Similar patterns occurred elsewhere. In Australia, peasants from Italy and Greece fitted this bill. In the northern industrial cities of the USA, blacks had arrived from the rural south during the war. In northern European countries, labour was attracted from southern and eastern Europe. And in each case women, who had entered the workforce during wartime when there was a shortage of male bodies, were pushed out again.

4. For an understanding of the ways in which the modern (welfare) state has been an agent of injury, the works of Michel Foucault are seminal. But for a twist, see also Wendy Brown, *States of Injury: Power and Freedom in Late Modernity* (1995). Brown shows how the regulatory demands of the state encourage the formation of political identities not only founded on injury but invested in maintaining an injured status.

5. The remaining costs of around £200 million were footed by a combination of private sector and European Union funds.

6. I return to the problematic of the contradictory state of multiculturalism in Chapter 4.

7. Writings by academics about Birmingham's efforts at revitalization have typically been hypercritical, applying the concept of 'the entrepreneurial city' in dismissive tones, without addressing the question of practical alternatives. Birmingham's residents are, in a sense, more critically discriminating, able to say, yes, this is good, this revitalization, we're proud of our new downtown, but it's not enough. How about doing something for the neighbourhoods?

8. I use the terms 'western cities' and 'western democracies' interchangeably with 'the North', 'advanced industrial societies', 'developed', and 'first world'.

9. The findings were published as *Building Cohesive Communities: A Report of the Ministerial Group on Public Order and Community Cohesion* (London: Home Office, 2001).

10. *The Vancouver Sun*, 23 April 2002, p.A13.

11. *International Herald Tribune*, 5 May 2002, p.1.

12. *The Vancouver Sun*, 1 June 2002, p.A17.

13. This is presumably to avoid more of the recent bad publicity about the living conditions of refugees in remote camps on the Australian continent, where there have been hunger strikes, charges of abuse, and so on.

14. For a brilliant articulation of this notion, in the context of a scathing critique of Australian multiculturalism, see the work of the Lebanese-Australian anthropologist Ghassan Hage, *White Nation: Fantasies of White Supremacy in a Multicultural Society* (1998).

15. Terrorism, and the 'war' against it have introduced a wild card by raising the spectre of a new era of nihilistic anarchism. It remains to be seen, in the wake of the terrorist attacks on the USA on September 11th, whether 'national security' will trump all other policy considerations for an indeterminate period, or whether the medium-term imperatives of an aging, and potentially declining, population will shift the immigration debate in new directions.

16. For instance, the act of planning a highway through a small Aboriginal reserve on the outskirts of Broome was seen by one Native Title claimant as comparable to the nineteenth-century practice of murdering Aboriginal people (Jackson, 1998: 226).

17. In Australia, for instance, the majority of lands returned to Aboriginal ownership since the 1970s have been in central and northern Australia, far from the urbanized coastal regions.

18. As described in Jacobs (1996), the Waugal serpent lives on the high ground, where the State Parliament House now stands. As he travelled across the country, he created the Swan River, and other features on the land. The site of the former brewery was one of Waugal's resting places.

19. Among the pioneering works of the 1980s were Wekerle, Peterson and Morley (1980), Hayden (1981, 1984), Stimpson, Dixler, Nelson and Yatrakis (1981), Birch (1983), Mackenzie (1984), Leavitt (1986), Andrew and Milroy (1988).

20. The sources are too numerous to list in the usual way in the text. For an overview of these debates and an extensive bibliography, see Sandercock and Forsyth (1990, 1992) and Sandercock (1995a).

21. Each of these movements deserves a chapter, but there is a blossoming literature on each. For example, on gay space and urban politics and planning, see Kenney (2001); on the environmental movement, see Gottlieb (1993), and for its connections with planning issues, see Newman and Kenworthy (1999); on disability and the city, see Gleeson (1998, 1999).

22. Haussmann in fact provided a model for the CIAM planner: technocrat, engineer, 'surgeon', incorruptible and autocratic.

23. For the parallel attitude of confidence in master plans and rational process models in the UK, see Keeble (1952) and Gower Davies (1972). Keeble later became a Professor of Planning in Australia, and transported these ideas with him.

24. These are an extension of the argument of Friedmann and Kuester (1994).

25. These objections will be dealt with more thoroughly in Chapter 3.

26. I talk more about the importance of the city of memory, of desire, and of spirit in the final chapter.

27. Roughly mid-way between these two, my

own study of the history of planning in Australia, *Cities for Sale: Property, Politics and Planning* (1st edition 1975, 2nd edition 1990) made the same 'discovery' for Australian planning culture.

28. For leading me to this insight I am indebted to my doctoral student Andrew Jackson, whose Master's thesis on the history and historiography of statistics in Australia (Jackson, 2002) led me to Latour, and thus to thinking about his statement, 'we have never been modern'.

29. I follow Mouffe (2000), Amin (2000) and Hillier (2002) in drawing attention to the need to move beyond the Habermasian ideal concept of rational consensus, to acknowledge the possibility of the permanence of conflict, a conflict arising from the vibrant clash between empowered publics, which can only ever produce fragile and temporary resolutions. Such a shift insists on more attention to the power games in which planning decision-making is inevitably immersed. Chapter 4 develops this concept.

CHAPTER 2: REWRITING PLANNING HISTORY

1. Mel Scott's book was, literally, an official history, in that it was commissioned by the American Institute of Planners on the occasion of the 50th anniversary of the Institute.

2. My own history of Australian city planning from the 1890s to the 1970s, *Cities for Sale: Property, Politics and Urban Planning* (1975), followed this same pattern and adopted more or less the same sets of assumptions, which I subsequently critiqued in the Introduction to the second edition (Sandercock, 1990).

3. The notion of planning 'as a heterosexist project' has been well argued by Frisch (2002).

4. The same lag was evident in architectural history until the late 1990s, but since then there have been a number of significant contributions to the rewriting of that field around the theme of difference. See Lokko (2000), Borden and Rendell (2000), Borden, Kerr, Rendell and Pivaro (2001).

CHAPTER 3: WHO KNOWS? EXPLORING
PLANNING KNOWLEDGES

1. 'Country' is an Aboriginal English term that refers to the collective identity shared by a group of people, their land (and sea) estate and all the natural and supranatural phenomena contained within that estate (Porter, 2002: 16).

2. For a brilliant refutation of this position, and an argument for the 'intelligence of the emotions', see Nussbaum (2001).

3. And in so doing, appears to put himself at odds with advocates of the 'communicative turn', (Forester, Healey, Innes, and others), whom he criticizes for paying too little attention to power and being too focused on consensus.

4. For a brief discussion of the significance of each of these 'schools', see Sandercock 1998a.

5. Foucault did such an analysis for the emergent professions of the eighteenth and nineteenth centuries. Christine Boyer's *Dreaming the Rational City* (1983) is a self-proclaimed Foucauldian analysis, although to this reader it comes across as more of a Marxist account of planning history. Bent Flyvbjerg's micropolitical analysis of power and planning in Aalborg is explicit about its debt to Foucault (Flyvbjerg, 1998). Jean Hillier (2002) draws on Foucault and other French theorists in her analysis of the power dynamics of contemporary planning practice.

6. Porter's research with indigenous groups in south-eastern Australia provides a perfect example of how 'planning's micro-technologies of power operate to domesticate indigenous knowledge and aspirations and ultimately maintain the authority of state planning knowledge' (Porter, 2002: 7).

7. There has been increasing recognition of the validity and importance of murals and graffiti from both community-based and official sources. In Los Angeles, the 'Great Wall of Los Angeles', a mural in the Tujunga Flood Control Channel in North Hollywood, was a seven-year

(1976–83) participatory project which originated in the Mexican-American community, but grew to include African American, Asian and white muralists, and is regarded as a people's history of the city. City power brokers are now concerned with the preservation/restoration of these murals, given their potential for cultural tourism (Tannenbaum, 2002). From a community development perspective, the work of the Rock Solid Foundation in Victoria, British Columbia, in trying to direct young people away from violence, has focused on establishing an 'outdoor gallery' for graffiti artists (the Trackside Art Gallery), located along a railway right of way between two rows of warehouses in an industrial park. The specific intent is to increase the profile of graffiti as a communicative art form (visit *www.rocksolid.bc.ca*).

8. In Chapter 8, I will build on this epistemology of multiplicity to develop the idea of *planning as performed story*, and to discuss the ways in which stories and story telling are central to planning and provide the core of a planning imagination for the 21st century.

CHAPTER 4: MONGREL CITIES

1. The following description is taken from James Tully's account of the sculpture (Tully, 1995: 17–18).

2. Strangely, Donald sidesteps racism, the dark side of cultural difference. Even 'assimilated' Jews in pre-war Europe remained Other, and anti-semitism was always latent. The same still goes for 'Blacks' today, not only in the USA, but also in Canada, the UK and even Brazil. I have a black student in my class at UBC who has lived in Canada for 25 years. Recently (November 2002), he was interrogated on the street by a complete stranger, who asked him where he was from. My student answered, 'Vancouver'. 'No, no,' pressed the stranger, 'where are you really from?' My student answered that he was born in Africa, to which the stranger replied, 'You should go back there. We don't want you here.'

3. There was less serious disorder in a number of other places and many more towns, mainly in the north, were identified by police as being at 'significant risk of serious disorder'. The 'disorders' involved hundreds of mainly young people, inflicted injuries on over 400 police, and caused millions of pounds worth of damages (Home Office, 2001: 7).

4. In addition to the Rogers Report (Urban Task Force, 1999) already noted, the writings of Richard Sennett and Iris Young have been much quoted in support of this view of the efficacy of public space.

5. Amin is not dismissive of urban planning efforts to make public spaces more inclusive, safe, and pleasant, and does not diminish the achievements of cities like Leicester or Vancouver in publicizing their commitments to multiculturalism by using public sites to support minority voices, ethnic pluralism, and alternative local histories. His point is rather (and I agree) to caution against raised expectations from the uses of public space for intercultural dialogue and understanding, 'for even in the most carefully designed and inclusive spaces, the marginalized and the prejudiced stay away' (Amin, 2002: 11).

6. For much of my interpretation in this section I am indebted to the work of William Connolly (1991, 1995) and Julia Kristeva (1991).

7. 'Culturally embedded' in the sense that we grow up and live within a culturally structured world, organize our lives and social relations within its system of meaning and significance, and place some value on our cultural identity (Parekh, 2000: 336).

8. Or what Cornell West called 'the new cultural politics of difference' (West, 1990), or James Tully calls the 'politics of cultural recognition' (Tully, 1995).

9. Or as previously dominated groups such as gays and lesbians, women, people with disabilities, decide to engage in a politics of identity/difference, a politics of place-claiming and place-making (Kenney, 2001).

10. See Hage (1998), on Australia; Hesse (2000) and Hall (2000), on the UK; Bannerji (1995, 2000), on Canada.

11. See Chantal Mouffe's discussion of this dilemma in her case for an agonistic democratic politics in *The Democratic Paradox* (2000).

12. Before writing the third draft of this section, I discovered (thanks to Patsy Healey)

Bhikhu Parekh's contribution to the debate, *Rethinking Multiculturalism* (2000), which paral- lels my own thinking. I have incorporated some of his insights.

CHAPTER 5: HOME, NATION, AND STRANGER

1. By late 2002 Haider was no longer head of the FP and the FP is no longer in the coalition.

2. In some academic writing the term 'the Other' has become a shorthand for all of those who are not part of the dominant culture and who are or have been marginalized or excluded. In the interest of a broader readership, I will use 'strangers' or 'outsiders' rather than Other.

3. Much of what follows draws on Sandercock (2002).

4. The classic definition of diaspora is a narrative organized around a homeland, a displacement, and a horizon of return. The classical exemplars of diaspora are the Jews, but recent literature attempts to widen the notion (see Sayyid, 2000; Saint-Blancat, 2002).

5. As is happening in the Berlin neighbourhood of Kreuzberg, for example. When I visited a primary school there in May 2002 there was, on average, only one ethnically German child in each class: the rest of the children were from Turkish, North African and other immigrant groups. The school principal explained that 'German Germans' who still lived in the neighbourhood were not sending their children to the neighbourhood schools.

6. Friedmann's essay, written at the request of the editors of the *Journal of the American Planning Association* in the weeks immediately after September 11th, sets out four topics that he believes are integral to this vision of the Open City: reducing the urban footprint; drafting charters of local citizenship; meeting basic human needs; and working towards new forms of governance at the level of cities and regions (Friedmann, 2002a: 238).

7. Just as in Johannesburg, another city of fear, commercial, financial and retail services have moved out of the downtown and into large centres in homogeneous white middle- and upper-class neighbourhoods like Sandton, and walled communities are being constructed adjacent to these new centres.

8. Phil Harrison 'The role of planners in shaping urban spaces', Urban Futures Conference, Johannesburg, July 2000.

9. Here I'm gratefully drawing on PhD research by Antje Nahnsen of the Carl von Ossietzky University in Germany, as presented at the Urban Futures Conference in Johannesburg, July 2000.

10. Anthropologist Sally Engle Merry (1981) concluded her study of 'urban danger' in Philadelphia by arguing that people tend to think strangers are criminals; eventually, crime becomes a device, an idiom, for thinking about the stranger.

11. Iveson (2000) presents a vivid case study of paranoia about 'youth' in the tranquil west coast Australian city of Perth, where the JAG (Juvenile Aid Group) Team of the metropolitan police force used their powers under child welfare legislation to remove young people not accompanied by their families from the downtown area, in order to make the streets of the city safe for families. One of the catalysts for this draconian practice was the anxieties of shopkeepers, who regarded 'youth' as undermining perceptions of the safety of the city.

12. At a workshop that I was involved in at the University of Iowa in June 2000 on the social sustainability of American cities, one participant, a private detective who works in Oakland, described the fear displayed by tough kids from very tough neighbourhoods once they are outside their own turf. They are very aware of being perceived as 'alien' and as threatening, and therefore of the likelihood of attracting 'preemptive violence', or of being stopped by police 'for being black while driving a car' (Barthels, 2003).

13. For a more hopeful story from Brazil, see Abers (2000), who describes just such an approach, under the leadership of the Workers Party, in the Brazilian city of Porto Alegre, specifically its participatory municipal budget process.

14. See Sandercock (2000a) for an extended discussion of such dialogical/therapeutic approaches to resolving conflicting fears and desires in the city. Chapter 7 develops that discussion further.

CHAPTER 6: THERE IS NO HIDING PLACE

1. This is not meant to deny the counter-hegemonic, or radical, potential of planning, which is the subject of Part III.

2. For an excellent study of the ways in which urban planning has developed, historically, as a heterosexist project antagonistic towards alternative sexualities, see Frisch (2002).

3. An inability on the part of western societies to understand, acknowledge, or accept what is sacred to indigenous societies produces an ongoing source of conflict between the two, which manifests itself frequently in planning disputes (see Jackson, 1998).

4. Chapter 7 tells such a story of the poor Black residents of East St Louis, and their successful struggle to regenerate their abandoned community.

5. See Westin (1996) for Sweden's failure in this respect.

6. Information about Erasmus 2001 was drawn from the website: www.erasmus2001.nl

7. Some of the publications from this research include Dunn et al. (2001a, 2001b); Thompson et al. (1998); Thompson (2003). What follows in this section draws primarily from Thompson (2003).

8. As remarkably harmonious as Canadian society undoubtedly is, and in no small part thanks to multicultural policy, there are nevertheless three significant criticisms of that policy that have emerged over the past three decades. One comes from indigenous communities who argue that their claims (which go beyond calls for 'cultural recognition', to demands for land and sovereignty) cannot be accommodated within a multicultural political framework. A second comes primarily from within 'ethnic communities' and is critical of multicultural policy insofar as it focuses on ethnicity as a primary identification, and encourages ethnic separatism and competition (Bisoondath, 2002). Some of these critics also object that it is only non-whites who are presumed to have an ethnicity, and, further, that ethnicity is only one of many ways of defining a sense of self and of belonging. A third criticism has been that the apparent tolerance expressed in multicultural-ism has actually masked an ongoing and institutionalized racism in Canadian society directed at non-whites (Bannerji, 1995, 2000; Hill, 2001; Henry et al., 2000).

9. In the following discussion of the CNH I draw gratefully on the Masters thesis of Steven Dang, *Creating Cosmopolis: The End of Mainstream* (Dang, 2002), and on conversations with Nathan Edeleson, senior planner with the City of Vancouver Planning Department, and Norma-Jean McLaren, cross-cultural relations consultant.

10. The organization has now diversified its funding sources and developed partnerships with other service providers. There are now over 100 collaborative partners and 30 separate funding agencies provide over 60 different grants.

11. In 1999 it received the City of Vancouver Cultural Harmony Award for having 'consistently demonstrated through its programs and actions a strong commitment to cultural diversity and community harmony' and for developing 'broad programming that brings people of different cultures and backgrounds together' (Dang, 2002: 73).

12. The aboriginal community, for example, has always been seen as needy. People did not see the resources in that culture until residents suggested an arts initiative that invited indigenous artists to do some carving for the façade of the new premises. Through the carving, and participation in other activities, people began to see what Aboriginal people could contribute to the community (Dang, 2002: 85).

13. In the early 1990s, over 1000 residents took part in the planning and construction of the CNH's main facility on Joyce Street. Representatives of various communities, based on age, ability, ethnicity, gender, and socio-economic circumstances, all left their mark on the design of the facility and the policies that govern its operation (Dang, 2002: 89).

14. This approach has been particularly successful in assessing needs among youth and seniors. 'Seniors asking seniors' was one such project, another is an ongoing community youth mapping exercise (Dang, 2002: 77).

15. All communication and information is provided in six languages: English, Chinese, Hindi, Punjabi, Spanish, and Vietnamese. These languages were decided on the basis of actual numbers of speakers in the community, and the likelihood of speakers not to understand one of the other languages.

16. These included banning redlining, doing housing audits to test for diversity, strictly enforcing housing codes, invoking the 'exempt location' clause of the fair housing legislation, licensing and inspecting multi-family buildings, and initiating housing rehabilitation programmes, and ensuring that no outside realtors were allowed to do business in Oak Park (Martin and Warner, 2000; Breems, 2002).

CHAPTER 7: TRANSFORMATIVE PLANNING PRACTICES

1. I take this notion from Pierre Bourdieu, who argues that it is central to all human action of any complexity, and that it enables an infinite number of 'moves' to be made, adapted to the infinite number of possible situations that no rule, however complex, can foresee. I thank Bent Flyvbjerg (2001: 136) for opening my eyes to this interesting way of characterizing practice. The good planner, or 'virtuoso social actor', is thus analogous to a great jazz musician or soccer player, with a repertoire of 'moves' and an instinct, which can be called judgement, about when to use certain moves. Flyvbjerg develops an excellent argument that this 'judgement' (or *phronesis*), in the case of professions like planning, is a form of applied ethics.

2. I first explored this case study in a paper in *Planning Theory and Practice* (Sandercock, 2000a). In this version the analysis has been further developed.

3. Sarkissian was actually working with a team of consultants headed by John O'Grady, a landscape architect and planner from a Sydney firm. Sarkissian was managing the consultation process. The following account is based primarily on discussions with the consultant, Dr Wendy Sarkissian, in October 1999 and October 2002.

4. In describing the mediation practice of Shirley Solomon, working on a dispute between Native Americans and a county government in the state of Washington, John Forester notes that 'the ceremonial design of innovative public policy conversation can be an important signal to all parties that they are about to engage in a different – fresh and non-threatening – kind of exploratory conversation in a different, deliberately designed setting' (Forester, 2000: 151). Solomon moved from the first stage, of creating a safe space, to a second stage, creating a sacred space in which the whole idea was of 'getting to higher ground' (Solomon, in Forester, 2000: 152). Solomon's story, like Sarkissian's, teaches us not only about caution in the face of explosive histories, but also about the place of story telling in setting the stage for beginnings of reconciliation (see Chapter 8).

5. Advocates of approaching the planning endeavour as a communicative action, involving talking, listening, argumentation, shaping attention, and persuasive story telling, include Healey (1992, 1997), Forester (1989, 1999), Innes (1995, 1996, 1998), Innes and Booher (1999), Hoch (1994), and Throgmorton (1996). I build on this work in Chapter 8 in developing an argument for the importance of story in planning practice and research.

6. The distinguished philosopher Martha Nussbaum has contributed most to this argument in her *Upheavals of Thought* (2001), the subtitle of which is '*On the intelligence of the emotions*'. See also Michelle LeBaron (2002).

7. In the field of conflict resolution there is a growing interest in ways of handling cross-cultural conflicts. LeBaron's work (2002) is path-breaking for that field in shifting attention away from material and communication issues to the deeper symbolic/emotional issues. For cross-cultural training methods see Fowler and Mumford (1999).

8. This approach might be described as 'when talk works', which is the title of an excellent collection of essays from the mediation field (Kolb, 1994).

9. For the story of East St Louis I am indebted to papers by Ken Reardon (1998, 2003) and for

conversations with Ken in June 2000. One of the things I want to convey in re-telling his story, is his own exceptional role in this community revitalization.

10. I am indebted to a paper by three University of Birmingham economic geographers (Henry, McEwan and Pollard, 2000) for this insight and for the discussion that follows.

11. I am grateful to Patsy Healey for sharing with me this unpublished paper and for drawing my attention to 'the New Institutionalism'.

12. The discursive heat that has been generated in planning journals, arguing the relative merits of the communicative approach versus some more critical and radical model, seems largely irrelevant when we consider these stories. Communicative and therapeutic work was intrinsic to the process of change in East St Louis, embodied in Ken Reardon as well as Miss Ceola Davis. The empowerment approach depends on a *process* that draws on these skills. And in Redfern, political mobilization was the necessary precondition for the work of communicative and therapeutic planning.

CHAPTER 8: THE POWER OF STORY IN PLANNING

1. Here I'm alluding to the title of Trinh Minh-ha's book, *Woman Native Other* (1989). Minh-ha is a writer, composer and film-maker. I was alarmed to hear that as recently as five years ago at my university (University of British Columbia) a Native woman who proposed to do her Masters thesis by focusing on the stories of her people was told that that was not an appropriate topic or methodology.

2. Barbara Eckstein and Jim Throgmorton conceived and convened a wonderful small workshop at the University of Iowa in summer 2000 on the role of stories in sustaining America's cities. The papers presented at the workshop are published in Eckstein and Throgmorton (2003). My own thinking about this issue benefited greatly from my participation in that workshop, and from the insights of Barbara and Jim.

3. In his comprehensive critique of mainstream social science, Flyvbjerg (2001: 137) argues that 'narratology' is a valuable but underrated research method compared with the more favoured quantitative approaches. 'Narratology, understood as the question of "how best to get an honest story honestly told", is more important than epistemology and ontology.' Flyvbjerg is an advocate of the case study method, with its thick description of character and events, its microscopic detail. His mission is to persuade social scientists of the virtues of this method. Similarly, my mission here is to persuade planners of the transformative possibilities of story. Flyvbjerg perhaps downplays the difficulties of getting 'an honest story honestly told'. I want to highlight some of these difficulties in this chapter.

4. This is why I have always been interested in 'gossip' as an everyday way of knowing/ interpreting the world, in which people exchange apparently small (but not trivial) stories and search out commonalities and differences, as a way of making sense of their world (see Spacks, 1985).

5. Bob Beauregard reminded me of the importance of this element, which he gleaned from a comment by one of his (and my) favourite novelists, Russell Banks.

6. Doug Aberley is a Vancouver-based practitioner who uses elaborate community mapping techniques in his work with indigenous communities. Maeve Lydon is the founder and director of Common Ground Community Mapping Project, a non-profit organization in Victoria, BC, that provides mapping and learning resources for schools, neighbourhoods and communities who want to undertake sustainable community development and planning projects. See Lydon (2002).

7. See Susskind, McKearnan and Thomas-Larmer, 1999; LeBaron, 2002; Fowler and Mumford, 1999; Thiagarajan and Parker, 1999.

8. Eckstein's advice is invaluable: 'if one listens to others' stories with ears tuned to how their stories will serve one's own story telling, how they will fit in one's grander narrative, then one risks not hearing them at all' (Eckstein, 2003).

9. As he did at the University of Iowa story telling workshop convened by Barbara Eckstein and Jim Throgmorton in Summer, 2000.

10. Rosa Parks was the African American woman who, in Alabama in 1955, refused to move to the back of the bus when white folks boarded. This act of civil disobedience turned into a year-long boycott of the bus service by Blacks, and gave birth to the Civil Rights Movement.

11. The School of Community and Regional Planning at the University of New Mexico explicitly bases its pedagogy on this Freirian model.

12. Marris cites Herbert Gans' *The Urban Villagers*, and Michael Young and Peter Willmott's *Family and Kinship in East London* as good examples.

13. The classic value-rational questions are 'Where are we going? Is it desirable? What should be done?' (Flyvbjerg, 2001: 130). For Aristotle, the most important task of social and political studies was to develop society's value rationality vis-à-vis its scientific and technical rationality (*ibid.*: 53). Flyvbjerg argues that for the past 200 years value-rationality has been eclipsed by technical or instrumental rationality. Critics of policy analysis or 'policy science' as a field have argued that it has ignored questions of value (Friedmann, 1987), but in recent years there has been growing interest in value-focused decision-making processes (see Keeney, 1996).

14. The eight volumes of edited transcripts, arranged by substantive content (e.g. 'Mediation in Practice: Profiles of Community and Environmental Mediators') are available from the Department of City and Regional Planning at Cornell University.

15. In *Towards Cosmopolis* I told the stories of two similarly extraordinary teachers, who connect students with communities: Gilda Haas in Los Angeles and Mel King in Boston. (Sandercock 1998a, Chapter 6).

16. That is, as a city welcoming of newcomers, with or without the legal papers.

17. For some hair-raising examples of how planners have used their data dishonestly and deceptively, see Flyvbjerg, Holm and Buhl (2002).

CHAPTER 9: CITY SONGLINES

1. This is an adaptation of Patsy Healey's (1997) definition of planning as managing our co-existence in shared space.

2. I concluded *Towards Cosmopolis* with an Appendix that outlined the five 'literacies' that would produce better planners: technical, analytical, multicultural, ecological, and design literacies. This chapter goes beyond that discussion of basic literacies, into a new planning imagination.

3. The Singaporean architect and scholar William Lim has written eloquently on the importance of this project for Asian countries (Lim, 2001, 2003). Mike Douglass has shown how the changing social realities of Asian countries, including demographic changes, challenge existing concepts of national identity and citizenship in Asia (Douglass, 1999, 2002).

4. See King, 1981; Leavitt and Saegert, 1990; Sandercock, 1998a, Chapter 6; Reardon, 2003.

5. Or, as Gibson-Graham (1996) puts it: it's important to take seriously the 'performativity of social representations', the ways in which they are implicated in the worlds they represent.

6. I could have said a Nietzschean scepticism, acknowledging the 'human, all too human' lament of Nietzsche. The 'enemy' is, in part, ourselves. Beware of those who think they have all the answers.

7. It was certainly there in the writings of Walter Benjamin about Paris in the 'arcades project' in the 1920s and 30s (see Buck-Morss, 1989).

8. Iain Borden's wonderful writings on skateboarding are a good illustration of this point (Borden, 2001).

REFERENCES

ABERS, Rebecca (2000). *Inventing Local Democracy: Grassroots Politics in Brasil.* Boulder, Colorado: Lynne Riener Publishers.

ABU-LUGHOD, Janet (1998). 'Civil/Uncivil Society: Confusing Form with Content', in M. Douglass and J. Friedmann (eds). *Cities for Citizens.* Chichester: John Wiley and Sons.

ADORNO, T. and M. Horkheimer (1982). *Dialectic of Enlightenment.* New York: Continuum (original 1944).

ALBROW, M. (1997). 'Travelling Beyond Local Cultures: Socioscapes in a Global City', in J. Eade (ed). *Living the Global City. Globalization as a Local Process.* London: Routledge.

ALIBHAI-BROWN, Yasmin (2000). 'Diversity versus Multiculturalism', *The Daily Telegraph*, 23 May.

ALIBHAI-BROWN, Yasmin (2002). *After Multiculturalism.* London: Routledge.

ALIBHAI-BROWN, Yasmin (2001). 'Mr. Blunkett Has Insulted All of Us', *The Independent*, 10 December.

AMEYAW, S. (2000). 'Appreciative planning: an approach to planning with diverse ethnic and cultural groups', in M. Burayidi (ed.). *Urban Planning in a Multicultural Society.* Westport, CT: Praeger.

AMIN, Ash, ed. (1994). *Post-Fordism. A Reader.* Oxford: Blackwell.

AMIN, Ash (1997). 'Placing Globalization', *Theory, Culture and Society.* 14: 123–37.

AMIN, Ash (2002). *Ethnicity and the Multicultural City. Living with Diversity.* Report for the Department of Transport, Local Government and the Regions. Durham: University of Durham.

ANDERSON, Kay (1991). *Vancouver's Chinatown: Racial Discourse in Canada, 1875–1980.* Toronto: McGill Queens University Press.

ANDREW, Caroline and Beth Moore Milroy, eds (1988). *Life Spaces: Gender, Household, Employment.* Vancouver: University of British Columbia Press.

ANZALDÚA, Gloria (1987). *Borderlands/La Frontera: The New Mestiza.* San Francisco, CA: Aunt Lute Books.

ANZALDÚA, Gloria, ed. (1990). *Making Face, Making Soul. Haciendo Caras.* San Francisco, CA: Aunt Lute Books.

ANZALDÚA, Gloria and Cherry Moraga, ed. (1983). *This Bridge Called My Back.* New York: Kitchen Table: Women of Color Press.

APPADURAI, A. (1990). 'Disjuncture and Difference in the Global Cultural Economy', *Public Culture*, 2, 2: 1–32.

APPLEBY, Joyce, Lynn Hunt and Margaret Jacob (1994). *Telling the Truth About History.* New York: W. W. Norton & Co.

ARNSTEIN, Sherry (1969). 'A Ladder of Citizen Participation', *Journal of the American Institute of Planners*, 35, 4: 45–54.

BANNERJI, H. (1995). *Thinking Through.* Toronto: Women's Press.

BANNERJI, H. (2000). *The Dark Side of the Nation: Essays on Multiculturalism, Nationalism and Gender.* Toronto: Canadian Scholars' Press, Inc.

BARTHELS, J. (2003). 'The Meanest Streets', in B. Eckstein and J. Throgmorton (eds). *Story and Sustainability: Planning, Practice, and Possibility for American Cities.* Cambridge, MA: MIT Press.

BAUM, H. (1999). 'Forgetting to Plan', *Journal of Planning Education and Research*, 19, 1: 2–14.

BAUM, H. (2000). 'Culture Matters – But it Shouldn't Matter too Much', in M.

Burayidi (ed). *Urban Planning in a Multicultural Society*. Westport, CT: Praeger.

BEAUREGARD, R. A. (1989). 'Between Modernity and Postmodernity: the Ambiguous Position of US Planning', *Environment and Planning D: Society and Space*, 7, 381–95.

BEAUREGARD, R. A. (1991). 'Without a Net: Modernist Planning and the Postmodern Abyss', *Journal of Planning Education and Research*, 10, 3: 189–94.

BEAUREGARD, R. A. (1998). 'Subversive Histories: Texts From South Africa', in Leonie Sandercock (ed.). *Making the Invisible Visible: A Multicultural History of Planning*. Berkeley: University of California Press.

BEAUREGARD, R. A. (1998a). 'Writing the Planner', *Journal of Planning Education and Research*, 18, 2: 93–101.

BEAUREGARD, R. A. (1993). *Voices of Decline. The Postwar Fate of US Cities*. Cambridge, MA: Blackwell.

BECK, U. (1998). *Democracy Without Enemies*. London: Polity Press.

BELENKY, Mary Field, Blythe Clinchy, Nancy Goldberger and Jill Tarule (1986). *Women's Ways of Knowing: The Development of Self, Voice, and Mind*. New York: Basic Books.

BENHABIB, Seyla (1995). 'Cultural Complexity, Moral Interdependence, and the Global Dialogical Community', in Martha Nussbaum and Jonathan Glover (eds). *Women, Culture and Development*. Oxford: Clarendon Press.

BERMAN, Marshall (1982). *All That Is Solid Melts Into Air*. New York: Simon and Schuster.

BERNSTEIN, Richard (1985). *Beyond Objectivism and Relativism. Science, Hermeneutics, and Praxis*. Philadelphia: Temple University Press.

BHABHA, Homi K. (1991). 'Introduction: Narrating the Nation', in Homi K. Bhabha (ed.). *Nation and Narration*. London: Routledge.

BHABHA, Homi K. (1994). *The Location of Culture*. London: Routledge.

BHATTACHARYYA, G. (1999). 'Metropolis of the Midlands', Mimeo. Department of Sociology and Cultural Studies, University of Birmingham.

BIRCH, Eugenie (1983). 'From Civic Worker to City Planner: Women and Planning 1890–1980', in Donald Krueckeberg (ed.). *The American Planner*. New York: Methuen.

BISOONDATH, N. (2002). *Selling Illusions: The Cult of Multiculturalism in Canada*. Toronto: Penguin Books.

BODIE-GENDROT, Sophie (2000). *The Social Control of Cities?* Cambridge: Blackwell.

BORDEN, Iain (2001). *Skateboarding, Space and the City: Architecture and the Body*. New York: Berg.

BORDEN, Iain and Jane Rendell, eds (2000). *InterSections. Architectural Histories and Critical Theories*. London: Routledge.

BORDEN, I., J. Kerr, J. Rendell, with A. Pivaro (eds). 2001. *The Unknown City. Contesting Architecture and Social Space*. Cambridge, MA: MIT Press.

BOURDIEU, P. 1977. *Outline of a Theory of Practice*. Cambridge: Cambridge University Press.

BOYER, Christine (1983). *Dreaming the Rational City. The Myth of American City Planning*. Cambridge, MA: MIT Press.

BREEMS, Kara (2002). 'The Struggle for Diverse Neighborhoods', Directed Studies Paper, School of Community and Regional Planning, University of British Columbia.

BROCK, Samara (2002). 'A Very Merry Scary Day', Term Paper, PLAN502, School of Community and Regional Planning, UBC.

BROWN, Wendy (1995). *States of Injury: Power and Freedom in Late Modernity*. Princeton, NJ: Princeton University Press.

BUCK-MORSS, Susan (1989). *The Dialectics of Seeing: Walter Benjamin and the Arcades Project*. Cambridge, MA: MIT Press.

BURAYIDI, M. (ed.) (2000). *Urban Planning in a Multicultural Society*. Westport, CT: Praeger.

BURAYIDI, M. (2000a). 'Urban Planning as a Multicultural Cannon', in M. Burayidi (ed.). *Urban Planning in a Multicultural Society*. Westport, CT: Praeger.

CALDEIRA, T. (1999). 'Fortified Enclaves: The New Urban Segregation', in J. Holston (ed.). *Cities and Citizenship*. Durham: Duke University Press.

CAPRA, Fritjof (1975). *The Tao of Physics*. Berkeley: Shambhala.

CARO, Robert (1975). *The Power Broker: Robert Moses and the Fall of New York*. New York: Albert Knopf.

CASTELLS, Manuel (1976). *The Urban Question*. London: Edward Arnold.

CASTELLS, Manuel (1996). *The Rise of the Network Society*. Oxford: Blackwell.

CASTELLS, Manuel (1997). *The Power of Identity*. Oxford: Blackwell.

CASTLES, Stephen and Mark J. Miller (1998). *The Age of Migration*, 2nd ed. New York: The Guilford Press.

CHAN, Sucheng ed. (1991). *Entry Denied: Exclusion and the Chinese Community in America, 1882–1943*. Philadelphia: Temple University Press.

CHATWIN, B. (1987). *The Songlines*. New York: Viking.

CHAUNCEY, George (1994). *Gay New York: Gender, Urban Culture, and the Making of the Gay Male World 1890–1940*. New York: Basic Books.

CHRISTENSEN, K. S. (1993). 'Teaching Savvy', *Journal of Planning Education and Research*, 12: 202–12.

CHRISTIAN, Barbara (1988). 'The Race for Theory', *Feminist Studies*, 14: 67–9.

CODE, Lorraine (1991). *What Can She Know?* Ithaca: Cornell University Press.

COHEN, Jean L. and Andrew Arato (1994). *Civil Society and Political Theory*. Cambridge, MA: MIT Press.

COLLINS, Patricia Hill (1990). *Black Feminist Thought: Knowledge, Consciousness and the Politics of Empowerment*. Boston: Unwin Hyman.

COLOMINA, Beatriz (ed.). *Sexuality and Space*. Princeton Papers on Architecture, Princeton, NJ: Princeton Architectural Press.

Community Cohesion Unit (2001). *Building Cohesive Communities*. London: Home Office.

CONNOLLY, William (1991). *Identity/Difference*. Ithaca: Cornell University Press.

CONNOLLY, William (1995). *The Ethos of Pluralization*. Minneapolis: University of Minnesota Press.

COOK, Judith and Mary Fonow (1986). 'Knowledge and Women's Interests: Issues of Epistemology and Methodology in Feminist Sociological Research', *Sociological Inquiry*, 56, 1: 2–29.

COULT, T. and B. Kershaw, eds (1990). *Engineers of the Imagination. The Welfare State Handbook*. London: Methuen Drama.

CROSS, M. and M. Keith, eds (1993). *Racism, the City and the State*. London: Routledge.

DALE, N. (1999). 'Cross-cultural Community-based Planning: Negotiating the Future of Haida Gwaii', in L. Susskind, S. McKearnan and J. Thomas-Larner, eds. *The Consensus Building Handbook*. Thousand Oaks, CA: Sage.

DANG, S. (2002). *Creating Cosmopolis: The End of Mainstream*. Unpublished Masters Thesis, School of Community and Regional Planning, University of British Columbia.

DAVIDOFF, Paul (1965). 'Advocacy and Pluralism in Planning', *Journal of the American Institute of Planning*, 31, 4: 331–8.

DAVIS, Mike (1990). *City of Quartz. Excavating the Future in Los Angeles*. New York: Verso.

DEAR, M. J. (1986). 'Postmodernism and Planning', *Environment and Planning D. Society and Space*, 4, 4: 367–84.

DE BONO, E. (1971). *The Use of Lateral Thinking*. London: Pelican.

DE BONO, E. (1996). *Serious Creativity*. London: HarperCollins Business.

D'EMILIO, J. (1983). *Sexual Politics/Sexual Communities*. Chicago: University of Chicago Press.

DENOON, D., M. Hudson, G. McCormack and T. Morris-Suzuki, eds (1996). *Multicultural Japan*. Cambridge: Cambridge University Press.

DONALD, J. (1999). *Imagining the Modern City*. London: The Athlone Press.

DOUGLASS, M. (1999). 'Unbundling National Identity – Global Migration and the Advent of Multicultural Societies in East Asia', *Asian Perspectives*, 23, 3: 79–128.

DOUGLASS, M. (2002). 'Below Replacement Fertility and International Migration. Challenges to National Identity and Citizenship in Pacific Asia'. Paper presented to International Workshop on Fertility Decline and the Family in Asia: Prospects, Consequences, and Policies, National University of Singapore, 10–12 April 2002.

DOUGLASS, Michael and J. Friedmann, eds (1998). *Cities for Citizens: Planning and the Rise of Civil Society in a Global Age*. London: John Wiley and Sons.

DOUGLASS, M. and Glenda Roberts, eds (2000). *Japan and Global Migration: Foreign Workers and the Advent of a Multicultural Society*. London: Routledge.

DRYZEK, J. (1990). *Discursive Democracy: Politics, Policy, and Political Science*. Cambridge: Cambridge University Press.

DUBROW, Gail Lee (1991). *Preserving Her Heritage: American Landmarks of Women's History*. Unpublished PhD Dissertation, Urban Planning Program, UCLA.

DUBROW, Gail Lee (1992). 'Claiming Public Space for Women's History in Boston: A Proposal for Preservation, Public Art, and Public Historical Interpretation', *Frontiers: A Journal of Women's Studies*, 13, 1, 111–48.

DUBROW, Gail Lee (1998). 'Feminist and Multicultural Perspectives on Preservation Planning', in L. Sandercock, ed. *Making the Invisible Visible*. Berkeley: UC Press.

DUBROW, Gail Lee and Jennifer Goodman, eds (2002). *Restoring Women's History through Historic Preservation*. Baltimore: Johns Hopkins University Press.

DUBROW, Gail, with Donna Graves (2002). *Sento at Sixth and Main*. Seattle: Seattle Arts Commission.

DUNN, K., Hanna, B. and S. Thompson (2001a). 'The Local Politics of Difference: An Examination of Inter-communal Relations Policy in Australian Local Government', *Environment and Planning A*, 33, 1577–95.

DUNN, K., Thompson, S., Hanna, B., and I. Burnley (2001b). 'The Institution of Multiculturalism within Local Government in Australia', *Urban Studies*, 38 (13), 2477–94.

DUNSTAN, G. and W. Sarkissian (1994). 'Goonawarra: Core Story as Methodology in Interpreting a Community Study', in W. Sarkissian and K. Walsh (eds). *Community Participation in Practice. Casebook*. Perth: Institute of Sustainability Policy, Murdoch University.

ECKSTEIN, B. (2003). 'Making Space: Stories in the Practice of Planning', in B. Eckstein and J. Throgmorton, eds. *Story and Sustainability: Planning, Practice, and Possibility for American Cities*. Cambridge, MA: MIT Press.

ECKSTEIN, B. and J. Throgmorton, eds (2003). *Story and Sustainability: Planning, Practice, and Possibility for American Cities*. Cambridge, MA: MIT Press.

EDGINGTON, D. and T. Hutton (2002). 'Multiculturalism and Local Government in Greater Vancouver', RIIM Working Paper Series, No. 02–06, University of British Columbia.

ELLIN, Nan (1997). Postmodern Urbanism. Oxford: Blackwell.

ELLYARD, P. (2001). *Ideas for the New Millen-*

nium. 2nd ed. Melbourne: Melbourne University Press.

EPSTEIN, Dora (1998). 'Afraid/NOT: Psychoanalytic Directions for the Tradition of Planning Historiography', in Leonie Sandercock, ed. *Making the Invisible Visible: A Multicultural History of Planning*. Berkeley: University of California Press.

Ethnic Affairs Commission of New South Wales (1993). *New South Wales Charter of Principles for a Culturally Diverse Society*. Sydney: Ethnic Affairs Commission of New South Wales.

FADERMAN, L. (1991). *Odd Girls and Twilight Lovers: A History of Lesbian Life in Twentieth-century America*. New York: Penguin.

FAINSTEIN, Susan (1994). *The City Builders: Property, Politics and Planning in London and New York*. Oxford: Blackwell.

FALUDI, Andreas (1973). *Planning Theory*. Oxford: Pergamon Press.

FALUDI, Andreas (1986). *Critical Rationalism and Planning Methodology*. London: Pion.

FENSTER, Tovi (1999a). 'On Particularism and Universalism in Modernist Planning: Mapping the Boundaries of Social Change', *Plurimondi*, 2, pp. 147–68.

FENSTER, Tovi, ed. (1999b). *Gender, Planning, and Human Rights*. London: Routledge.

FINCHER, Ruth and Jane Jacobs, eds (1998). *Cities of Difference*. New York: Guilford.

FINNEGAN, R. (1998). *Tales of the City. A Study of Narrative and Urban Life*. Cambridge: Cambridge University Press.

FITZGERALD, Joan and William Howard (1993). *Discovering an African American Planning History*. Unpublished paper, presented to American Collegiate Schools of Planning Conference, Philadelphia.

FLYVBJERG, B. (1992). 'Aristotle, Foucault and Progressive Phronesis', *Planning Theory*, 7/8, 65–83.

FLYVBJERG, B. (1998). *Rationality and Power*. Chicago: University of Chicago Press.

FLYVBJERG, B. (2001). *Making Social Science Matter*. Cambridge: Cambridge University Press.

FLYVBJERG, B. (2002). 'Bringing Power to Planning Research: One Researcher's Praxis Story', *Journal of Planning Education and Research*, 21, 4: 353–66.

FLYVBJERG, B., Mette Skamris Holm, and Soren Buhl (2002). 'Underestimating Costs in Public Works Projects: Error or Lie?', *Journal of the American Planning Association*, 68, 3: 279–96.

FOGELSON, Robert M. (1967). *The Fragmented Metropolis. Los Angeles, 1850–1930*. Cambridge, MA: Harvard University Press.

FOGLESONG, Richard (1986). *Planning the Capitalist City. The Colonial Era to the 1920s*. Princeton, NJ: Princeton University Press.

FORESTER, John (1989). *Planning in the Face of Power*. Berkeley: University of California Press.

FORESTER, John (1991). 'On Critical Practice: The Politics of Storytelling and the Priority of Practical Judgement', The Clarkson Lecture, SUNY at Buffalo.

FORESTER, John (1999). *The Deliberative Practitioner*. Cambridge, MA: MIT Press.

FORESTER, John (2000). 'Multicultural Planning in Deed: Lessons from the Mediation Practice of Shirley Solomon and Larry Sherman', in M. Burayidi, ed. *Urban Planning in a Multicultural Society*. Westport, CT: Praeger.

FORESTER, J., J. Pitt, and J. Welsh, eds (1993). *Profiles of Participatory Action Researchers*. Ithaca: Department of City and Regional Planning, Cornell University.

FOUCAULT, Michel (1979). *Discipline and Punish. The Birth of the Prison*. New York: Vintage Books.

FOUCAULT, M. (1984). The Birth of the Clinic: An Archaeology of Medical Perception. New York: Vintage Books.

FOUCAULT, M. (1990). *The History of Sexuality*. Vol. 1. New York: Vintage Books.

FOWLER, Sandra and Monica Mumford, eds (1999). *Intercultural Sourcebook: Cross-Cultural Training Methods*. Vol. 2. Yarmouth, Maine: Intercultural Press.

FRIEDMANN, John (1973). *Retracking America*. New York: Doubleday Anchor.

FRIEDMANN, John (1986). 'The World City Hypothesis,' *Development and Change*, 17, 1: 69–84.

FRIEDMANN, John (1987). *Planning in the Public Domain: From Knowledge to Action*. Princeton, NJ: Princeton University Press.

FRIEDMANN, John (1988). *Life Space and Economic Space: Essays in Third World Planning*. New Brunswick, NJ: Transaction Books.

FRIEDMANN, John (1992). *Empowerment. The Politics of Alternative Development*. Oxford: Blackwell.

FRIEDMANN, John (1996). 'The Core Curriculum in Planning Revisited', *Journal of Planning Education and Research*, 15: 89–104.

FRIEDMANN, John (1997). 'World City Futures: The Role of Urban and Regional Policies in the Asia Pacific Region', Department of Geography, Chinese University of Hong Kong.

FRIEDMANN, John (2002). *The Prospect of Cities*. Minneapolis: University of Minnesota Press.

FRIEDMANN, John (2002a). 'City of Fear or Open City?' *Journal of the American Planning Association*, 68, 3: 237–43.

FRIEDMANN, John and Carol Kuester (1994). 'Planning Education for the Late Twentieth Century: An Initial Inquiry', I, 14, 1, 55–64.

FRIEDMANN, John and Ute Angelika Lehrer (1997). 'Urban Policy Responses to Foreign In-Migration. The Case of Frankfurt-am-Main', *Journal of the American Planning Association*, 63: 1 (Winter), 61–78.

FRISCH, M. (2002). 'Planning as a Heterosexist Project', *Journal of Planning Education and Research*, 21, 3: 254–66.

GADAMER, H. G. (1976). *Philosophical Hermeneutics*. Ed. and trans, D. Linge. Berkeley: University of California Press.

GALLEGO-DIAZ, S. (2002). 'Excessive Immigration Provokes Crime', *El Pais*, 16 May, pp. 4–5.

GIBSON-GRAHAM, J.-K. (1996). *The End of Capitalism (As We Knew It)*. Oxford: Blackwell.

GILKES, Cheryl (1988). 'Building in Many Places: Multiple Commitments and Ideologies in Black Women's Community Work', in Sandra Bookman and Elaine Morgen, eds. *Women and the Politics of Empowerment*. Philadelphia: Temple University Press.

GILROY, P. (2000). *Between Camps*. London: Penguin.

GLEESON, B. (1998). 'Justice and the Disabling City', in R. Fincher and J. Jacobs, eds. *Cities of Difference*. London: Guilford Press.

GLEESON, B. (1999). *Geographies of Disability*. London: Routledge.

GÓMEZ-PEÑA, Guillermo (1993). *Warrior for Gringostroika*. Saint Paul, Minnesota: Graywolf Press.

GOTTLIEB, Robert (1993). *Forcing the Spring. The Transformation of the American Environmental Movement*. Covelo, CA: Island Press.

GOWER DAVIES, J. (1972). *The Evangelistic Bureaucrat*. London: Tavistock.

GRASSBY, A. (1973). *A Multicultural Society for the Future* Canberra: Department of Immigration/Australian Government Publishing Service.

GRIGSBY, J. Eugene (1994). 'In Planning There Is No Such Thing as a "Race Neutral" Policy', *Journal of the American Planning Association*, 60, 2: 240–41.

GROSZ, Elizabeth (1993). *Volatile Bodies.* Bloomington: Indiana University Press.

GUHA, Ranajit and Guyatri Chakravorty Spivak, eds (1988). *Selected Subaltern Studies.* New York: Oxford University Press.

GUINIER, L. and G. Torres (2002). *The Miner's Canary. Enlisting Race, Resisting Power, Transforming Democracy.* Cambridge, MA: Harvard University Press.

HABERMAS, J. (1984). *The Theory of Communicative Action.* Trans. T. McCarthy. Boston: Beacon Press.

HABERMAS, J. (1990). *Moral Consciousness and Communicative Action.* Trans. C. Lenhardt and S. Weber Nicholson. Oxford: Polity Press.

HAGE, Ghassan (1998). *White Nation: Fantasies of White Supremacy in a Multicultural Society.* Sydney: Pluto Press.

HALL, Peter (1988). *Cities of Tomorrow. An Intellectual History of Urban Planning and Design in the Twentieth Century.* London: Blackwell.

HALL, Peter, and C. Landry (1997). *Innovative and Sustainable Cities.* Dublin: European Foundation for the Improvement of Living and Working Conditions.

HALL, Stuart (2000). 'Conclusion: The Multicultural Question', in B. Hesse, ed. *Un/settled Multiculturalisms.* London: Zed Books.

HAMDI, Nabeel and Reinhard Goethert (1997). *Action Planning for Cities: A Guide to Community Practice.* Chichester: John Wiley.

HARDING, Sandra and Merrill Hintikka, eds (1983). *Discovering Reality: Feminist Perspectives on Epistemology, Metaphysics, Methodology, and Philosophy of Science.* Dortrecht, Holland: D. Reidel.

HARDING, Sandra (1986). *The Science Question in Feminism.* Ithaca: Cornell University Press.

HARDING, Sandra, ed. (1987). *Feminism and Methodology.* Bloomington: Indiana University Press.

HARVEY, David (1973). *Social Justice and the City.* London: Edward Arnold.

HARVEY, David (1989). *The Condition of Postmodernity.* London: Blackwell.

HAYDEN, Dolores (1980). 'What Would a Non-Sexist City be Like?', in Catherine Stimpson *et al. Women and the American City.* Chicago: University of Chicago Press.

HAYDEN, Dolores (1981). *The Grand Domestic Revolution.* Cambridge, MA: MIT Press.

HAYDEN, Dolores (1984). *Redesigning the American Dream.* New York: W. W. Norton.

HAYDEN, Dolores (1995). *The Power of Place. Urban Landscapes as Public History.* Cambridge, MA: MIT Press.

HEALEY, Patsy *et al.* (1988). *Land use Planning and the Mediation of Urban Change: The British Planning System in Practice.* Cambridge: Cambridge University Press.

HEALEY, Patsy (1992). 'A Planner's Day: Knowledge and Action in Communicative Practice', *Journal of the American Planning Association,* 58: 9–20.

HEALEY, Patsy (1997). *Collaborative Planning.* London: Macmillan.

HEALEY, Patsy (2003). 'The New Institutionalism and the Transformative Goals of Planning', paper for Niraj Verma, ed. *Institutions and Planning* (forthcoming)

HEKMAN, Susan (1990). *Gender and Knowledge. Elements of a Postmodern Feminism.* Boston: Northeastern University Press.

HENRY, F. *et al.* (2000). *The Color of Democracy: Racism in Canadian Society.* Toronto: Harcourt Canada.

HENRY, N., C. McEwan and J. Pollard. (2000). 'Globalization From Below: Birmingham – Postcolonial Workshop of the World?', Working Paper WPTC-2K-08, School of Geography, University of Birmingham.

Heskin, Allan (1991). *The Struggle for Community.* Boulder, CO: Westview Press.

Hesse, Barnor, ed. (2000). *Un/settled Multiculturalisms.* London: Zed Books.

Hesse, B. (2000). 'Introduction: Un/settled Multiculturalisms', in B. Hesse, ed. *Un/settled Multiculturalisms.* London: Zed Books.

Hii, Yvonne (2002). 'The Fool's Journey', (unpublished) Term Paper, PLAN 502, School of Community and Regional Planning, UBC.

Hill, L. (2001). *Black Berry, Sweet Juice: On Being Black and White in Canada.* Toronto: Harper Collins.

Hillier, Jean (2002). *Shadows of Power. An Allegory of Prudence in Land-Use Planning.* London: Routledge.

Hilton, Isabel (2002). 'Orange Alert', *New Yorker,* 1 July, 38–44.

Hoch, C. (1994). *What Planners Do: Power, Politics and Persuasion.* Chicago: American Planning Association.

Holston, James (1989). *The Modernist City. An Anthropological Critique of Brasilia.* Chicago: University of Chicago Press.

Holston, James (1998). 'Spaces of Insurgent Citizenship', in Leonie Sandercock, ed. *Making the Invisible Visible: A Multicultural Planning History.* Berkeley: University of California Press.

Home Office (2001). *Building Cohesive Communities: A Report of the Ministerial Group on Public Order and Community Cohesion.* London: Home Office.

hooks, bell (1984). *Feminist Theory: From Margin to Centre.* Boston: South End Press.

hooks, bell (1989). *Talking Back.* Boston: South End Press.

hooks, bell (1990). *Yearning: Race, Gender, and Cultural Politics.* Boston, MA: South End Press.

hooks, bell (1994). 'House, 20 June 1994', *Assemblage,* 24, 22–9.

hooks, bell and Cornell West (1991). *Breaking Bread: Insurgent Black Intellectual Life.* Boston, MA: South End Press.

Hooper, Barbara (1992). 'Split at the Roots': A Critique of the Philosophical and Political Sources of Modern Planning Doctrine. *Frontiers,* XIII, 1: 45–80.

Hooper, Barbara (1998). 'The Poem of Male Desires: Female Bodies, Modernity, and "Paris: Capital of the Nineteenth Century"', in Leonie Sandercock, ed. *Making the Invisible Visible: A Multicultural History of Planning.* Berkeley: University of California Press.

Hooper, Barbara (2002). *Performativities of Space: Bodies, Cities, Texts.* Unpublished PhD Dissertation, Department of Urban Planning, UCLA.

Houston, Jean (1982). *The Possible Human.* Los Angeles: Tarcher.

Houston, Jean (1987). *The Search for the Beloved: Journeys in Sacred Psychology.* Los Angeles: Tarcher.

Hunt, Lynn, ed. (1989). *The New Cultural History: Essays by Aletta Biersack.* Berkeley: University of California Press.

Huxley, M. and O. Yiftachel (2000). 'New Paradigm or Old Myopia? Unsettling the Communicative Turn in Planning Theory', *Journal of Planning Education and Research,* 19, 3: 101–10.

Innes, Judith (1995). 'Planning Theory's Emerging Paradigm: Communicative Action and Interactive Practice', *Journal of Planning Education and Research,* 14, 3 (Spring): 183–90.

Innes, Judith (1996). 'Planning through Consensus Building', *Journal of the American Planning Association,* 62, 4 (Autumn): 460–72.

Innes, Judith (1998). 'Information in Communicative Planning', *Journal of the American Planning Association,* 64, 1: 52–63.

Innes, Judith and D. Booher (1999). 'Consensus as Role Playing and Bricolage', *Jour-*

nal of the American Planning Association, 65, 1: 9–26.

ISIN. E., ed. (1999). 'Special Issues on Cities and Citizenship', Citizenship Studies, 3, 2.

IVESON, K. (2000). 'Beyond Designer Diversity', Urban Policy and Research, 18, 2: 219–38.

JACKSON, Sue (1998). Geographies of Coexistence: Native Title, Cultural Difference and the Decolonization of Planning in North Australia. Unpublished PhD Dissertation, School of Earth Sciences, Macquarie University, Sydney.

JACKSON, A. (2002). The Statistical Complex. Unpublished Masters in Urban Planning Thesis. University of Melbourne, Faculty of Architecture and Planning.

JACOBS, J. (1962). The Death and Life of Great American Cities. London: Jonathan Cape.

JACOBS, Jane M. (1996). Edge of Empire. Post-colonialism and the City. London: Routledge.

JAGGAR, Alison and Susan Bordo, eds (1989). Gender/Body/Knowledge. New Brunswick, NJ: Rutgers University Press.

JAMESON, Fredric (1991). Postmodernism or the Cultural Logic of Late Capitalism. London: Verso.

JOJOLA, Theodore (1998). 'Indigenous Planning: Clans, Intertribal Confederations and the History of the All Indian Pueblo Council', in Leonie Sandercock, ed. Making the Invisible Visible: A Multicultural History of Planning. Berkeley: University of California Press.

KARST, Kenneth (1986). 'Paths to Belonging: The Constitution and Cultural Identity', North Carolina Law Review, 64 (Jan): 303–77.

KAYDEN, J. and C. Haar, eds (1989). Zoning and the American Dream. Chicago: Planners Press.

KEEBLE, L. (1952). Principles and Practice of Town and Country Planning. London: Estates Gazette.

KEENEY, R. (1996). Value-Focused Thinking: A Path to Creative Decision-making. Cambridge, MA: Harvard University Press.

KELLER, Evelyn Fox (1983). A Feeling for the Organism. New York: Freeman.

KELLER, Evelyn Fox (1985). Reflections on Gender and Science. New Haven: Yale University Press.

KELLY, Joan Gadol (1984). Women, History, and Theory. Chicago: University of Chicago Press.

KENNEY, Moira (1995). 'Remember, Stonewall was a Riot: Understanding Gay and Lesbian Experience in the City', Planning Theory, 13, 73–88.

KENNEY, Moira (2001). Mapping Gay LA: The Intersection of Place and Politics. Philadelphia: Temple University Press.

KERSHAW, B. (1990). 'Techniques of Survival – Statements of Hope', in T. Coult and B. Kershaw, eds. Engineers of the Imagination. London: Methuen Drama.

KHAKEE, A., P. Somma and H. Thomas, eds (1999). Urban Renewal, Ethnicity and Social Exclusion in Europe. Aldershot: Ashgate.

KHAKEE, Abdul, and Huw Thomas (1995). 'Ethnic Minorities and the Planning System in Britain and Sweden', European Planning Studies, 3, 4: 489–510.

KIMBALL, S. and J. Garrison (1999). 'Hermeneutic Listening in Multicultural Conversations', in Victoria Fu and A. Stremmel, eds. Affirming Diversity through Democratic Conversations. Columbus, Ohio: Merrill.

KING, A. D. (1976). Colonial Urban Development: Culture, Social Power, and Environment. London: Routledge and Kegan Paul.

KING, A. D. (1990). Urbanism, Colonialism, and the World Economy. London: Routledge.

KING, Mel (1981). Chain of Change. Boston: South End Press.

KNOX, Paul and Peter J. Taylor (1995). World

Cities in a World System. Cambridge: Cambridge University Press.

KOLB, Deborah, and Associates. (1994). *When Talk Works.* San Francisco: Jossey Bass.

KONG, L. (1993). 'Ideological Hegemony and the Political Symbolism of Religious Buildings in Singapore', *Environment and Planning D: Society and Space*, 11, 1: 23–46.

KONRAD, George (1977). *The City Builder.* New York: Harcourt Brace Jovanovich.

KRISHNARAYAN, V. and H. Thomas (1993). *Ethnic Minorities and the Planning System.* London: Royal Town Planning Institute.

KRISTEVA, Julia (1991). *Strangers to Ourselves.* New York: Columbia University Press. Trans. Leon S. Roudiez.

KRUECKEBERG, Donald, ed. (1983a). *Introduction to Planning History in the United States.* New Brunswick, NJ: Center for Urban Policy Research.

KRUECKEBERG, Donald, ed. (1983b). *The American Planner: Biographies and Recollections.* New York: Methuen.

KRUGER, B. and P. Mariani, eds (1989). *Remaking History.* Seattle: Bay Press.

KUHN, Thomas (1961). *The Structure of Scientific Revolutions.* Chicago: University of Chicago Press.

KYMLICKA, Will (1995). *Multicultural Citizenship: A Liberal Theory of Minority Rights.* Oxford: Oxford University Press.

KYMLICKA, Will and W. Norman (1994). 'Return of the Citizen: A Survey of recent Work on Citizenship Theory', *Ethics*, 104, 2: 352–81.

LANDRY, C. (2000). *The Creative City. A Toolkit for Urban Innovation.* London: Earthscan.

LATOUR, Bruno (1993). *We Have Never Been Modern* (trans. Catherine Porter), Cambridge, MA: Harvard University Press.

LEAVITT, Jacqueline (1980). 'The History, Status, and Concerns of Women Planners', in Catherine Stimpson *et al.*, eds. *Women and*

the American City. Chicago: University of Chicago Press.

LEAVITT, Jacqueline (1986). 'Feminist Advocacy Planning in the 1980s', in Barry Checkoway, ed. *Strategic Perspectives in Planning Practice.* Lexington, MA: Lexington Books.

LEAVITT, Jacqueline (1994). 'Planning in an Age of Rebellion: Guidelines to Activist Research and Applied Planning', *Planning Theory*, 10/11, 111–30.

LEAVITT, Jacqueline and Susan Saegert (1990). *From Abandonment to Hope: Community Households in Harlem.* New York: Columbia University Press.

LeBARON, Michelle (2002). *Bridging Troubled Waters.* San Francisco: Jossey Bass.

LEE, Bill (1986). *Pragmatics of Community Organization.* Mississauga, Ontario: Common Act Press.

LERNER, Gerda (1976). 'Placing Women in History: A 1975 Perspective', in Berenice Carroll, ed. *Liberating Women's History: Theoretical and Critical Essays.* Urbana: University of Illinois Press.

LIGHT, I. (2002). 'Immigrant Place Entrepreneurs in Los Angeles, 1970–1999', *International Journal of Urban and Regional Research*, 26, 2: 215–28.

LIM, William (2001). *Alternatives in Transition. The Postmodern, Glocality and Social Justice.* Singapore: Select Publishing.

LIM, William (2003). *Alternative (Post)-Modernity.* Singapore: Select Publishing (forthcoming).

LOFTMAN, P. and B. Nevin (1996). 'Prestige Urban Regeneration Projects: Socioeconomic Impacts', in Gerrard, A. J. and T. R. Slater, eds. *Managing a Conurbation: Birmingham and its Region.* Studley: Brewin Books.

LOKKO, Lesley Naa Norle, ed. (2000). *White Papers, Black Marks. Architecture, Race, Culture.* London: The Athlone Press.

LYDON, M. (2002). *(Re)presenting the Living Landscape: Exploring Community Mapping as a Tool for Transformative Learning and Planning.* Unpublished Masters Thesis, Department of Environmental Studies, University of Victoria, British Columbia.

LYNCH, Kevin (1972). *What Time Is This Place?* Cambridge, MA: MIT Press.

LYOTARD, J. F. (1984). *The Postmodern Condition.* Manchester: Manchester University Press.

MABIN, A. and D. Smit (1997). 'Reconstructing South Africa's Cities? The Making of Urban Planning 1900–2000', *Planning Perspectives*, 12: 193–223.

MacINTYRE, Alasdair (1981). *After Virtue.* Notre Dame: University of Notre Dame Press.

MACKENZIE, Susan (1984). 'Catching Up With Ourselves: Ideas on Developing Gender Sensitive Theory in the Environmental Disciplines', *Women and Environments*, 5, 3, 16–18.

MACNAUGHTON, Alison (2001). 'Constable Tom Woods – The Unlikely Planner', Term Paper for PLAN 502, School of Community and Regional Planning, University of British Columbia.

MAHTANI, Minelle (2002). 'Interrogating the Hyphen-nation: Canadian Multicultural Policy and "Mixed Race" Identities', *Social Identities*, 8, 1: 67–90.

MANDELBAUM, S. (1991). 'Telling Stories', *Journal of Planning Education and Research*, 10, 1: 209–14.

MANNHEIM, K. (1949). *Ideology and Utopia.* New York: Harcourt Brace (first published 1928).

MARCUSE, Peter (1980). 'Housing in Early City Planning', *Journal of Urban History.* 6: 2 (February) 153–71.

MARCUSE, Peter (1994). 'Not Chaos, but Walls: Postmodernism and the Partitioned City', in Sophie Watson and Katherine Gibson, eds, *Postmodern Cities and Spaces.* Oxford: Blackwell.

MARRIS, Peter (1974). *Loss and Change.* London: Routledge of Kegan Paul.

MARRIS, Peter (1996). *The Politics of Uncertainty.* London: Routledge.

MARRIS, P. (1997). *Witnesses, Engineers, and Storytellers: Using Research for Social Policy and Action.* Maryland: University of Maryland, Urban Studies and Planning Program.

MARRIS, Peter (1998). 'Planning and Civil Society in the Twenty-first Century: An Introduction', in M. Douglass and J. Friedmann, eds. *Cities for Citizens.* London: Wiley.

MARTIN, Judith and Sam Bass Warner, Jr (2000). 'Local initiative and Metropolitan Repetition: Chicago 1972–1990', in R. Fishman, ed. *The American Planning Tradition.* Washington, DC: Woodrow Wilson Center Press.

MASSEY, D. and N. Denton (1993). *American Apartheid: Segregation and the Making of the Underclass.* Cambridge, MA: Harvard University Press.

MAYAKOVSKY, V. (1975). *The Bedbug and Selected Poetry*, trans. Max Hayward and George Reavey. Bloomington: Indiana University Press.

MERCHANT, Carol (1980). *The Death of Nature.* San Francisco: Harper and Rowe.

MERRY, Sally Engle (1981). *Urban Danger: Life in a Neighborhood of Strangers.* Philadelphia: Temple University Press.

MEYER, P. and C. R. Reaves (2000). 'Objectives and Values: Planning for Multicultural Groups rather than Multiple Constituencies', in M. Burayidi, ed. *Urban Planning in a Multicultural Society.* Westport, CT: Praeger.

MIER, R. (1993). *Social Justice and Local Development Policy.* Newbury Park, CA: Sage.

MILROY, B. and M. Wallace (2001). 'Ethnoracial Diversity and Planning Practices in the Greater Toronto Area', *Plan Canada*, 41, 3: 31–3.

MINH-HA, Trinh (1989). *Woman Native Other.* Bloomington: Indiana University Press.

MOUFFE, Chantal (2000). *The Democratic Paradox.* London: Verso.

MUMFORD, Lewis (1961). *The City in History.* New York: Harcourt, Brace and World.

NARAYAN, Uma (1989). 'The Project of Feminist Epistemology: Perspectives from a Non-western Feminist', in Alison Jaggar and Susan Bordo, eds. *Gender/Body/Knowledge.* New Brunswick, NJ: Rutgers University Press.

NARSOO, Stephen (2001). *The History of Power, Space and Knowledge in Bertrams: Towards New Epistemologies of Planning in South Africa.* Unpublished BSc Thesis, Department of Town and Regional Planning, University of Witwatersrand, Johannesburg.

NEWMAN, P. and J. Kenworthy (1999). *Sustainability and Cities. Overcoming Automobile Dependence.* Washington, DC: Island Press.

NICHOLSON, Linda, ed. (1990). *Feminism/Postmodernism.* London: Routledge.

NIELSEN, J., ed. (1989). *Feminist Research Methods.* Boulder, Colorado: Westview Press.

NIRWAN, D. (1997). 'Against Purity: Reflections of an Indonesian Writer', in D. Y. H. Wu, H. McQueen, Y. Yamamoto, eds. *Emerging Pluralism in Asia and the Pacific.* Hong Kong: Hong Kong Institute of Asia-Pacific Studies.

NUSSBAUM, Martha (1990). *Love's Knowledge. Essays on Philosophy and Literature.* New York: Oxford University Press.

NUSSBAUM, Martha (2001). *Upheavals of Thought. The Intelligence of Emotions.* Cambridge: Cambridge University Press.

OLDS, K. (2001). *Globalization and Urban Change. Capital, Culture, and Pacific Rim Megaprojects.* Oxford: Oxford University Press.

PAPADEMETRIOU, Demetri (2002). *Reflections on International Migration and its Future.* The J. Douglas Gibson Lecture. Kingston, Ontario: Queens University, School of Policy Studies.

PAREKH, B. (2000). *Rethinking Multiculturalism.* London: Macmillan.

PARK, R. (1967). *On Social Control and Collective Behavior.* Chicago: University of Chicago Press.

PASCOE, R. (1992). 'Place and Community: The Construction of an Italo-Australian Space', in S. Castles, C. Alcorso, G. Rando, and E. Vasta, eds. *Australia's Italians: Culture and Community in a Changing Society.* Sydney: Allen and Unwin.

PATEMAN, Carole (1988). *The Sexual Contract.* Cambridge: Polity Press.

PATEMAN, Carole (1989). *The Disorder of Women: Democracy, Feminism and Political Theory.* Stanford: Stanford University Press.

PEATTIE, Lisa (1987). *Planning: Rethinking Cindad Guayana.* Ann Arbor: University of Michigan Press.

PERLOFF, Harvey (1957). *Education for Planning: City, State and Regional.* Baltimore: The Johns Hopkins Press.

POLANYI, Michael (1962). *Personal Knowledge: Towards a Post-Critical Philosophy.* New York: Harper and Rowe (orig. 1958).

POPPER, K. R. (1975). *Objective Knowledge: An Evolutionary Approach.* Oxford: Clarendon Press (orig. 1972).

PORTER, Elizabeth (2002). 'Indigenous Planning Knowledge/s: The Possibility of Planning as an Inclusionary Practice in Protected Area Planning in South-east Australia', paper presented to Association of Collegiate Schools of Planning Annual Conference, Baltimore, November 21–24.

QADEER, M. (1994). 'Urban Planning and Multiculturalism in Ontario, Canada', in H.

Thomas and V. Krishnarayan, eds. *Race, Equality and Planning: Policies and Procedures.* Avebury: Aldershot.

QADEER, M. (1997). 'Pluralistic Planning for Multicultural Cities', *Journal of the American Planning Association*, 63, 4: 481–94.

RABINOW, Paul (1984). *The Foucault Reader.* New York: Pantheon.

RABINOW, Paul (1989). *French Modern. Norms and Forms of the Social Environment.* Cambridge, MA: MIT Press.

RATCLIFFE, P. (1999). 'Ethnicity, Sociocultural Change, and Housing Needs', *Journal of Planning Education and Research*, 19, 2: 135–43.

REAGON, Bernice (1981). 'Coalition Politics: Turning the Century', in B. Smith, ed. *Home Girls: A Black Feminist Anthology.* New York: Kitchen Table, Women of Color Press.

REARDON, K. (1998). 'Enhancing the Capacity of Community-based Organizations in East St. Louis', *Journal of Planning Education and Research*, 17, 4: 323–33.

REARDON, K. (2003). 'Ceola's Vision, Our Blessing: The Story of an Evolving Community/University Partnership in East St. Louis, Illinois', in B. Eckstein and J. Throgmorton, eds. *Story and Sustainability. Planning, Practice, and Possibility for American Cities.* Cambridge, MA: MIT Press.

REIN, M. and D. Schön (1977). 'Problem-setting in Policy Research', in C. Weiss, ed. *Using Social Research for Public Policy.* Lexington, MA: Lexington Books.

REPS, John (1965). *The Making of Urban America.* Princeton, NJ: Princeton University Press.

REYES, Eric (1993). *Queer Spaces: The Spaces of Lesbians and Gay Men of Color in Los Angeles*, unpublished Masters thesis, Graduate School of Architecture and Urban Planning, UCLA.

RHODES, R. (2001). 'Ken Lum's Outsider Art', *The Globe and Mail* (Toronto), 12 May, V3.

RITTEL, H. and M. Webber (1973). 'Dilemmas in a General Theory of Planning', *Policy Sciences*, 4, 155–69.

ROBINS, K. (1995). 'Collective Emotion and Urban Culture', in P. Healey *et al.*, eds. *Managing Cities: The New Urban Context.* Chichester: Wiley and Sons.

ROCCO, R. (2000). 'Associational Rights-claims, Civil Society and Place', in E. Isin, ed. *Democracy, Citizenship and the Global City.* London: Routledge.

ROCHE, M. (1992). *Rethinking Citizenship.* Cambridge: Polity Press.

ROMO, Ricardo (1983). *East Los Angeles: History of a Barrio.* Austin: University of Texas Press.

RORTY, Richard (1979). *Philosophy and the Mirror of Nature.* Princeton, NJ: Princeton University Press.

ROTELLA, C. (1998). *October Cities.* Berkeley: University of California Press.

RUDDICK, Sara (1989). *Maternal Thinking: Towards a Policy of Peace.* New York: Ballantine.

RUSHDIE, Salman (1992). *Imaginary Homelands.* London: Granta Books.

SAINT-BLANCAT, Chantal (2002). 'Islam in Diaspora: Between Reterritorialization and Extraterritoriality', *International Journal of Urban and Regional Research*, 26, 1: 138–52.

SANDERCOCK, Leonie (1975). *Cities for Sale: Property, Politics and Urban Planning.* Melbourne: Melbourne University Press.

SANDERCOCK, Leonie (1975b). *Public Participation in Planning.* Adelaide: South Australian Government Printer.

SANDERCOCK, Leonie (1978). 'Citizen Participation in Planning: The New Conservatism', in P. Troy, ed. *Federal Power in Australian Cities.* Sydney: Hale and Iremonger.

SANDERCOCK, Leonie (1982). 'Producing Planners or Educating Urbanists?', in

Stephen Murray-Smith, ed. *Melbourne Studies in Education.* Melbourne: Melbourne University Press.

SANDERCOCK, Leonie (1990). *Property, Politics, and Urban Planning: A History of Australian City Planning, 1890–1990,* 2nd ed. New Brunswick, NJ: Transaction Publishers.

SANDERCOCK, Leonie (1995a). 'Voices from the Borderlands: A Meditation on a Metaphor', *Journal of Planning Education and Research,* 14, 2: 77–88.

SANDERCOCK, Leonie (1995b). 'Introduction', in Leonie Sandercock, ed. 'Making the Invisible Visible: New Historiographies for Planning'. *Planning Theory,* 13: 10–33. Milan: Franco Angeli.

SANDERCOCK, Leonie, ed. (1995c). 'Making the Invisible Visible: New Historiographies for Planning' special issue, *Planning Theory,* 13. Milan: Franco Angeli.

SANDERCOCK, Leonie (1996). 'The Docklands: Melbourne's Next Goldrush', *The Age,* 28 November.

SANDERCOCK, Leonie, ed. (1998). *Making the Invisible Visible: Insurgent Planning Histories.* Berkeley: University of California Press.

SANDERCOCK, Leonie (1998a). *Towards Cosmopolis. Planning for Multicultural Cities.* Chichester: Wiley.

SANDERCOCK, Leonie (2002). 'Difference, Fear, and Habitus: A Political Economy of Urban Fears', in Jean Hillier and Emma Rooksby, eds. *Habitus: A Sense of Place.* Aldershot: Ashgate.

SANDERCOCK, Leonie (2000a). 'When Strangers Become Neighbors: Managing Cities of Difference', *Planning Theory and Practice,* 1, 1: 13–30.

SANDERCOCK, Leonie (2000b). 'Cities of (In)Difference and the Challenge for Planning', *DISP* [Dokumente und Informationen zur Schweizerischen Orts-, Regional- und Landesplanung: Documents and Information on Swiss Local, Regional and State Planning], no. 140, January 2000, 7–15.

SANDERCOCK, Leonie and Ann Forsyth (1990). *Gender: A New Agenda for Planning Theory,* Working Paper 521. Berkeley: Institute of Urban and Regional Development, University of California.

SANDERCOCK, Leonie and Ann Forsyth (1992). 'A Gender Agenda: New Directions for Planning Theory', *Journal of the American Planning Association,* 58, 1 (Winter): 49–59.

SANDERCOCK, L. and B. Kliger (1998a). 'Multiculturalism and the Planning System, Part One', *The Australian Planner* 15, 3: 127–32.

SANDERCOCK, L. and B. Kliger (1998b). 'Multiculturalism and the Planning System, Part Two', *The Australian Planner* 15, 4: 223–7.

SARKISSIAN, Wendy and Donald Perlgut, eds (1995). *Community Participation Handbook,* 2nd ed., Institute for Science and Technology Policy, Murdoch University.

SASSEN, Saskia (1991). *The Global City: New York, London, Tokyo.* Princeton, NJ: Princeton University Press.

SASSEN, Saskia (1995). 'On Concentration and Centrality in the Global City', in Paul Knox and Peter Taylor, eds. *World Cities in a World System.* Cambridge: Cambridge University Press.

SASSEN, Saskia (1996). 'Whose City Is It? Globalization and the Formation of New Claims', *Public Culture,* 8: 205–23.

SASSEN, Saskia (2000). *Guests and Aliens.* New York: The New Press.

SASSEN, Saskia, ed. (2002). *Global Networks: Linked Cities.* London: Routledge.

SAYYID, S. (2000). 'Beyond Westphalia: Nations and Diasporas – The Case of the Muslim Umma', B. Hesse, ed. *Un/settled Multiculturalisms.* London: Zed Books.

SCHAFFER, Daniel, ed. (1988). *Two Centuries*

of American Planning. Baltimore: The Johns Hopkins University Press.

Schön, Donald (1983). *The Reflective Practitioner*. New York: Basic Books.

Scott, Allen J., ed. (2001). *Global City-regions. Trends, Theory, Policy*. Oxford: Oxford University Press.

Scott, James C. (1998). *Seeing Like a State. How Certain Schemes to Improve the Human Condition Have Failed*. New Haven: Yale University Press.

Scott, Mel (1969). *American City Planning since 1890*. Berkeley: University of California Press.

Sennett, Richard (1970). *The Uses of Disorder*. New York: Knopf.

Sennett, Richard (1990). *The Conscience of the Eye*. New York: Norton.

Sennett, Richard (1994). *Flesh and Stone: The Body and the City in Western Civilization*. New York: Norton.

Shiva, Vandana (1988). *Staying Alive: Women, Ecology and Development*. London: Zed Books.

Simon, Herbert (1976). *Administrative Behavior*, 3rd ed., New York: Free Press (orig. 1945).

Siemiatycki, M. and E. Isin (1997). 'Immigration, Diversity and Urban Citizenship in Toronto', *Canadian Journal of Regional Science*, Spring–summer, 73–102.

Sinatra, Jim and Phin Murphy, eds (1999). *Listen to the People, Listen to the Land*. Melbourne: Melbourne University Press.

Slater, T. R. (1996). 'Birmingham's Black and South Asian Population', in Gerrard, A. and T. R. Slater, eds. *Managing a Conurbation: Birmingham and Its Region*. Studley: Brewin Books.

Spacks, Patricia (1985). *Gossip*. Chicago: University of Chicago Press.

Spelman, Elizabeth (1988). *Inessential Woman. Problems of Exclusion in Feminist Thought*. Boston: Beacon Press.

Spender, Dale (1980). *Man-made Language*. London: Routledge & Kegan Paul.

Soja, Edward W. (1989). *Postmodern Geographies*. London: Verso.

Soja, Edward W. (1996). *Thirdspace: Journeys to Los Angeles and other Real-and-Imagined Places*. Oxford: Blackwell.

Sorkin, Michael, ed. (1992) *Variations on a Theme Park*. New York: Noonday.

Spain, Daphne (1992). *Gendered Spaces*. Chapel Hill: University of North Carolina Press.

Stanner, W. E. H. (1979). *White Man Got No Dreaming: Essays, 1938–1973*. Canberra: ANU Press.

Stimpson, Catherine, Elsa Dixler, Martha Nelson and Kathryn Yatrakis, eds. (1981). *Women and the American City*. Chicago: University of Chicago Press.

Sudjic, Deyan (1992). *The Hundred Mile City*. London: André Deutsch.

Susskind, L. and J. Cruikshank (1987). *Breaking the Impasse: Consensual Approaches to Resolving Public Disputes*. New York: Basic Books.

Susskind, L., S. McKearnan and J. Thomas-Larmer, eds. (1999). *The Consensus Building Handbook*. Thousand Oaks, CA: Sage.

Tacey, David (1995). *Edge of the Sacred*. Melbourne: Harper Collins.

Takaki, Ronald (1993). *A Different Mirror: A History of Multicultural America*. New York: Little, Brown & Co.

Tannenbaum, B. (2002). 'Where Miles of Murals Preach a People's Gospel', *Sunday New York Times*, 26 May, AR 29.

Tchen, John Kuo Wei (1990). 'The Chinatown-Harlem Initiative: Building Multicultural Understanding in New York City', in Jeremy Brecher and Tim Costello, eds. *Building Bridges: The Emerging Grassroots Coalition of Labor and Community*. New York: Monthly Review Press.

Thiagarajan, S. and G. Parker, eds (1999).

Teamwork and Teamplay. San Francisco: Jossey-Bass.

THIONG'O, N. (1986). *Decolonising the Mind: The Politics of Language in African Literature*. London: James Currey.

THOMAS, H. (1995a). 'Ethnic Minorities and Planning', *The Built and Natural Environment*, 6: 4–8.

THOMAS, H. (1995b). ' "Race", Public Policy, and Planning', *Planning Perspectives*, 10, 2: 123–48.

THOMAS, H. (1997). 'Ethnic Minorities and the Planning System. A Study Revisited', *Town Planning Review*, 68, 2: 195–211.

THOMAS, Huw and V. Krishnarayan, eds (1994). *Race Equality and Planning: Policies and Procedures*. Aldershot: Ashgate.

THOMAS, June Manning (1994). 'Planning History and the Black Urban Experience: Linkages and Contemporary Implications', *Journal of Planning Education and Research*, 14, 1: 1–10.

THOMAS, June Manning (1998). 'Race and Empowerment: Necessary Theoretical Constructs for Understanding US Planning History', in Leonie Sandercock, ed. *Making the Invisible Visible: A Multicultural History of Planning*. Berkeley: University of California Press.

THOMAS, June Manning and Marsha Ritzdorf, eds (1997). *Urban Planning and the African American Community. In the Shadows*. Thousand Oaks: Sage.

THOMPSON, S. (2003). 'Planning and Multiculturalism: A Reflection on Australian Local Practice', *Planning Theory and Practice*, 4, 3 (forthcoming).

THOMPSON, S., Dunn, K., Burnley, I., Murphy, P. and Hanna, B. (1998). *Multiculturalism and Local Governance: A National Perspective*. Sydney: New South Wales Department of Local Government/Ethnic Affairs Commission of New South Wales/University of New South Wales.

THROGMORTON, J. (1991). 'The Rhetoric of Policy Analysis', *Policy Sciences*, 24, 153–79.

THROGMORTON, J. (1996). *Planning as Persuasive Storytelling*. Chicago: University of Chicago Press.

TULLY, James (1995). *Strange Multiplicity. Constitutionalism in an Age of Diversity*. Cambridge: Cambridge University Press.

TURNER, B., ed. (1993). *Citizenship and Social Theory*. London: Sage.

Urban Task Force (1999). *Towards an Urban Renaissance*. London: E. & F. N. Spon.

VOSE, C. (1967). *Caucasians Only: The Supreme Court, the NAACP, and the Restrictive Covenenant Cases*. Berkeley: University of California Press.

WALLACE, M. and B. Milroy (1999). 'Intersecting Claims: Planning in Canada's Cities', in T. Fenster, ed. *Gender, Planning, and Human Rights*. London: Routledge.

WATSON, S. and A. McGillivray (1995). 'Planninng in a Multicultural Environment: A Challenge for the Nineties', in P. Troy, ed. *Australian Cities: Issues, Strategies and Policies for Urban Australia in the 1990s*. Cambridge: Cambridge University Press.

WATSON, Vanessa (2002). *Change and Continuity in Spatial Planning. Metropolitan Planning in Cape Town under Political Transition*. London: Routledge.

WEISMAN, Lesley Kanes (1992). *Discrimination by Design*. Urbana, Illinois: University of Illinois Press.

WEKERLE, Gerda, Rebecca Peterson, and David Morley, eds (1980). *New Space for Women*. Boulder, CO: Westview Press.

WEKERLE, Gerda and Linda Peake (1997). 'New Social Movements and Women's Urban Activism', in J. Caulfield and Linda Peake, eds. *Critical Perspectives on Canadian Urbanism*. Toronto: University of Toronto Press.

WERTHEIM, Margaret (1995). *Pythagoras'*

Trousers. God, the New Physics, and the Gender Wars. New York: Times Books.

WEST, Cornell (1990). 'The New Cultural Politics of Difference', in R. Ferguson, M. Gever, T T. Minh-ha, and C. West, eds. *Out There: Marginalization and Contemporary Cultures.* Cambridge MA: MIT Press.

WESTIN, C. (1996). 'Equality, Freedom of Choice, and Partnership: Multicultural Policy in Sweden', in R. Baubock, A. Heller, A. Zollberg, eds. *The Challenge of Diversity.* Aldershot: Avesbury.

WESTKOTT, Nancy (1979). 'Feminist Criticism of the Social Sciences', *Harvard Educational Review*, 49, 4: 422–30.

WILSON, Elizabeth (1991). *The Sphinx in the City: Urban Life, the Control of Disorder, and Women.* Berkeley: University of California Press.

WILSON, Elizabeth (1992). 'The Invisible Flaneur', *New Left Review*, 191 (Jan–Feb), 90–110.

WILSON, William Julius (1987). *The Truly Disadvantaged: The Inner City, the Underclass and Public Policy.* Chicago: University of Chicago Press.

WINIKOFF, Tamara, ed. (1995). *Places not Spaces. Placemaking in Australia.* Sydney: Envirobooks Publishing.

WIRKA, Susan (1989). *A Foremother of Planning: Mary Kingsbury Simkhovitch and the First National Conference on City Planning, 1899–1909.* Unpublished Masters thesis, Graduate School of Architecture and Urban Planning, UCLA.

WIRKA, Susan (1994). 'Introduction to Mary Simkhovitch's Housing Chapter', in Donald Kreuckeberg, ed. *The American Planner: Biographies and Recollections*, 2nd ed., New Brunswick, NJ: Center for Urban Policy Research, Rutgers University.

WITTGENSTEIN, L. (1971). *On Certainty*, ed. G. Anscombe and G. H. von Wright. New York: Harper Torchbooks.

WOODS, Clyde (1998). *Development Arrested. The Blues and Plantation Power in the Mississippi Delta.* New York: Verso.

WU, D. Y. H., H. McQueen, Y. Yamamoto, eds (1997). *Emerging Pluralism in Asia and the Pacific.* Hong Kong: Hong Kong Institute of Asia-Pacific Studies.

YEATMAN, Anna (1994). *Postmodern Revisionings of the Political.* London: Routledge.

YIFTACHEL, Oren (1992). *Planning a Mixed Region in Israel: The Political Geography of Arab-Jewish Relations in the Galilee.* Aldershot: Avesbury.

YIFTACHEL, Oren (1994). 'The Dark Side of Modernism: Planning as Control of an Ethnic Minority', in Sophie Watson and Katherine Gibson, eds. *Postmodern Cities and Spaces.* Oxford: Blackwell.

YIFTACHEL, Oren (1996). 'The Internal Frontier: Territorial Control and Ethnic Relations', *Regional Studies*, 30: 5, 493–508.

YIFTACHEL, Oren (2000). 'Social Control, Urban Planning and Ethno-Class Relations: Mizrahim in Israel's Development Towns', *International Journal of Urban and Regional Research*, 24, 2: 417–34.

YIFTACHEL, Oren (2001). 'Introduction: Outlining the Power of Planning', in O. Yiftachel, I. Alexander, D. Hedgecock, J. Little, eds. *The Power of Planning: Spaces of Control and Transformation.* The Hague: Kluwer Academic Press.

YOUNG, Iris (1990). *Justice and the Politics of Difference.* Princeton, NJ: Princeton University Press.

YOUNG, M. and P. Willmott (1957). *Family and Kinship in East London.* London: Routledge Kegan Paul.

ZHANG, Li (2001). *Strangers in the City.* Stanford, CA: Stanford University Press.

ZUKIN, S. (1996). *The Cultures of Cities.* New York: Blackwell.

INDEX

Note: Page entries in **bold** represent whole chapters.
Entries in *italics* represent works of art, books, film titles.

Printed in the United States
101076LV00001B/15/A